THROUGH
the
FAERIE GLASS

ABOUT THE AUTHOR

Kenny Klein (California) is a musician, performer, and lecturer who has been active in the Pagan community and on the Renaissance festival and folk music circuits for over twenty years. He has recorded numerous CDs of music and performs year round. Visit him online at www.kennyklein.net.

THROUGH
the
FAERIE GLASS

A Look at the Realm of
Unseen and Enchanted Beings

KENNY KLEIN

Llewellyn Publications
Woodbury, Minnesota

First Edition
First Printing, 2010

Cover art © Esao Andrews
Cover design by Lisa Novak
Editing by Rosemary Wallner
Llewellyn is a registered trademark of Llewellyn Worldwide, Ltd.

The Annotated Brothers Grimm, notes by Maria Tatar,. Reprinted with permission from W. W. Norton & Company, New York, 2004.

The Celtic Twilight by W.B. Yeats. Reprinted with permission from Dover 2004, unabridged replication of the work first published by A. H. Bullen, London, 1902.

English & Scottish Popular Ballads by J. F. Child. Reprinted with permission from Dover Publications, Inc. New York Dover (2003) unabridged replication of the works originally published by Houghton, Mifflin and Company, Boston, MA between 1882 and 1898.

The Great Oak and Brother Sister; Little Mos-woman, the story of a (Fairy) Tale by Aado Lintrop. Reprinted with permission from Electronic Journal of Folklore, 1997.

A History of Private Life, Volume I, From Pagan Rome to Byzantium. Paul Veyne, ed., Translated by Arthur Goldhammer. Reprinted with permission from Harvard University Press, Cambridge MA, 1992.

The Mabinogion, translated with an introduction by Jeffrey Gantz. Reprinted with permission from Penguin Classics, 1976.

Library of Congress Cataloging-in-Publication Data (Pending)
ISBN: 978-0-7387-1883-5

Llewellyn Publications
A Division of Llewellyn Worldwide, Ltd.
2143 Wooddale Drive, Dept. 978-0-7387-1883-5
Woodbury, Minnesota 55125-2989, U.S.A.
www.llewellyn.com

Printed in the United States of America

CONTENTS

Chapter 11
The End . . . 265

No matter what one doubts one never doubts the Faeries,
for, as the man with the Mohawk Indian on his arm said to me,
"they stand to reason."
—W. B. YEATS, *The Celtic Twilight*

Chapter 1

ONCE UPON A TIME: FAERIES

You'll begin the story, as these stories often begin, like this: "Once upon a time, in a beautiful land far far away, there dwelt some lovely little Fairies."

So you want to talk about Faeries? Cute, sweet, lovely Faerie creatures? Well, I hate to be the one to change your opinion, but Faeries are scary. Yes, that's what I said: Faeries are scary, awesome, frightful creatures.

You'll argue with me. No, no, you'll say. They're adorable, happy beings, about the size of my hand. (Maybe a little bigger sometimes, you'll add.) They have pretty wings, and they hum when they fly, or they tinkle, like a bell (wasn't one of them named for that?). They are ephemeral, mercurial, flitting from flower to flower, astoundingly happy in their brief, tiny lives. Mr. Barrie said so. And those two little girls in England saw them, and could speak to them. The man who wrote Sherlock Holmes would never lie to me!

I love Faeries, you'll say. They make the world a bright, happy place.

That is certainly what you'll say. You've read the books. You've seen the movies, heard the stories, perused the pretty pictures on calendars and posters.

But are you sure?

All these things you tell me, all of your ideas about who the Kindly Ones are, and aren't, are the impression of Faeries you probably gleaned from the nineteenth-century authors J. M. Barrie and Arthur Conan Doyle, from painters such as Amy Brown and Brian Froud, and from illustrators Arthur Rackham and Kate Greenaway. Your safe, fantasy-laced view of these creatures makes you believe they are magical and giggly. You may imagine them flying into your house through an open window, and nestling in the sock drawer. Mischievous but lovely; tiny and adorable.

In the social circles I inhabit, pretty, dimple-cheeked young women go to Renaissance festivals wearing Faerie wings and acting like flitting Elves. They sport green bodices with plastic leaves hanging from their waist, and green fishnet tights ending in the irony of Converse All Stars. They walk through the faire catching every eye, capturing hearts, a stunning picture of Otherworldly beauty. At night, when they've shut off their computers, finished their LARPs, and traded their bodice for an old, ratty Rutgers sweatshirt, they dream of journeying to a magical land where handsome Faerie men romance them. Perhaps you, yourself, have worn those wings, played those LARPs, dreamed that dream?

Perhaps as a child you read the Blue and Pink Fairy books, and saw the Flower Fairy artwork of Cicely Mary Barker, or those insipid Anne Geddes creations—winged babies, grasping at green stalks and sitting prettily on tulip petals. Bright-cheeked children, standing impishly on the green, tender leaves of a dandelion. You wanted to join them, to be tiny in size and to dance on a honeysuckle. When your mother tucked you in and kissed you goodnight, you imagined bright-eyed Fairy children dancing above your bed.

But listen, it's not like that. I'm here to tell you that Faeries are scary.

In the oldest of folk songs, stories, myth and lore, the people who knew the Faerie world paint a very different picture of the Fey than the ones people regard today. The legends contain warnings. The legends tell of fright, horror, the displacement of time, the confusion of finding a shriveled creature where last you left a pretty, sleeping babe. The songs tell of heartache and longing, of young women taken by a Faerie lover, now absent; young women who will never look with love or brightness at this disappointing mortal world again.

There are best-case and worst-case scenarios in these ancient tales.

At best, Faeries are mischievous pranksters that prey on the hapless traveler or the unsuspecting milkmaid. They are Leprechauns that tease humans with a wonderful pot of gold coins. Oh, the bounty, the delirious joy! Until the coins turn to old, dried leaves in the breaking light of day.

They are Robin Goodfellow, whom Shakespeare says:

frights the maidens of the villagery;
Skim milk, and sometimes labour in the quern
And bootless make the breathless housewife churn;
And sometime make the drink to bear no barm;
Mislead night-wanderers, laughing at their harm?
Those that Hobgoblin call you and sweet Puck . . .
(Shakespeare, A *Midsummer Night's Dream*, Act II,
Scene I, 34–40)

Oh yes; sad for the victim of their torment, but funny from a distance. But that's at best.

At worst, they are Tam Lin, who robs young women of "either their mantles of green, or else their maidenhead." They are Jenny Green Teeth, who spirits children away from the calm banks of the river and drowns them in turgid waters. They are Selkies, who seduce mortals and then leave them to mourn over their lover's disappearance into the frothy sea. They are L'Annawnshee, who inspires poets to brilliance, but whose bards lead short, tortured lives. They are the will-o'-the-wisp, who lures travelers from the roads on dark, gusty nights, until they lose their way and run desperately through the night forest, to be bound up in Mab's train.

And there is Mab, the Faerie Queen, who haunted the swirling visions of Shakespeare and Edmund Spenser, Her poets. Dark and beautiful She is, The Queen of Night, riding her great white horse with its red ears through the tangled forest, capturing spirits killed in the harvest and the hunt, and any stray human spirits that might be haplessly in the way. Mab, for whom the grain is left rotting in the corners of the field, for whom the first mead and ale is poured frothing on the ground, for whom the Seven Year King is sacrificed.

No, these are not the stories you read as a child, safe and warm in your bedroom, under layers of down quilts. These are not the stories you grew up with, written down by jovial men with warm smiles, whose activities in secret societies were not discussed in proper British circles. These are not the images you saw in bright colors, by prim Victorian artists who were delighted by the smiles on children's faces.

These are the stories told by the smoky hearth on a cold Samhain night, in a small cottage on the heath, where every sound of rustling hawthorn and ghostly wind just might have been the Pookah's call. These are stories woven into the songs of minstrels who traveled wearily on midnight roads, seeking shelter and coin in noisy pubs, in towns whose names were only dimly recalled from year to frozen year. These were poems told in hushed tones by gray-bearded bards, whose tormented sleep aside whispering waters gave them visions of the Good People. Their hands trembled slightly as they struck harp string, their eyes darted furtively from corner to corner of the great hall, as they prepared to tell the tale of Llew Llaw Gyffes, or recite the *Saga of Thorstein*.

Through these oldest of sources, the sagas, the lays, the bardic tales half-remembered, let us search for the true character of the Fey.

Through songs brought back from the Scottish moors, let us hear of Janet, heir to Carter Hall, who was seduced by a Faerie changeling fallen in battle. From the poems of a London actor, let us know of the cruel pranks of Puck, changing at will from hoofed human wanderer, to pony, to wren. From the tales of the Irish bards, let us learn of the Daoine Sidhe, doomed to lurk in the deep earth below County Ulster. From the oldest Pagan lore, let us hear of the Seven Year King, whose life was given to Her, the Faerie Queen.

But I warn you, your mind's eye will no longer see those cheery creatures on their flower petal beds. You will no longer look at computer-enhanced babies on dandelions with a passing smile as you search the aisles of that huge bookstore-café-record shop on a lazy afternoon. You will come to search the night forest for a hint, a sign, that frightening creatures live close by, waiting, lurking.

And if your name should happen to be Janet, you might think carefully before picking that lovely red rose.

A NOTE ON COLLECTING FAERIE LORE

We know about Faeries because people have learned of them, through bitter experience, and left a record of their dealings with the Good People. Nowadays, scientists and historians like records that are neatly written and have little footnotes and asterisks and that kind of thing. But the record of the Fey is not like that. The record of the Faeries has been preserved through folklore.

Folklore involves folk songs, stories, legends and myths; not the sort of things scientists and historians like to collect. So over the years, especially in the modern age, scientists and historians pooh-pooh Faerie lore, claiming the folkloric record is silly, unreliable and blatantly untrue. In modern usage, words that mean sacred stories and inner truths, words like *myth* and *legend*, have come to be equated with lies and mistruths. This is not at all what *myth* or *legend* means. Myths are sacred stories that hold deep truths, although these truths are not always literal truths. Legends are stories, songs, even plays that carry a seed of that which deeply touches our lives in the most spiritual way.

So Faerie lore has been preserved in these myths, lore and legends, surviving industrialism, wars, education and science, preserved to be discovered by those of us who believe.

In referencing the mythic record, I will speak about the work of certain individuals who helped gather and preserve this lore. None of these people made up the stories—they are stories that come from sources so old no one remembers the authors, and they are referred to as "traditional." But these individuals have created collections of the stories, songs and myths in published forms, so that people today may rediscover them. Below is a summary of a few sources mentioned in this book.

In the late nineteenth century, the idle rich of England, Germany and France roamed about the countryside and collected the songs, stories and folk wisdom of the common people. Many of the most enduring folklore come from this trend. The Brothers Jacob and Wilhelm Grimm are probably the best known of these collectors. They wandered through Germany and France, gathering old stories and writing them down, giving Walt Disney his best material. The Grimms' collection has elements of every type: Faerie lore, myth, folk theater and traditional storytelling. While the term "Fairy tales" is a bit of a misnomer when applied to the Grimms, because most of the stories don't involve actual Faeries, the elements and themes in each story are often carried down from much older lore, and provide a glimpse of the most ancient Faerie interactions with humans. I refer to the Grimms' collection quite a bit while discussing Faeries, because I think that important elements of Faerie lore are preserved in the stories they collected.

Another well-known collector was Francis James Child, whose work *The English and Scottish Popular Ballads* is probably the greatest compendium of traditional folk music we have and are likely ever to have. A Harvard professor, Child began collecting Scottish and

English folk songs, or ballads (a term meaning a folk song that tells a story—modern musicians have come to use the term to mean any slow song) and filling the Harvard library with them. Child gathered many versions of each ballad, annotated each and numbered them according to subject matter or theme. In the final years of the nineteenth century, he published this enormous folkloric collection, with his notes and histories of each song. So when I refer to a song as a Child ballad, this does not mean it is a song for children, but that it was collected from the folk of Scotland and England by F. J. himself. And when a song bears his name and a number, such as Child #37 (there are 305 in all), it simply refers to the order in which Child saw fit to place the song into his collection.

Another great collector was Cecil Sharp, who followed the English ballads to America. An Englishman who had lived briefly in Australia, Sharp was interested in how English ballads were sung in other parts of the English-speaking world. He believed that by the early twentieth century the ballads of England and Scotland had changed with use in their native countries, but had remained more pristine in America, Australia and Canada. He felt that a longing for "the old country" had caused immigrants to the New World to keep their folklore pure, especially in remote places like the American Appalachians. So he traveled across the Atlantic during the years of World War I and collected dances, songs and stories in rural America.

Finally, there have been musicians like myself who have devoted themselves to preserving and performing songs of the Fey, often changing them in musical style and presentation to reflect the tastes of the times. Two very good examples are the English bands Fairport Convention, probably the first English band to perform British folk music in an American-inspired psychedelic rock style; and Steeleye Span, a Fairport offshoot with a more pop-music approach to folk songs and Faerie lore. These bands collected their songs from much older traditional sources, as do most folk musicians, and made the material their own in terms of performance and style. Both bands were a huge influence on several generations of musicians, Renaissance faire goers, Pagans and geeks.

Using all of these sources—as well as more obscure ones such as folk songs learned wherever possible, Greek and Roman tales, Norse sagas and other European sources—gives us a view of the Faeries as they have been known throughout time, and throughout our experience of them.

One final note: Scholars and collectors who see the study of the Fey as a quaint science, a study of country peoples' odd beliefs, have written many books on Faerie lore. I am not one of those authors. While this book looks at the Kindly Ones through every angle of folklore, scholarship and myth, it does so from the point of view that they are real. They are out there, and you will learn the things you need to know to interact with them in the best, safest possible ways. Though when it comes to Faeries, you never can foresee certain things happening.

WHO ARE THE FAERIES?

Winged creatures. Imps, Sprites, Hobgoblins. Puck in his forest bower creating mischief for hapless wanderers. The Selkie King, Hell Hounds, Jenny Green Teeth. Queen Mab leading the Wild Ride on Samhain eve.

Everything we know about historic Faeries comes to us from folklore. Ancient people who lived in England and Scotland, France and Belgium, Ireland and the far-off Shetlands; Vikings of the North; the Saami; the Khanty; and the Bog People left records of their beliefs and their knowledge in the form of stories and songs. These bodies of lore have been passed down over centuries, from Pagans to Christians, Jews and Muslims, changing with the evolution of language, shifting with morals and beliefs, until here, now, they reach us. To know who Faeries are, and what they mean to us, we need to look carefully at the folkloric record with the eyes of a scholar, a poet and a Pagan who believes in these creatures.

First, what are the characteristics of these creatures? The many things learned from folklore include:

- The Faeries, or Fey, live close to nature. Their homes are often hollow hills or mounds, and they dance in rings of mushrooms or stones. They haunt overgrown ruins (Carter Hall) and tangled green places (Huntley Bank, the forests of old New York). The desecration of nature can summon them—the plucking of a rose, for instance.

- They spend a good deal of time devoting themselves to the arts: dancing, making music and song. In the case of Irish Faeries, they are often warlike.

- Faeries can hurt or help humans, but there seems little evidence as to why they choose to do one or the other. A particular Faerie might go out of its way to help a human, and then turn around and harm another human for no apparent reason. But like the little girl with the little curl, when they are helpful they are very helpful. The same goes for the aforementioned harm.

- They fear iron. Being gifted with signs of human civilization or society can cause their banishment: a gift of clothes, for instance, will frighten them off. All Harry Potter fans know this.

- They can appear as many elements of the natural world: human, animal, floral. Bird-like, fox-like, insect-like, seal-skinned, fishy, leafy, watery, earthy; these are all guises the Good People have taken.

- Their food and drink are harmful to humans, and even speaking to them can bring unpleasant consequences. This does not stop humans from doing so.

- They can be lusty, and they seem to desire romance and sex as much as humans do (or perhaps a good deal more). Often their embrace is harmful or deadly. In other cases, it spells heartache to mortals.

- Some Faeries are portrayed as immortal, some as long-lived, some subject to harm and death as much as mortals are. It depends on the Faerie.
- They have a sense of humor, and often a sense of honor. They speak various human languages but also have languages of their own. They ride horses as well as bugs, foxes, cows and fish.

You're nodding at all of these facts. You agree. You've heard the stories, and you still think they're cute. Shall we go on? Good. Let's take a look at who Faeries might truly be and where their stories come from. Let's sort out history from legend. Let's eliminate the medieval mush, the Renaissance troubadour romance, the Victorian politeness, and get to the bottom of the question of Faeries.

Let's first look at the oldest sources for Faerie lore: the names we know these creatures by.

Fairy and Pixie, whose names evoke the images of tiny Sprites dancing in green meadows, actually may refer to a race of people or magical beings that our European ancestors found when they arrived. People have known (or at least suspected) that another race shared our world since the dawn of time. The mythic record is peopled from time beyond memory with these creatures of glade and stream. Picts, Elves, Dwarves and Trolls may be these races of beings that came to be known by the Saxons, Celts, English and Germans.

The Scandinavians who first settled the frozen lands of northern Europe and Germany came there centuries ago from the Asian plains. Their mythology spoke of an ancient race of Devas, or demi-Gods, called the Peries. There are many stories of these fair ones in Persian mythology—Otherworldly beings that fought wars and whose impossibly beautiful women seduced men (sound familiar?). By the time the Vikings got to Europe, their stories included a race called the Feen or Feinin, the Fair Ones (Fairies, Faeries). They had probably encountered a race of fair-skinned creatures in Europe whom they took to be the Peries or Faeries of Asian Plains folklore; a race of people or beings much older than themselves, and very light of hair and complexion.

When Celts first came to the isles we now call Ireland, Scotland, England and Wales, they encountered the same curious race of people. Old by Celtic standards, these were either people who lived close to nature or a race of enchanted beings. They had Stone Age technology (the Celts had already moved well into the Bronze and Iron Ages), and they feared the Celts' iron weapons and fixtures.

They lived in caves or beneath hills, so the Celts called them The Sidhe (Shee), "the Hill People." They were also called the Picts, and that's where we get the word *Pixie*. They covered themselves with blue woad, culled from the *Isatis tinctoria* plant native to their lands, and the Celts learned this trick from them and in time used the paint themselves. This colorful body painting may have influenced a belief that Faeries are blue and live among plants. The oldest stories of Faeries are mixed in with or inspired by stories of this ancient race. Magical, mysterious and subtle, we do not know for sure if these were humans like us, true Faeries, or some other creatures that have fallen into the mythic or legendary domain. But we do know they interacted with Celts and Germans on occasion, taught secrets to certain individuals, hunted, and were found to be lovely and seductive—all of the qualities of the Fey.

Over time, stories of the Picts became mixed with religious Pagan mythology. When the isles became Christian, people refused to give up the worship of Gods and Goddesses, spirits and apparitions. Many of the Goddesses became saints, such as Brigit. But many others became Faeries. Mab was the name of a Goddess in English lore. In order to continue her worship, the people of the forests may have simply given her a new title, the Faerie Queen. Likewise the Tuatha De Danaan, the great Gods of Ireland, fell into Faerie lore. Many times the name of a Goddess or God seems to have been applied to a Faerie or spirit that haunted a local region. This may be true of Mab, and of Odin as well.

By the Middle Ages, Europe was Christian. The Church waged a war against the Pagan beliefs that had existed for thousands of years previously. For believers to escape the suspicion of heresy, Faeries had to be given a Christian back story. No longer creatures of forest and glade, the Faeries' cover story went like this: Faeries were angels who had not taken sides during the war in Heaven. Since they did not side with Satan, they were not consigned to Hell; not siding with God meant they could not remain in Heaven. So they were relegated to a world between Heaven and Hell, the Faerie world, in the same plane as our Earth. And for their disloyalty, every seven years the Faerie Queen must pay a tithe to Hell, a human life, to maintain this covenant.

Many Pagan myths fell under this cloak of respectability, preserved for countless generations by this seemingly naïve belief in the Fey. Mab's legends, the Seven Year King, Oak and Holly, the sacred stewardship of certain lands, the Mummer's Plays and the Hero's Journey, Bird lore and Leaf lore, all fell into the swirling mythic vortex of Faerie lore and legend.

Finally there is the record of true Faeries, creatures that humans have come to know as watchers of the ways, denizens of the forest glades, swimmers on the sea, the mischief makers, the malicious and the seductive. Selkies, Imps, Sprites, Nymphs, Leprechauns, Gnomes, Banshees, Fauns and Flower Faeries all fall into this set of Fey creatures. They walk the same Earth we do, yet few see them, and fewer know them. They keep hidden, they lurk, they watch us and study our ways. They are ever-present and can ruin our lives with trickery, malice or their beauty.

People tend to speak of the Fey creatures that affect their lives the most. For Celtic fishermen, it was the Selkies, Seal Maidens that followed their boats and came ashore in human form. For Germans along the Rhine, frosty Elves and the seductive Lorelie haunt their songs and tales. The Mermaid dwells in the sagas of Copenhagen, surviving into the modern world through the tales of Hans Christian Andersen. To the Greeks and Italians, it is seductive Nymphs of the field and forest. For those who live in the English woods, it is Herne, Puck and Robin Goodfellow, all names of forest Gods melded into the body of Faerie lore or applied to woodland spirits. For the Irish of the shores and meadows, the Leprechaun, taunting humans with wealth, the thing they most desire. And for the Highland Scots, in the terrifying night moors, Reynardine seduces their young women, devouring their bodies when he has had his sexual pleasure of them. (How's that for cute and spritely?) People also tend to use names that reflect a good opinion of the Fey, like the Good People, or the Kindly Ones. These euphemisms are meant to deter the Fey from harming humans and their families.

The Faerie lore explored in this book is a combination of these three elements: memories of an ancient race, perhaps enchanted, who lived close to nature and who were seen as emissaries of the natural world; Gods and Goddesses whose worship lives still among the common people in the form of Faerie stories and songs; and the Faeries themselves, a race of beings that inhabit our world but remain hidden, ever watchful, interacting with mortals when their fancy takes them to do so. In many cases, two or even all three of these elements may apply to the same creature.

By the nineteenth century, industrialism had destroyed a life close to nature for most English and Americans. Many longed for a simpler time and desired images and stories of the rustic life. They also longed for tales of magic as the simple supernatural beliefs of their grandparents were replaced with toil and pragmatism. Stories of Faeries became a quaint look into beliefs of rural people. The cultured began to collect these stories, lest they die out from memory, and saw Faeries as a ripe fruit for inclusion in their fantasy novels. J. M. Barrie envisioned a child's world where Faeries, Native Americans and pirates all held the attention of runaway boys. He further presented us with a secret world in London itself, where Faeries roamed Kensington Gardens, collecting boys who had run away or become lost. George MacDonald introduced us to a Faerie world beyond the fields, which mortals could enter to fight evil. It was at this time that Faeries became regarded as diminutive, tiny creatures we could smile upon and that were "cute" in our eyes.

One well-regarded author, Arthur Conan Doyle, went so far as to believe two young women who claimed to see little dancing Faeries in the English countryside, and who produced photographs of themselves with tiny, winged creatures prancing about them. Doyle pronounced these photos genuine, though later investigation and interviews proved them fakes. But Doyle's patronage of these girls helped to create in the common mind the popular image of tiny, dancing, winged Sprites.

Faerie stories told in this civilized world of nonbelievers became cautionary: they helped exemplify to young women the tragedies that would befall them if they did not "keep it in their bloomers." Like the young woman who meets Reynardine on a high mountaintop, or the poor maid seduced by the Selkie, women were warned through these stories that Faeries, like sexual urges, were wild and perilous; young Victorian ladies must keep their passions from destroying them, or fall prey to these erotic, malicious creatures that exemplified the worst passions of men. (This theme was further seen in other fantasy works of the era such as *Dr. Jekyll and Mr. Hyde* and *The Portrait of Dorian Gray*.)

So let's begin. Let us separate out the stories of Picts and Goddesses from the stories of the Fey. Let us look at the magical, the mystic, the historic and the sacred. Let's start with the characteristics of the Good People, who are dangerous to dance with, or eat with, or even to speak with. Let us consider stories of enchanted ale, enchanted food and enchanted speech. Stories of time and iron.

TIME

Where are you? What place is this?

You were asleep last night in the forest. It's coming back to you, as sun creeps into the wooded glade that surrounds you, reflecting off of vine and leaf. You were walking home, as usual, and there you saw them—tiny men playing at ninepins. It is, of course, your favorite game. When they asked you to join, you could not refuse.

They offered you small beer and ale. It tasted quite good. You've never tasted beer that delicious. It seemed to quench every thirst you had ever had. It went to your head, and the world began to spin.

You recall it now. You fell asleep, here in the forest.

But where is the little glade where the tiny men had set up their pins? Now it seems overgrown, covered in ivy. And why can't you move your arms? You tug and feel roots rip from earth and loam. Your arms are encased in greenery. Your legs too. You pull as hard as you can and free yourself. You sit up, your head aching.

The forest is thick and deep. Much thicker than you remember it. Where is the path you were taking home? It should be just over here, behind the tall oak. You search, but you find it's overgrown with ferns.

The village is just over this rise in the hill. You walk toward it. There is smoke rising from chimneys. Soon you will be home.

Curious . . . the village looks different. There are houses closer to the woods, houses you don't remember ever seeing before. And women walk past you whom you do not recognize, in clothes that seem strange and of an odd fashion. What is happening?

Remember the story of Rip Van Winkle? According to Washington Irving, Rip wanders the forests of the Mid-Hudson region of New York State (a very Faerie-enchanted place, I can tell you from experience), when he meets with some tiny fellows playing ninepins (a sort of bowling game). He drinks their beer (big mistake!), and falls asleep. When he wakes up, decades have passed.

Ossian, the son of Finn Mac Coul, has a similar experience. He rides off over the Western Ocean with Niamh of the Golden Hair, to Tir N'an Og, the Land of the Young. It's nice there for seven years, but he begins to long for Ireland. So off he goes, back over the Western Ocean on the magical white horse. But upon his return, he learns that three hundred years have passed in his island home.

We see it again in the *Mabinogion*, a medieval collection of much older Welsh lore and legend that mixes Arthurian stories, Welsh folk tales and stories of Gods and heroes. In one section, or branch, a band of Gods/heroes feast for what seems like several nights, grieving over fallen friends who fought a great war. The birds of the horse creature Rhiannon sing to them, and they speak at length with the severed head of Bran, their leader. But one day a member of their party opens a forbidden door, and they must return to the mundane world. Once there, they learn that eighty years have passed.

In Faerie lore, there is always a question of the passage of time. In almost every story of a journey into the lands of the Fey, times passes differently in that twilight land than it does here in our green fields. In *The Chronicles of Narnia*, C. S. Lewis borrowed from this tradition, sending his children heroes home from that magical realm through a wardrobe where they learn that while two decades have passed in Narnia, no time has elapsed in England.

Why this insistence that time passes differently in Faerie Lands? That travelers to and fro are caught in a time-space jigsaw puzzle? Perhaps, some might say, because the Faerie Land exists in a different dimension. Portals exist between the two realities, especially where rings of mushrooms grow or under hollow hills. Only the hardened time and space traveler can weather the change in time, the way only a trained astronaut can withstand G-force pressures. Those untrained, or unsuspecting, like Rip Van Winkle, suffer the dire consequences. It also helps not to eat the food.

The passage to Faerie is always spoken of as involving a passage over water or some other, ghastlier liquid. Travelers to the land of the Fey must ride over an ocean, a river of blood or nine putrid rivers of stagnant water. There is always a long voyage, in many stories fourteen days and nights. This seems to imply a passage through dimensions or through some sort of portal between worlds.

In many stories, the passage through this portal seems real, as in a physical journey. In others it seems to be what Wiccans call astral projection, a journey of consciousness.

As mentioned above, both the words *Faerie* and *Pixie* come from an ancient, mysterious race, the Picts. There are many theories about the Picts: they were Celts, they were not Celts, they painted their skin, they tattooed their skin, they were human, they were enchanted beings. They were, in the end, a mysterious people with ways close to nature. The Picts, like Australian Aboriginals and South American Indians, had a dream time, a group consciousness of time altered by a trance state. Individual Celts who came to know Pictish ways gradually and by tiny steps might have taken the substances or learned the trance techniques of their Pictish hosts and experienced this dream time. Coming back to themselves, they found that time had passed much more quickly in the waking world, and this passage of time was related in stories of the Fair Folk.

Imagine you are a young Celt, strong and brave, eager to prove yourself in battle and in the harvest. Your father's father and your mother's mother left the mountains of France (or whatever they might have called that native land of theirs), pushed by Frankish or Viking incursion, to this green land that you now call home. Tara. Eire. The Emerald Isle.

You've heard legends of the fair-faced ones who paint themselves blue, who live by rock and wood, and who shun metal tools. A few months ago, while wandering the forests, you spotted one. A young hunter like yourself, taking aim with a spear upon a young doe. You watched as his skill with that javelin brought down the deer.

You felt brave. Sheathing your iron knife, pushing your quiver of bronze-tipped arrows aside, you approached. The meeting was tense at first. Language was a barrier. But in a short time you showed this talented hunter that you were friendly. A language of hand signs arose between you—every hunter knows a set of hand signs.

You brought bread next time, to share, and he was there, happy to see you. One day you made to show him your iron knife, but he shrank back, fearing this technology. He explained as best he could that his people thought this new material cursed, ripped from the precious Earth by some sort of blasphemous magic. You sheathed the blade, eager to keep your new friend content. You would consider, in the future, how best to get your companion over this strange fear.

Now weeks had passed, maybe months, and you have been invited to his hearth, to meet his people, his parents, his sisters. The Fair Ones have determined that a bond between their people and yours would be advantageous, and they hope you will find his sisters charming and comely. You are excited at this prospect. The girls of your village seem plain and boring to you now that this idea has been put in your head.

Your friend bids you follow, and you do. You travel far into the forest, along a trail hardly visible to your eyes, but the young Pict knows the path well. There, in a murky glade, you see smoke rising from a small fire. A group of men sit around the flame, speaking in hushed tones. They are pale, like the young hunter, and wear only loin cloths. Their cheeks are ruddy and their hair the color of rusted iron. Their faces seem somber to you. They have old woad marks on their white skin. They stand to greet you as you enter the glade. They offer you meat, and you bow and accept, careful not to pull out your iron knife to cut it.

Now a group of women appear, dressed in skirts made of leather, their chests bare, their breasts smaller than those of Celtic women. You are not used to seeing girls with their chests bare, and you feel both excited and embarrassed. But these are their ways, and you smile and greet these women of the Picts.

Two of them are smiling shyly at you. They are beautiful. Their cheeks are deep red against the milky white of their skin, and their hair is the murky auburn of their tribesmen's, bound up in spiral braids on either side of their high foreheads. You feel a pang of desire as you watch them walk gracefully by. The girls of your village do not hold themselves like these thin, willowy, graceful girls. Maybe, as some in your village say, these girls actually have some enchantment within them that makes them so unspeakably lovely.

In time you find the tension has gone, and there is now laughter and song. Two of the women play pipes. It is the most compelling, enchanting music you have ever heard. The melodies lull you, drifting in and out of keys you know, moving into strange modes you've never heard before. A woman sings, in the jangled language of her people that sounds like twittering birdsong and soft moans held long and deep.

Now the evening is dark black, and one of the young women sits beside you. She offers you a long wooden tube with a wide bowl at the end. You look around and notice that all the men seem to have these, and that the women are holding glowing embers above the bowl while the men take long breaths from the tube.

You try it. Smoke fills your lungs and you cough. The girl beside you covers her mouth with her hand, but you see she is giggling.

Your pride is at stake, so you take another puff. The smoke is acrid and tangy like metal. Your head begins to swim. The music fills you, and the girl beside you seems to have eyes as big as the owl's. She smiles, and you can't help laughing. You laugh more and begin speaking in your Celtic bardic language the story of Danaan. The men smile and slap your shoulder. You talk on, embellishing the tale, seeing the shapes you describe. Vivid they seem, large and colorful. The girl beside you is a pillar of your desire, and she laughs with you, easily and softly. The stars twinkle above you.

You wake in bright morning. A few men of the Pictish village sleep beside you, near the embers of the fire. The women are baking bread nearby. You don't see the girl you sat near last night.

You are offered bread and honey, and you realize you are very hungry. After eating and drinking, you stand and stretch. You feel very tense, your muscles tight. You look around, wondering about the girl you sat beside. You ask one of the women in your halting Pictish, and she smiles, telling you that all of the girls are off gathering berries.

Your friend appears and points to himself and to the trail. He is offering to walk with you back to your village. You nod.

Through the deep forest, the murky wood, to the meadows you know. Your village is now a short walk ahead, and you bid your friend thanks and make plans to meet again. You go on alone, hoping to shoot a duck or a grouse before you arrive home with strange stories to tell.

When you catch sight of home, with the grouse in hand, your family shouts and runs to greet you.

"We were so worried," your mother says. Your sisters all frown at you.

"Why?" you ask.

"You've been gone a week!" they cry. "We thought those Faeries killed you and ate you!"

You consider. A week? How could this be? You arrived at their village yester eve, as the sun hung low in the sky. A week ago? How could that have happened?

At least, that is one explanation. Of course, there are many stories of the time difference that cannot be accounted for by this theory. Some think that the Fey enter our world through an inter-dimensional portal, an anomaly in time and space; or that Faerie metabolism is very quick, and once accustomed to life in the Faerie world, human metabolism speeds to the rate of one's hosts. Then again, maybe time is just different in the Faerie world. As you look at the folkloric record in the chapters ahead, you'll see many examples of travel between this world and the realm of the Kindly Ones. Is one theory better than another? Who knows? All things are possible with the Fey, and while some stories may refer to a dream time, others involve a trip across rivers of blood.

IRON

Faeries are uncomfortable with iron, and stories tell of banishing a Faerie by allowing the creature to touch an iron object. When entering a Faerie place, a piece of iron stuck in the door frame, perhaps a nail or a pocketknife, prevents the Fey from shutting one in. Nails in a headboard of the bed protect women with babies from Faerie harm. Placing a knife in a hunted animal while carrying it home prevents Faeries from putting their weight on the carcass (I told you Faeries are not nice).

The common practice of nailing a horseshoe above a door was originally meant not to bring luck but to guard against Faeries and other "evil" spirits. Horseshoes are made by smiths, and since smiths work in iron, it is believed Faeries will not bother with them. There is in fact a custom throughout the Isles that "black men," light-skinned men whose skin is darkened to black by their work, bring good luck, which is a way of saying that they prevent harm from Faeries. Such occupations include blacksmiths and chimney sweeps. Each New Year's Eve, it is custom to have one's house visited by a "black man" for protection from enchantment and spirits.

In *Superstitions of the Highlands and Islands of Scotland*, John Gregorson Campbell writes:

> The great protection against the Elfin race (and this is perhaps the most noticeable point of the whole superstition) is Iron, or preferably steel (cruaidh). The metal in any form, a sword, a knife, a pair of scissors, a needle, a nail . . . a fish hook, is all powerful. Playing the Jew's harp (tromb) kept the Elfin women at a distance from the hunter, because the tongue of the instrument is of steel. So also a shoemaker's awl in the door-post of his bothy [home] kept a glastig from entering. (Campbell 1900, 46)

Glastigs are Faeries that seduce hunters of deer by taking the form of a beautiful maid only to suck the victim's blood. In the story of *The Four Hunters and the Four Glastigs*, the four hunters are stalking a herd of deer when the Glastigs seduce them. Only one hunter survives the attack, and he does this by playing a Jew's harp, or "tromb," a metal musical instrument played with the mouth. When the Glastig sees she cannot have the hunter, she mocks him, saying:

Good is the music of the tromb
Saving the one note in its train
Its owner likes it in his mouth
In preference to any maid

There are many other stories of Glastigs in the Scottish Highlands. In one, the hunter, Big Young Donald, saves himself by swearing to hunt only stags and never hinds. Other stories mention that the Glastig has the hindquarters of a goat, but she keeps these hidden under her skirts or, if naked, under her long golden hair.

Iron is used as a Faerie imprisonment in several of the Grimms' stories. In *Iron John* or *Iron Hans*, the title character is a wild man who guards a golden well and is covered with fur said to be the color of iron. He is captured and imprisoned in an iron cage, with a key of the same metal, but is freed by the king's son. The prince is rewarded several times by gifts of armor and iron weapons, which allow him to win a war and thereby the hand of a princess. The wild man, having divested himself of all of his iron, is transformed into a king, and explains that he had been under an enchantment.

In *The Iron Stove*, another tale collected by the Grimms, a king's son is imprisoned in a large iron stove in a forest. He may only be freed by a princess, and when two girls who are not the princess attempt to bore through the iron to free him, they fail. But when the princess tries, she succeeds immediately. After he is freed, the stove itself runs away over the mountains.

In the original story of *The Frog Prince*, the prince's servant Henry (Heinrich) is so sad while the prince is a frog that he has three iron bands placed about his heart. When the prince is kissed back into human form (or in the original, squashed against a wall by the princess, which turns him back), he hears a series of three cracking sounds, which he believes are the wheels of his coach breaking. Henry tells him it is the bands around his heart breaking off. We are to understand that while Henry's master is imprisoned in a frog's likeness, his own heart is imprisoned in iron. The breaking of the iron bands frees his heart to feel emotion again.

In each of these Grimms' stories, iron is used to imprison a magical creature, or in Heinrich's case, to keep his heart bound (imprisoned) while his master is victim to an enchantment. In each case, removing the iron frees the creature or allows an enchantment to be lifted. In each story, only a particular person, who has power within the Faerie world or power over iron, may remove the iron from the inflicted person or creature. This is why smiths (people who have power over iron) are immune to Faerie harm, and why iron is used as a protection—mortals who possess iron are seen as having power to use it.

The notion that the Picts had a Stone Age technology and were frightened of the Celts' advanced weapons and tools would explain at least part of the notion that Fairies are affected by the metal. In her book *The Vanishing People*, Katherine Briggs relates an Irish folk story about a woman who lives in the deep forest and is visited each day by a woman of "the Vanishing People," or a Faerie. The Faerie woman is delighted by the Celtic woman's copper kettle, and the Celt allows the Faerie to borrow it each day.

A day comes, however, when the Celt is not at home, and a relative greets the Faerie woman. Not knowing the protocol, the relative offers an iron kettle instead of the copper one. The Faerie woman leaves, and never returns.

If the Faerie woman is a Pict, one of the last of the Vanishing People, she would be pleased to use a kettle to heat water, rather than a skin or a hollowed stone. A copper kettle might be enough like raw ore for her to be comfortable with using it. But when handed an iron kettle, the "killing metal" of swords and axes, she felt horrified, and never returned.

Of course there are other theories: Being of the most natural earth, Faeries abhor the making or shaping of ore and stone, other than by wind and rain. They never use shaped ore and prefer to use natural implements found in or given by nature. We can see by the story of the Glastig that the Fey fear or are horrified by any object made of shaped iron. We do not know if it's the ore itself, or the shaping of it, that horrifies them. But it's likely it is the shaping of it, especially since Faeries will not go near a blacksmith. It is likely that the Good People simply abhor the process of smith craft, because it is so antithetical to their natural world and nature-rich environment. The shaping of iron is considered the act that brought humans from the Stone Age to the modern age, and separated them from their Faerie neighbors. The ore may lay at the center of that rift, a constant reminder to the Kindly Ones of the gap between themselves and humans. Anyone seen as controlling, handling or shaping iron is blasphemous in their eyes.

WHAT DO FAERIES LOOK LIKE?

Many depictions of Faeries exist in our modern culture. Some are cute, like the little Faeries painted by Cicely Mary Barker and Kate Greenaway, adorable children in green clothes with colorful wings. Amy Brown's Faeries are presentable Goth girls with bat wings, sitting idly in trees and on flowers, wearing clothes they bought from Hot Topic at some tiny Faerie mall. I've recently seen painted Playboy bunnies with butterfly wings that I was meant to believe were Fey.

Then there are paintings by nineteenth-century illustrators such as Arthur Rackham and Edmund Dulac, depicting impish creatures with pointed ears and long, nimble fingers. Puck and Ariel flying through the forest night, laughing like giddy schoolboys.

Let's look at the record of folklore and decipher what is true and what is not regarding Faerie manifestation.

Some Fey seem very human in appearance. The Selkie King (when in human form), the Queen of Elfland, and the Faerie Queen all seem human enough to need no particular description of their physical features. Reynardine the fox man is ruddy and red-haired when in human form, but that could be said of many Scots. The Lorelie, Nymphs and Sirens are all perfectly human and so beautiful in appearance that sailors and wanderers are drawn close enough to be pulled beneath the waters, dying for their attraction to these gorgeous Faerie maids.

The Fey are masters of disguise. Many take on human form to interact with us, while reverting back to a ghastlier appearance when in the company of their own kind. They may appear in the forms of animals, plants, clouds or stones. These forms help them to interact with us, or to hide from our view. Either way, we seldom see Faeries, and only those with the "Faerie sight" may see their true forms (see chapter 2 and the story of True Thomas, who had the gift of the Faerie Sight, and Tam Lin).

There are tales of beings completely nonhuman in appearance: Dwarves, Sprites, Goblins and Pookahs to name a few. These creatures are products of a different world, tied to nature, and appear as tiny men, like the Dwarves in Rip Van Winkle or Rumplestiltskin, or as impish creatures, like Puck or Ariel. Puck comes from the Pookah, Irish and English Faeries whose name derives from the Greek *booka*, "goat" or "pastoral animal." Their impish beards may have reminded people of that creature. According to the Church, the goat was the creature of Satan, so Goblins would have been associated with that animal. Puck's legacy in Shakespeare's writings seems to be a combination of Faerie stories and myths of local Gods. Robin Goodfellow is a name for Herne, the God of the English Forests. Puck, like any Pookah, could change into a goat, horse, dog or rabbit. In one story, Puck takes revenge on a miserly, bitter man by appearing as a horse, and then disappearing from under the man while he is riding.

In this world of Faerie/Gods, disguises are common. The *Mabinogion* tells the story of Arawn, the king of Annwn, who appears as a mortal hunter when he tempts Pwyll to fell the white stage he is hunting. He asks Pwyll to take his place in a battle with his enemy

Havgan, who himself is disguised as an armored knight. The same story is in *Sir Gawain and the Green Knight*, a story from the Arthurian legend.

In Arthur's own story, Merlin enchants Arthur's father, Uther Pendragon, to appear in the disguise of his enemy Gorlois in order to sleep with Gorlois's wife, Ygrain. In a similar way, when Arthur is crowned king, his own sister Morgan Le Fay (Morgan of the Faeries, a Faerie woman and queen of the Isle of Apples) disguises herself as a maiden to sleep with Arthur and bear his son, Mordred.

A similar story from Ireland is of Niamh of the Golden Hair, who takes mortal form to seduce Ossian, son of Finn Mac Coul. Niamh is very like the figure of Morgan; she is a Faerie woman and queen of Tir N'an Og, the Isle of the Young (very like Avalon, the Isle of Apples).

Nymphs take many shapes. Many are associated with water, and can appear as clouds, rain, streams or brooks. Others are animal in form, like the Fauns or Satyrs associated with Nymphs. Many are tied to trees and flowers. All may take the appearance of female humans; some will appear as young girls, and others as sexually blossoming young woman.

BIG OR SMALL?

Across the folkloric record is evidence for Faeries being both large and small.

In the song "The Wee Wee Man" (see Child 1965, #38), the narrator meets a Faerie or Dwarf that is described as both tiny and very strong. He lives in a Faerie mound, the type of place where the Fey are said to live throughout the mythic record. Here is the song as Child collected it:

Twas down by Carterhaugh, father
Between the water and the wall
There I met with a wee wee man
And he was the least that ever I saw.

His length was scarce a finger's length
And thick and nimble was his knee
Between his eyes a flea could go
Between his shoulders inches three.

His beard was long and white as a swan
His robe was neither green nor grey
He clapped his hands, down came the mist
And he sank and he sainted clean away.

He's lifted up a stone, six feet in height
And flung it farther than I could see
And though I'd been a-trying bold
I'd never had lifted it to my knee.

"Wee wee man, that thou art strong,
Tell me where thy dwelling be."
"It's down beneath yon bonny green bower
Though you must come with me and see."

We roved on and we sped on
Until we came to a bonny green hall
The room was made of the beaten gold
And pure as crystal was the wall.

There were pipers playing on every stair
And ladies dancing in glistering green
He clapped his hands, down came the mist
And the man in the hall no more was seen.

Carterhaugh, or Carter Hall, mentioned in the first verse, is a
place named in several songs as haunted by the Fey (for example, in
the story of Tam Lin, a changeling). The narrator is traveling by Carterhaugh when he sees a tiny man, described as "a finger's length," yet
strong enough to pick up a stone "six feet in height." Upon questioning, the narrator learns that the Faerie man lives beneath a "bonny
green bower," or under a Faerie mound. The human is taken there

and sees that the walls are made of gold (a hint at the Irish Leprechaun tale of the "pot of gold" at the end of the rainbow).

This notion of a tiny strong Faerie man, a Gnome or Dwarf, is found across the northern edge of the world. In Baltic folklore, there's a song abut a miniscule Herculean Dwarf that cuts down the World Tree, the great Tree of Life at the center of creation. Here is a verse:

> The little man rose from the sea
> His height was about a thumb
> Or he was three fingers tall
> He honed his axe
> Fire flashed from the blade
> (Lintrop 2001, volume 16)

Notice the last line of the song that mentions a honed axe. This "Little Man" of Norse mythology is usually a forester, smith or iron worker, who burrows into the earth for ore to make axes and tools. In Finnish and Siberian myth, the Underworld is said to be inhabited by these tiny people. Dwarves are the name often given to these tiny Norse Faeries, like the Dwarves in Snow White that mine the earth for precious stones. As diggers and burrowers, these tiny men are associated with sleep and death (hibernation) as well as the Underworld.

The tiny Faerie exists in Irish folklore too, living in the earth beneath mounds and hills. The Leprechaun is tiny (like the Wee Wee Man) and unusually cunning and strong. He controls another ore of the deep earth, gold, and often makes devious promises concerning this treasure. The Leprechaun can shape gold into coins and jewelry, but often the precious metal will turn to old leaves or sticks in the Faerie's absence.

Mab, the English Fairy Queen, is variously seen as both large and small. In Shakespeare's Romeo and Juliet, Mercutio describes Mab as tiny:

> O, then, I see Queen Mab hath been with you.
> She is the Faeries' midwife, and she comes

In shape no bigger than an agate-stone
On the fore-finger of an alderman,
Drawn with a team of little atomies
Over men's noses as they lie asleep;
Her chariot is an empty hazel-nut
Made by the joiner squirrel or old grub,
Time out o' mind the Faeries' coachmakers.
Her wagon-spokes made of long spinners' legs,
The cover of the wings of grasshoppers,
The traces of the smallest spider's web,
The collars of the moonshine's watery beams,
Her whip of cricket's bone, the lash of film,
Her wagoner a small grey-coated gnat,
Not so big as a round little worm
Prick'd from the lazy finger of a maid;
(Shakespeare, *Romeo and Juliet*, Act I, Scene 5, 53–66)

Yet in the song "True Thomas" (Child #37), the Faerie Queen is described as human size or larger. Thomas calls her "the Queen of Heaven," referring to her goddesslike stature. She rides a great white steed and seems to tower over Thomas. And in A *Midsummer Night's Dream*, Shakespeare uses another name for the Faerie Queen, Titania, and depicts her and her husband, Oberon, as being tall and statuesque, though they are surrounded by Faeries of various sizes. (In Act 2, Puck tells a Faerie that the King's Elves "creep into acorn cups and hide them there" when Oberon and Titania fight.)

Niamh of the Golden Hair is also described as human size. The Queen of Tir N'an Og, the Land of the Young in Irish lore, Niamh appears to the hero Ossian as a human woman playing a harp, whose singing is so beautiful Ossian cannot resist leaving Ireland with her for her homeland of Tir N'an Og, across the Western Ocean.

Human-sized Faeries and Elves mating with humans is a very common event in Faerie stories. Selkies crawl out of their seal skins as human women and men and marry or simply impregnate mortals.

In the Norwegian *Thidreksaga*, written down in the thirteenth century, a mortal queen learns that her lover is an Elf. She becomes pregnant by him and bears the hero Hogni. In another story, the *Saga of Thorstein*, an entire race of half-Elfin people reside in a town called Alfheim. These people are said to be uncommonly beautiful because of their mixed race.

Elves may even be large and fierce enough to wage out-and-out war on mortals. A Danish song tells of seven hundred Elves (or in some versions trolls) that attack a local farmer. The band Steeleye Span did an English-language version of the song that describes these grim trolls descending upon the farmer to eat his food and raze his land, angered by the farmer cutting down trees to create a field.

And a King Henry meets a Faerie woman whose "head hit the rooftop of the house" and whose "middle you could not span." A substantial woman indeed!

The Fey then are mercurial; born into certain forms that may vary among tall or short; more human in appearance or very inhuman in shape and size; impish and pointy or round and goatish. They also have the ability to change forms, especially imitating or taking on the characteristics of animals, plants, water and stones. They can appear royal and stately, or common and impudent. They may show us a human form, or a form we easily recognize, such as a common beast. Or they may take ghastlier, Otherworldly forms, leading us to create stories not only of Faeries but of ghosts, Imps, monsters, bogies and were-animals. They may be helpful enough, or take delight in our mishaps. They are frightened of things we take for granted, such as iron. But they can frighten us, and often do so with malice and pleasure. We can travel to their realm, and they to ours, though it seems easier for them to come here than for us to go there.

So we will look at each characteristic of the Fey, each of their ways, and especially how they have related to us and we to them throughout the folkloric record. Let us start with the journey to their world, which very few have taken, and fewer still have survived.

Chapter 2

THE JOURNEY TO FAERIE

Is there really a world surrounded by mist, lost in time, filled with magic? Where song and poetry fill the air? Where creatures we can only imagine roam the enchanted wood? Where denizens of legend inspire human dreaming? Is this place reachable, across the Western Ocean, or through a river of blood? What do we know about Faerie, and the journey mortals might take to get there?

Tir N'an Og, Avalon, Shangri La, the Isle of Women, the Athenian forest on Midsummer Eve; the Faerie world, close to ours and yet far away, is both a true place and an archetype, a real destination and a destination of the heart. For many of us it is a fantasy, a dream or an initiatory experience. For some stories of the journey to Faerie represent dreams, or the shamanic journey.

Many of us see the storyline as alluding to an archetype of human experience. Like the time discrepancy, a journey to the Faerie world might often be a journey into the dream state or a trance experience. Like Shakespeare's humans in A *Midsummer Night's Dream*, people might enter the mortal woods, and in an altered state, find the Faerie world to be alive therein. And, by the same token, find they awake in bright dawn in their own world once again.

chapter 1 explained how the Faerie world may allude to a trance experience shared with Picts and other aboriginal Europeans. Like Australian Aboriginals and Amazon Rainforest peoples, these earliest denizens of the European forests may have had a dream time experience shared with certain Celts over time as the two races came to know each other.

Yet throughout the folkloric record, humans seem to have traveled to a real Faerie world. Some are bidden by the inhabitants of that world to enter. Others stumble there haplessly. In all the stories, it is a perilous journey. Travelers to the Fey lands are given strict warnings, and disobedience of these could result in slavery or death. No, these are not the sweet Faeries in your bedtime stories.

Songs and stories tell us much about the journey to Faerie. Any human who undertakes the trek is warned of certain dangers. Namely, do not eat or drink anything offered by Faeries; this will bind you for all your days to their world. It's also a bad idea to speak to anyone in that land; this too will bind one to Faerie. And Faerie is just not the place you want to go if you're good looking. According to medieval legend, the devil gets a tithe from the Faerie Queen every seven years, and a human of beautiful form is His preferred meal. One of the best examples of the way to the Faerie Lands is the Scottish song "True Thomas."

TRUE THOMAS OR THOMAS THE RHYMER

"True Thomas," a Scottish tune dating back to at least the thirteenth century, tells of Thomas Learmont of Erceldoune, a poet and bard who is called away to Elfland by the Faerie Queen. Below is one version of the song. (These older songs can be found in dozens or even hundreds of variations. People sang them differently in different places, changing them over time. In the days long before recorded music, folk songs were ever changing. Folklorists call this the "Folk Process.") Being in a Scottish dialect, it may be hard to follow; a syn-

opsis of the story is provided at the end of the Scottish lyric that
Child collected and numbered 37, version C.

> True Thomas lay on Huntlie bank,
> A ferlie he spied wi' his eye,
> And there he saw a lady bright,
> Come riding down by the Eildon Tree.
>
> Her shirt was o' the grass-green silk,
> Her mantle o' the velvet fine,
> At ilka tett her horse's mane
> Hang fifty siller bells and nine.
>
> True Thomas, he pull'd aff his cap,
> And louted low down to his knee:
> 'All hail, thou mighty Queen of Heaven!
> For thy peer on earth I never did see.'
>
> 'Oh no, O no, Thomas,' she said,
> 'That name does not belong to me;
> I am but the queen of fair elfland,
> That am hither come to visit thee.'
>
> 'Harp and carp, Thomas,' she said,
> 'Harp and carp along wi me,
> And if ye dare to kiss my lips,
> Sure of your bodie I will be.'
>
> 'Betide me weal, betide me woe,
> That weird shall never daunton me';
> Syne he has kissed her rosy lips,
> All underneath the Eildon Tree.
>
> 'Now, ye maun go wi me,' she said,
> 'True Thomas, ye maun go wi me,
> And ye maun serve me seven years,
> Thro weal or woe, as chance to be.'

She mounted on her milk-white steed,
She's taken True Thomas up behind,
And aye wheneer her bride rung,
The steed flew swifter than the wind.

O they rade on, and farther on—
The steed gaed swifter than the wind—
Until they reached a desert wide,
And living land was left behind.

'Light down, light down, now, True Thomas,
And lean your head upon my knee;
Abide and rest a little space,
And I will shew you ferlies three.

'O see ye not yon narrow road,
So think beset with thorns and briers?
That is that path of righteousness,
Tho after it but few enquires.

'And see not ye that briad braid road
That lies across the lily leven?
That is the path of wickedness,
Tho some call it the road to heaven.

'And see not ye that bonny road,
That winds about the fernie brae?
That is the road to fair Elfland,
Where thou and I this night maun gae.

'But, Thomas, ye maun hold your tongue,
Whatever ye may hear or see,
For, if you speak word in Elflyn land,
Ye'll neer get back to your ain countrie.'

O they rade on, and farther on,
And they waded thro rivers aboon the knee,

And they saw neither sun nor moon,
But they heard the roaring of the sea.

It was mirk mirk night, and there was nae stern light,
and they waded thro red blude to the knee;
Fow a' the blude that's shed on earth
Rins thro the springs o that countrie.

Syne they came on to a garden green,
And she pu'd an apple frae a tree:
'Take this for thy wages, True Thomas,
It will give the tongue that can never lie.'

'My tongue is mine ain,' True Thomas said;
'A gudely gift ye wad gie to me!
I neither dought to buy nor sell,
At fair or tryst where I may be.

'I dought neither speak to prince or peer,
Nor ask of grace from fair ladye:'
'Now hold thy peace,' the lady said,
'For as I say, so must it be.'

He has gotten a coat of the even cloth,
And a pair of shoes of velvet green,
And till seven years were gane and past
True Thomas on earth was never seen.

In this ballad, we meet True Thomas, a title of the thirteenth-century Scottish soothsayer Thomas Learmont of Erceldoune. We know that Thomas was a real person who lived upon the Scots-English border, as he is mentioned in two charters dating 1260–1280 and 1294, which refer to "Thomas de Ercildounson, son and heir of Thome Rymour de Ercildoun."

When we make Thomas's acquaintance, he is sitting on Huntley Bank, a green and fertile place. Just the place one would expect to meet with a Fey. It was in fact a custom of musicians of the time to lie on riverbanks and beside streams in order to allow Nymphs or water Sprites to inspire them to write new tunes. Thomas was probably doing just that, and came to the Faerie Queen's notice in some way.

Thomas spies a "ferlie," a marvel. It is a "lady bright" (in some versions a "lady gay"), dressed in "the grass-green silk," and adorned by "Her mantle o' the velvet fine." Her horse's mane is dressed as well, with "fifty siller bells and nine." A great white horse whose mane is hung with silver bells is a characteristic of the Faerie Queen in many tales, and so it is here. Another Faerie characteristic is clothing that matches the forest colors or is sparkly and grand in some way.

Compare the vision of the Queen of Elfland to that of the Underworld Queen Rhiannon when she first appears to the mortal Pwyll in the *Mabinogion*, a medieval telling of much older Welsh myths. Like Thomas, Pwyll (pronounced "poodge"; yes, the Welsh speak funny) has brought himself to a deserted green spot, a mound, where he was told he would either receive a blow, or see a wonder:

> And upon the mound he sat. And while he sat there, they saw a lady, on a pure white horse of large size, with a garment of shining gold around her, coming along the highway that led from the mound; and the horse seemed to move at a slow and even pace, and to be coming up towards the mound. "My men," said Pwyll, "is there any among you who knows yonder lady?" "There is not, Lord," said they. "Go one of you and meet her, that we may know who she is." (Guest 1877, 344–345)

With the same medieval gallantry, Thomas greets the woman of his vision, by pulling off his cap and bowing, calling the woman "the Queen of Heaven." This is a title applied to Mary by the Catholics. But it is also an older title, applied by the Babylonians to the Goddess Ishtar, and by the Hebrews to their Goddess Lilith. The Saxon Britons had a similar Goddess, Oestara. The Catholic holiday Easter still bears her name, as the celebration of Christ risen from the tomb was originally superimposed over Her feast day. Modern Pagans still use Her name for their Spring Equinox festival. Oestara is linguistically tied to the Sumerian Ishtar, to the Egyptian Isis, to the Phoenician Astarte and to the Hebrew Asherah, all mother Goddesses associated with spring and fertility. Each of these Goddesses journeys into the Underworld or death world in the winter, and returns in spring to bring life back to the earth. Upon seeing the woman approaching him, Thomas assumes it is this mythic figure, the Queen of spring and of the Underworld.

The woman is quick to correct Thomas, saying "that name does not belong to me." She tells him in short order that she is the Queen of Elfland.

Then she asks Thomas to kiss her.

Now it would never behoove a mortal noblewoman of the Middle Ages to be so forward with a stranger. A woman of the Queen's character and bearing would never instigate a kiss with a man she had just come upon, so we understand that there is more here than just sexual desire. Thomas knows it too, and he knows that to kiss a denizen of Faerie may bring his destruction. He says, "Betide me weal, betide me woe/That weird shall never daunton me." Meaning "though it bless me or harm me, I shall not be daunted by the task." And he kisses her.

In doing so, he ties his destiny to her, giving her control over his fate. She tells him that, having tasted her kiss, "True Thomas, ye maun go wi me/And ye maun serve me seven years/Thro weal or woe, as chance to be." Thomas has by his desire made of himself her servant, indebted to her for seven years. Thomas must know, being a bard, that seven years is just the timeframe of the tithe to Hell. Yet he has given the Queen his kiss, and so perhaps his life. Wouldn't you, perhaps, in the same position?

Again, let us refer to the *Mabinogion* for a comparison. When the mortal Pwyll confronts Rhiannon, the Underworld Queen, she tells him boldly that she is to be his lover:

So the maiden stopped, and she threw back that part of her head-dress which covered her face. And she fixed her eyes upon him, and began to talk with him. "Lady," asked he, "whence comest thou, and whereunto dost thou journey?" "I journey on mine own errand," said she, "and right glad am I to see thee." "My greeting be unto thee," said he. Then he thought that the beauty of all the maidens, and all the ladies that he had ever seen, was as nothing compared to her beauty. "Lady," he said, "wilt thou tell me aught concerning thy purpose?" "I will tell thee," said she. "My chief quest was to seek thee." (Guest 1877, 346–347)

Again, a brazen statement for a medieval woman. As we will see again and again, stories of the Kindly Ones exhibit a wanton sexuality that people of the day would not have been comfortable expressing in human terms. In a certain sense, the journey to the Faerie world is a journey to an abandon of sexual mores, a descent into a sexual depravity that common life will not permit (I know what you're saying . . . "where do I sign up?"). We will see this often in Faerie stories. In a word, Faeries are the hussies of folklore, and their sexuality often spells destruction and death for mere mortals, who are their sexual playthings.

Now in her service, Thomas mounts the Queen's white steed behind her, placing her in control of the ride and of his life. They ride through a desert, where "living land" is "left behind." All this time the horse rides faster than the wind. They have left Thomas's land, Scotland, and have begun a slow descent to the Faerie world.

In a moment the Queen asks Thomas to dismount, so that she may show him the landscape. He lays his head upon her knee, a very intimate stance, and the Queen points out three roads before him. The road blazoned with thorns and briars is, she says, the road to Heaven, where few go. The nicer road, strewn with lilies, is the road to Hell. She tells him many find it a pleasing road. Finally she shows him the "bonny bonny road, that lies across the fernie brae," the meadow. That road will take them to Elfland. (The road to Elfland is strewn with meadow flowers, marking it as part of nature, and of the natural world that Faeries control.)

At this point the Queen warns Thomas sternly of one of the cardinal rules of journeys to Faerie: don't talk to anyone there, or you're in a heap of trouble. "But, Thomas, ye maun hold your tongue/Whatever ye may hear or see/For, if you speak word in Elflyn land/Ye'll neer get back to your ain countrie." Thomas is warned that if he speaks while in the Elf world, he's stuck there, doomed never to return to his own world.

So armed, Thomas finds himself riding "thro red blude [blood] to the knee" for fourteen days and fourteen nights. Not pleasant. Finally they come to a beautiful garden, where she offers Thomas an apple. Thomas is told that the apple will give him a gift, the ability to see and speak the truth.

It does not take a folkloric genius to see the parallel here to a certain Biblical story. But let us examine that story in light of Faerie lore and Paganism, and compare it to the saga of Thomas. It will be a short diversion, but an interesting one.

Now to begin with, Genesis 1 when read in Hebrew tells how Elohim, אלהים, created the Heavens and the Earth. Elohim is a plural name of God; literally, Gods. So we are told in Hebrew that The Gods created the Heavens and the Earth.

The story in Genesis 1 moves through the creation of waters, dry land, plants, animals and finally humans. Using the plural form of God, Gods, we read "Elohim [The Gods] created man in their own image. In the image of [the Gods] created He them. Male and female created [They] them." (KJV, Gen. 1:27)

ויברא אלהים האדם-את, בצלמו
לסבב אלהים ברא אתו:
זכר וגקבה, בדא אתם.

In Genesis 2, verse 4, the name of God suddenly changes. Yahweh (יהוה), the God of the Hebrews, creates his own man, one separate from the creation by the other collective Gods (the Elohim). He breathes life into a man made from dust (we are not told what the other people of the earth are made from) then sets this man into a bountiful garden on the Tigris and Euphrates Rivers, wherein he created animals and fruit-bearing trees. Yahweh makes a covenant with Adam (in Hebrew, a name loosely meaning "First Man"), forbidding him from eating certain fruit at the center of the Garden. In time, he puts the man to sleep and creates a woman from his rib. Yahweh then leaves the two to dwell undisturbed in the Garden.

So as Genesis begins, Eden is a place separate from the rest of the Creation, a place guarded over by a separate God who does not wish to take part in the Creation of the other Gods. In this sense, Eden is like the Faerie world, a place apart, on its own time and in its own space.

The Kabalists, Jewish mystics who study ancient Hebrew knowledge, see Eden just this way. To them Eden is both a place of trance state, and a physical place where the most devout might go. There is a story of three devout rabbis who, through prayer and trance, reach Eden. One sees the place and dies immediately. The second returns, but has lost his sanity. The third returns, but will never speak of what he has experienced. So it is a Kabalistic maxim that "for every three who enter the Garden, one will die, one will go mad, and one will return but never say what he has seen there." Likewise, for humans who visit Faerie, many die, and others return without their wits. Few come back whole, and those who do have the Faerie sight, the ability to see what no other mortals see. Hence they cannot speak of what they see, for no one understands this gift. This is echoed again in a bardic lay associated with Taliesin, the great Welsh bard: "Three times the loading of Prydwen we went there, Besides seven none returned from Caer Sidi." Here a great number sail to Caer Sidi, the castle of Faerie (or the Spinning Castle), but only seven return.

Now at this point in Genesis 2, Yahweh has never spoken to Eve. Eve, in fact, has never even seen Yahweh. Yahweh's covenant with Adam is enacted before Eve existed, and no one has spoken of it to her.

So when Eve meets the Serpent, she is unaware of any limitation upon her diet.

The Serpent is an interesting character in the Hebrew Bible. For centuries before the Hebrews came to dwell in Zion, the snake or serpent was a symbol of the Goddess, the Queen of Heaven. Rhea, a Babylonian Goddess, holds snakes in her outstretched hands, her breasts bared by her flowing garment. Hecate of Turkey is associated with the snake, as well as the horse and the dog.

The snake or serpent is a symbol of rebirth, because it sheds its skin and so recreates itself. While the serpent was sacred among the "other people" [than the Hebrews], the people of other Gods, the serpent was certainly associated by the ancient Hebrews with the Goddess Asherah and with the Goddess Lilith. Asherah was worshipped by the children of Israel from time immemorial, and is often mentioned in the Torah and in other Jewish scripture. And Lilith is often pictured as an owl woman with a serpent at her feet. So we ought to understand that when Eve (Hebrew *chavvah*, חוה or Arabic *hawwah*, "living one" or "source of life;" so Eve is associated with various life-giving Semitic Goddesses) is approached by the serpent, it is because the creature is a Goddess, the Queen of Heaven, who sees Eve, being woman, as of her own province here in male-dominated Eden. Because Eve has made no covenant with Yahweh, the serpent feels free to make her own covenant with the human woman, sealed with a bite of the fruit (Genesis just refers to "the fruit" and it is never stated with any certainty what fruit it actually might have been; modern European and American cultures assume it was an apple). That apple bears a gift for Eve; the knowledge that, like the Goddess, she is capable of creating life. That seems to be the inference of "the Tree of Knowledge."

Eve has no idea that Adam's covenant with Yahweh, made before she existed, forbids Adam from eating this Goddess-given fruit. She offers it to him in complete innocence. But doing so unleashes their sexual desire for each other, perhaps just what the serpent Goddess intended so that they could procreate and join the life-giving force of the natural world around them.

Like the serpent, the Queen of Elfland wears the colors of a verdant garden, green silk. She takes Thomas to a place that lies between heaven and Hell (like Yahweh's Garden), where she tempts him to seal the covenant engendered by their kiss, doing so by offering him a fruit, the ripe, voluptuous apple. Red as the cheek of a maiden flushed with excitement, round as a bosom. While she is not nude, as Eve had been, we have seen that the Queen of Elfland wears her sexuality overtly, brazenly and unapologetically. The apple is her sexual compact with Thomas, who, upon tasting it, will be enthralled by her completely. There will be no hope for him. He is hers to do with as she likes. Pay the tithe to Hell with him. Or return him to his own world. But while he may return to the mortal realms, as a result of eating "the fruit of knowledge," Thomas will ever have the Faerie sight, and never be able to speak a lie. He will always bear the mark of his journey to the Otherworld, and ever stand apart from other men.

The same temptation is in one of the stories the Grimms collected. When Snow White eats of a sensuous fruit (an apple in some versions, a tomato in others), she faints away, entering a half world that is much like the twilight of Faerie, where her experience of time loses its connection with our time. In this state she is susceptible to the advances of her savior, the prince. She could not have succumbed to her lover while she was awake in our world, her chastity guarded by the vigilant Dwarves. In another version of the story, called Briar Rose, the entire castle falls under the spell, and the girl's family and servants sleep with her for a hundred years.

Sleep is a state between life and death, where time passes unnoticed, and the sleeper receives prophecy in the form of dreams. Both Snow White and Briar Rose needed to enter the dream state, the state of the Faerie world, so that they could receive prophetic visions of their true lover/rescuer. In "True Thomas," he came out of his voyage with prophetic ability as well. Thomas is given the gift of true speech. (Don't worry. There is a lot more to say about Snow White.)

Thomas tells the Queen that he has always been truthful in his dealings with "prince or peer," but the Queen warns him to be silent with everyone in the mortal world: the same warning she gave him in the Faerie realm. From now on, speaking in the mortal world carries a bit of a curse: he must always tell the truth. Upon his return he is hailed as a soothsayer, and Thomas can never lie.

Seven years have passed in the Faerie world during Thomas's sojourn there, but before he can be claimed as the tithe to Hell, Thomas is returned to our mortal Earth. We are never told why the Elf Queen spares Thomas from the tithe. We can only assume that the sex was good. Or that she actually fell in love with the minstrel, enough that she could not bear to kill him.

⚬

Looking back for a moment at Asherah, Eve, the Serpent, Rhiannon and our Elf Queen, here are some points in which the Queen of Elf-land and the Serpent Goddess of Genesis bear a marked resemblance:

- Both are sexual and sensuous.
- Both are native to the wild places, the forest or the Garden.
- Both come unbidden. Thomas is simply sitting by Huntley Bank; Eve is simply wandering the Garden. Neither takes any action that would elicit a visit, other than both mortals being in a wild, green, natural place. Once they show up, each Otherworldly being sees their respective mortal as their own to claim.
- Both mortals are put in peril by the actions of their Otherworldly visitor: Eve risks the wrath of Yahweh, and death in childbirth. Thomas risks being given over as the tithe to Hell or dying in the Faerie Land without ever returning to the mortal world.
- Each mortal survives the encounter, making a covenant with their Otherworldly visitor, but each bears a lifelong curse and a

gift because of their covenant, one that is not normal or natural in their world. For Eve, the curse is pain in childbirth; the gift is knowledge of her body. Yahweh seems not to have intended women to experience pain while giving birth until placing this curse on Eve; on the other hand, the serpent's gift seems to have made Eve aware that she is capable of giving life. For Thomas, he is cursed with the Faerie sight, seeing a world that he blissfully knew, but like Adam, may never return to. His gift is "true speech," or prophecy, for which he becomes mega-famous.

The similarities between Thomas and Eve seem to point to a notion of the interaction between the Otherworld and the mortal world common to both British and Hebrew myth. That the Otherworld is lovely and perilous, and that a covenant can be made between our world and theirs is shown in both stories.

PWYLL'S COVENANT WITH THE UNDERWORLD

A similar story of the covenant between our world and the Faerie world is seen in the *Mabinogion*.

While there is an element of sexuality in this story, it begins with a covenant being made between two males, a man of our world (Pwyll) and a denizen if the Underworld, an antlered God of the hunt.

In the *Mabinogion*, Pwyll, prince of the Welsh kingdom Dyved, is hunting in his cantrev (kingdom) of Glyn Cuch with his pack of dogs. He sees a great stag being set upon by another pack of dogs. These dogs are white, with red ears.

While people in the United States are taught that black animals are of the Underworld, or perhaps of Hell, the British have always regarded white animals as Otherworldly. In all stories of Faerie and of the Gods of the Underworld, animals are seen as being white, with red ears and perhaps glowing red eyes. Pwyll should have had a clue almost immediately that these dogs were not of the mortal world. The *Mabinogion* says:

Then looked he at the colour of the dogs, staying not to look at the stag, and of all the hounds that he had seen in the world, he had never seen any that were like unto these. For their hair was of a brilliant shining white, and their ears were red; and as the whiteness of their bodies shone, so did the redness of their ears glisten. (Guest 1877, 340)

Pwyll then sets his own dogs onto the stag, chasing the white pack away. His dogs bring the stag down, and Pwyll celebrates his kill. But the celebration is short lived.

In an instant, looming before Pwyll is Arawn, a King of Annwn, the Welsh Underworld. He tells Pwyll that for the trespass of stealing his kill from him, Pwyll owes Arawn his life. But Arawn will take a less severe payment: Pwyll (whose name means "thought") must trade places with Arawn, serving as Lord of the Underworld for a year, and sleeping with Arawn's wife. In that time, Arawn will live as Pwyll in the mortal world. Arawn explains that all will perceive Pwyll as Arawn, and vice versa, so great is Arawn's magic. Further, Pwyll must fight Arawn's enemy, Havgan, and defeat him in order to return to the mortal world.

Pwyll agrees to the bargain and journeys for one year into the Underworld, or the land of death. However, there is one part of the bargain he will not keep: he does not have sex with Arawn's wife, but sleeps with his back to her each night. At the end of this year, he faces Havgan in battle, and deals him a great blow. Havgan begs for Pwyll to kill him, but Pwyll will not, which is as Arawn had instructed him. Havgan says that he will now die (this is a very similar passage to the battle scene in *Sir Gawain and the Green Knight*; the Green Knight is also an underworld lord who can only be defeated by a mortal opponent refraining from striking a killing blow).

When Pwyll returns to his own cantrev, he learns that Arawn has ruled wisely in his stead, and his people are prosperous. It is after his return that Pwyll falls in love with Rhiannon, the Faerie Queen-like horse woman.

Looking at the stories of Pwyll and of Thomas, you might catch a few marked similarities: In each, a ruler of the Underworld seeks out a mortal whom the ruler sees as his or hers to command. In the case of Pwyll, Arawn uses Pwyll's usurping of the stag as his excuse, but I really think that this was a ruse, designed to cause Pwyll to come under Arawn's command. Thomas, of course, seems marked by the Queen before the action of the story even begins. Conditions are made for the return of each mortal to his own lands. For Thomas, he must be ruled by the Queen, and speak to no one. For Pwyll, he must successfully battle Havgan. Only these actions will return the mortal's life to normal. When each mortal returns, he learns that some magical advantage has been bestowed upon him. For Thomas, he is a soothsayer, and may only speak the truth. For Pwyll, his kingdom has been blessed with prosperity, and he soon finds and falls in love with an Otherworldly wife, Rhiannon.

Patrick Ford, translator and scholar of the *Mabinogion*, has this interesting theory: that to cement the covenant between the two worlds, Pwyll was meant to have sex with Arawn's wife. Out of his sense of chivalry, Pwyll refrained from this, even though he found Arawn's wife quite lovely: "And with them came in likewise the Queen, who was the fairest woman that he had ever yet beheld." (Guest 1877, 342) But because of his failure to consummate a marriage with Arawn's wife, Pwyll was given another chance to seal the covenant, by marrying the Otherworldly woman Rhiannon. Now the bargain was certain, sealed with sexual fruit, just as it was in the story of Eve, and the tale of Snow White.

In each case, the Faerie ruler needed a human to serve some purpose in Faerie. Arawn needed a mortal warrior to defeat Havgan. Perhaps Arawn was impressed with Pwyll's ruthlessness or tenacity when the human chased the strange pack of dogs away, and commanded his own dogs to kill the stag. (The stag of course is a symbol of both Kingship, and of Arawn's identity as an antlered God of the hunt.) The Lord of the Death World, for whatever reason, was confident that a Mortal in his form, armed with the knowledge of Underworld magic, could defeat Arawn's enemy.

In the case of the Elvin Queen, we can only assume that Thomas was meant to be the tithe to Hell, but that she had a change of heart when the seven years had passed. There seems to be some genuine affection between the Queen and her human lover. She is patient with him, taking the time to explain to him the crossroads that lead to Heaven, Hell and Faerie, and she is sensual when she offers Thomas her sexuality in the form of the apple. Perhaps she is unable, after seven years spent together, to give the Devil her human lover as a sacrifice.

OSSIAN'S JOURNEY WITH NIAMH

Another instance of true love between mortal and Faerie is in the story of Ossian. Ossian is the son of Ireland's greatest hero, Finn Mac Coul. Ossian's name means "Little Deer," and he is named this due to the rather strange circumstances of his birth.

Finn Mac Coul, it seems, was hunting one day, when he saw a white doe. He made to loose an arrow upon the doe, but the doe spoke to Finn, saying, "Do not shoot me, but take me to your castle and you will behold a wonder."

Unused to being spoken to by forest creatures, Finn obliged the doe. Once inside the walls of Finn's castle, the doe turned to a lovely woman. She explained that she was Sadb, a daughter of Bodb the Red, a king of the Sidhe. A rival goddess had changed her into a deer, but the enchantment held no power in Finn's castle.

Upon seeing the doe shape-shift into this beauty, Finn did what any self-respecting Irish hero would have done, and in nine months, Ossian was born.

Fast forward two decades, give or take a week. Now a young man, Ossian is walking in the forest one day, when he hears harp music and a lovely voice, one whose singing seems to drive any other thought out of Ossian's mind. He searches, but though he can clearly hear the music, he cannot see the singer. Slowly a woman appears before him, sitting upon a hill playing her harp. It is Niamh of the Golden Hair.

The Gaelic poet Michael Comyn (born c. 1688), who, in the eighteenth century, rewove the ancient story into his own words, describes Niamh this way:

> A royal crown was on her head;
> And a brown mantle of precious silk,
> Spangled with stars of red gold,
> Covering her shoes down to the grass.
>
> A gold ring was hanging down
> From each yellow curl of her golden hair;
> Her eyes, blue, clear, and cloudless,
> Like a dew-drop on the top of the grass.
>
> Redder were her cheeks than the rose,
> Fairer was her visage than the swan upon the wave,
> And more sweet was the taste of her balsam lips
> Than honey mingled thro' red wine.
>
> A garment, wide, long, and smooth
> Covered the white steed,
> There was a comely saddle of red gold,
> And her right hand held a bridle with a golden bit.
>
> Four shoes well-shaped were under him,
> Of the yellow gold of the purest quality;
> A silver wreath was on the back of his head,
> And there was not in the world a steed better.
> (Squire 1905, 223)

Niamh explains to Ossian that she has come from Tir N'an Og, the Land of the Young, to take Ossian back to rule that land with her. Ossian is quickly convinced that this is a good idea, and climbs upon Niamh's magical white horse. They begin to ride over the Western Ocean (it is understood that this Faerie horse can ride on water). As they journey, Ossian sees a stag jumping from wave to wave, chased by a white dog with red ears. He later stops to fight a Fomor giant, an ancient foe of the Tuatha De Danaan (the Irish people of the Goddess Danaan or Dana) who has imprisoned a Tuatha woman. After a battle lasting several days, Ossian defeats the giant, and he and Niamh ride on.

Following a fortnight of riding, they come to the isle of Tir N'an Og. There Ossian feasts, hunts, and makes love to his bride for seven years, until one day he remembers Ireland and the Fenians, and grows homesick. He asks Niamh if he may take her magical white horse over the Western Ocean once again to visit his home.

But Niamh begs him not to go, for she is sure that he will never return to her. In time she relents, and Ossian rides off.

When Ossian returns to Ireland, he finds it populated by tiny people. He asks where the Fenians might be, and the people tell him that they are remembered only in legend, and that they died three hundred years ago. While seven years have passed in Tir N'an Og, three hundred years have passed in Ireland.

Ossian resolves to return to Niamh, but as he is leaving Ireland, he sees some of the tiny Irish struggling to lift a large stone. He tries to help them, and in doing so, falls from the saddle of his horse. Upon touching the ground, he becomes three hundred years old, and lays dying.

The legend says that this is how Saint Patrick finds him. Ossian recounts all of the tales of Finn Mac Coul and the Fenians to the saint, which is how we know them today. Finally, Saint Patrick asks Ossian "Before you leave this world, do you wish to convert to Christianity, so you'll go to Heaven?"

Ossian asks "Are the Fenians in Heaven?"

"No," Saint Patrick answers. "They were Pagan, so they went to Hell."

"Well," Ossian says. "If Heaven's not good enough for the Fenians, it's not good enough for me!" And saying so, Ossian dies.

There are some striking similarities between Ossian's tale and the other stories of the journey to Faerie Land. For one, the trip itself. Ossian must mount Niamh's magical white horse and bound over the Western Ocean. This is exactly like Thomas, who must mount the Faerie Queen's horse to journey to Elfland. Both mortals must ride for fourteen days and nights to reach the magical world.

The crossing of liquid seems a constant in the journey to the Faerie world. Ossian must spend his fourteen days crossing the Western Ocean. Thomas crossed "red blood to the knee." In the version of Thomas the Rhymer that we've looked at here, there are also references to "rivers aboon the knee," a reference not to blood but to water, like the Western Ocean.

In a similar Irish legend, Bran Mac Febal crossed the Western Ocean in a coracle, a small round boat, to come to the Isle of Women. He had been bidden to come there, like Ossian, by the queen of that land, who came to Ireland to claim him as her lover.

THE VOYAGE OF BRAN MAC FEBAL

The Voyage of Bran Mac Febal has a good deal of elements in common with both the story of Ossian, and the Arthurian legend of the Isle of Apples (Avalon). This story begins as Bran (which is Irish for Raven) is lulled to sleep in the forest by Otherworldly music. When he wakes he finds a silver branch lying next to him, from a tree he does not recognize. He takes this branch to his hall, where he assembles his men. A strange, beautiful woman appears, and begins to sing to the assembly of a land far away, the Isle of Women. Bran decides at that moment to sail to this land.

He gathers three groups of nine men to accompany him, and they set sail. After being at sea a short time, they meet Manannan Mac Lir, the sea God, riding his chariot. The God tells Bran he is not on the sea, but on a plain of flowers. He also says that there are many men in chariots riding here, but they are invisible.

Bran and his men sail on, until they see an island. The people of the Island of Joy come to the shore, but they are laughing and staring, and will not respond to Bran's call. One of Bran's men goes ashore, and he too begins laughing and staring. Bran's party leaves him there and sails on.

The men come to the Isle of Women, but after their experience at the Isle of Joy, the men are afraid to go ashore. The women of the isle throw Bran a magical line, and reel the men in. There the men pair off with the women, Bran with the Queen and his men with the other women. They feast and make love for one year. But one of Bran's men, Nechtan Mac Collbran, becomes desperately homesick. The party decides to return to Ireland.

After sailing home and reaching Ireland, the party sees that things there are very different. Centuries have passed since they left. Nechtan becomes upset, and jumps off the boat. As soon as he touches the shore, he turns to ashes.

From the boat, Bran and his men tell the Irish their story. They then set sail, never to be seen again.

This story has many of the same elements in the journey to Faerie and the return. First, like Ossian and Thomas, Bran is visited by an Otherworldly beauty, blessed with every characteristic of a Nymph (as we will see in chapter 6). The woman lulls Bran and his men into visiting her world, the Isle of Women (Eden, the Faerie world, Tir N'an Og).

During the journey, they reach a world where those who have seen the Otherworld go mad. One man shares this fate.

Finally they reach the Isle of Women. There they spend what seems like a year, though centuries pass in their world. When they grow homesick, they return, but die if they try to live among mortals. So like the three rabbis, one has gone mad, one has died, and Bran and his surviving men return but cannot share their experiences of the Isle of Women other than simply relating that they have journeyed there. Unable to live now in the mortal world, they sail off, disappearing forever. (For the full text of *The Voyage of Bran Mac Febal*, see the Appendix.)

WATER AND THE JOURNEY TO FAERIE

Water is a constant in the journey to Faerie. Another story from the *Mabinogion* is about Bendigai Vran, or Bran the Blessed, and his sister, Branwen. (If you notice a lot of men with this name, it's because Bran means "Raven" in both Welsh and Irish; Branwen means "White Raven.")

In this story, Bran the Blessed must cross the Irish Sea to rescue Branwen from an imprisonment in a kitchen galley, in a land where birds can speak. In fact, Bran becomes aware of Branwen's captivity when a wren flies from the enchanted land to Wales to tell him of his sister's plight. Bran, being "so large no house can contain him," forms a bridge by throwing himself across the Irish Sea so that his soldiers might cross.

In Greek myth, the dead cross a series of rivers to reach Hades, the land of Death, ferried across by Charon, the ferryman who charges a coin placed in the mouth of the corpse. Perhaps the best known of these rivers is the River Styx, which is said to wind nine times around Hades. In all there are five rivers: Acheron, the river of woe; Cocytus, the river of lamentation; Phlegethon, the river of fire; Lethe, the river of forgetfulness; and Styx, the river of hate. It was said that if a God broke an oath, he would be forced by Zeus to drink the water from the river Styx, which was so foul he would lose his voice for nine years (reminiscent of being unable to say what he had seen in the Land of the Dead, where he obviously must go to get this draught).

The Land of Death is ruled by a stern king, Hades. Hades can come into our world when he has a need, much like Arawn in the *Mabinogion*. For instance, Hades comes into our world to find and fall in love with Persephone, whom he first sees bathing in a stream of flowing water at Innes. He takes her to his land, forcing her mother, Demeter, to search for her. We learn that Persephone has eaten six pomegranate seeds in the Underworld, and so is bound to that land. Demeter argues with Hades for her daughter's return to Earth, and their ultimate bargain over Persephone creates the seasons of the year. Here is the theme of not eating food from the Enchanted Lands, or you'll be bound to that place.

While treading through the waters of Greek myth, there is also Europa. Courted by Zeus in the form of a white bull, Europa is transported from her home in Turkey across the Mediterranean by Zeus. She is told that the sons Zeus gives her will people a new land, which will be named for her. Again, the mother of Europe must cross water to come to this land of promise.

In each record of the journey to a land of enchantment, a river or sea must be crossed. In many cases, the myth draws upon a body of water that the storyteller might see and visit in our world: the Irish Sea, the Atlantic Ocean, the Mediterranean, or in Eve's case, the Tigris and Euphrates. In Estonian folklore, the Underworld is said to lie in the Northern Sea, and is peopled by tiny inhabitants who appear childlike. Finnish stories tell of a tiny enchanted man emerging from the sea. Siberian tales place the Otherworld in water too, at the mouth of the River Ob.

Water as an archetype looms large in Faerie lore. As a psychological element, the crossing of water in the journey to Faerie represents going into the unconsciousness, entering the Shamanic or trance experience. In a purely analogous view of these stories, the journey to Faerie is a journey through the psyche, a mystic trek through the dangerous landscape of the inner mind. But I do not believe that the stories we have inherited are purely analogous. I believe somewhere in space and time there is a real Faerie world, which mortals like Thomas have reached.

Putting archetype aside, how did water get into so many Faerie myths? Was it a historical fact? Could the original Faeries, the Picts, have been a seafaring people? Or dam builders, building moats around their villages against intrusion? Perhaps the Celts had to cross rivers to reach the Picts, and so a legend was born? Or did seers of the Celts share the vision of the Greeks and Egyptians, seeing the crossing of a great river before entering the Otherworld?

I think the Picts might have had some imprint on the journey to Faerie. But I think, more importantly, the trip over water represents the passage through the mist or veil between our world and the world of the Fey. This veil might indeed be a river or sea, or it might be a fog or mist, a wet transition taken over minutes, hours or even days or weeks.

Of all the four elements, water is possibly the most primal. It is the great cauldron in which all life was formed. The Torah reflects knowledge of this. Genesis 1 says, "The Earth was without form, and void, and the spirit of God [Elohim] moved across the face of the waters." (KJV, Gen. 1:2) In this chapter of Genesis (unlike the second account of Creation in Genesis 2), dry land appears from under the water, and life is formed first in water, then on land.

Later in Genesis, Yahweh decides to stage a new creation, on his own this time, and causes a great flood that only a chosen set of humans and animals survive. Perhaps the Elohim, including Yahweh, may only begin the creation of a world from water?

In Hebrew, water is symbolized by the letter *mem* (מ), and rain is *mayim* (starting and ending with *mem*). The word for the Gods, Elohim, ends with *mem*. To a student of Kabalah, each letter of the Hebrew alphabet has amazing magical powers, and the occurrence of *mem*, and its correspondence to the source of Creation and to the name of the Gods, would be of great importance in understanding the power of the Gods. So we understand that water is an important element in the magic of creation.

In the Tarot, each of the Major Arcana cards corresponds to a Hebrew letter, and the card associated with *Mem* is The Hanged Man. In this card, a man is suspended upside down (A. E. Waite, Paul Foster Case and other Tarot experts see him as the Fool, who appears in card 0). The suspension device above him is made of living wood, and is often depicted in the shape of the Hebrew letter *mem*.

One set of meanings of the card is the unconscious journey, the shaman's experience, and sacrifice. Odin hung in this position on

Ygdrassil, the World Tree (correlating to the Hebrew Tree of Life) to gain wisdom, as did the older Norse God Tewaz before him (both Odin, or Wodin, and Tewaz are remembered in our days of the week: Wodin in Wodinsday, Wednesday; and Tewaz in Tuesday). In this way the Hanged Man is both wisdom and sacrifice.

He is also introspection and reflection. Because the card is equated to the letter *Mem*, we can assume the Hanged Man hangs above a body of water. When something in the physical world hangs above water upside down, it is reflected in the water right-side-up. Through the Hanged Man's sacrifice, the world will be made right; by suspending himself upside down, he brings his life into order, right-side-up. Faerie water is a mirror of our world, reversing what we see as reality.

So in Kabalah, water represents both sacrifice and the emergence of wisdom from the unconscious mind. To truly see the world right ways up, one must suspend one's place in it, and view it askance, or upside down. When our mortal heroes cross the water, they leave their "normal" perceptions of our world behind. They come back with their sense of time skewed, and with abilities life in our world does not offer: in Thomas's case, the Faerie sight and truth telling. While Ossian is abnormally strong when he returns to our world, his time sense was completely flawed. And like the Kabalistic rabbis, he could never tell of what he had seen in that enchanted world, only of having been there. The same applies to Bran Mac Febal and his men.

Sacrifice as a meaning of *Mem*, the Hanged Man, is seen in Thomas taking the risk of being the tithe to Hell. Mortals are often called to Faerie to be sacrificed, first experiencing this divine, magical realm, then being given to Hell as an offering. Thomas, like Odin or Tewaz, goes willingly. "'Betide me weal, betide me woe/That weird shall never daunton me." Thomas says: Whether it brings me good or evil, this will not daunt me. Thomas is willing to die, if he can know the Faerie Land and the love of its Queen.

In the Tarot, water also represents emotion and intuition. Thomas's crossing water on the journey to Faerie gives him the gift of prophecy, the greatest expression of intuition. As far as emotion, from Tomas to Ossian to Bran Mac Febal, each mortal falls so deeply in love with his Faerie woman that he is willing to follow her into her far-off realm despite the risks. In fact, in the next few chapters the Faerie seductress appears in many stories and songs.

Many Faeries come to our world from the water. Selkies come from the sea. Lorelie, a seducer Faerie of Germany, emerges from the Rhine River. Many Nymphs are associated with rivers, streams, clouds and rainstorms. In each of these cases, the journey across water goes both ways, to and from Faerie.

Water reflects reality upside down, as with the Hanged Man card. The Faerie record is full of incidents of things being reversed the way reality is reversed when reflected in water. The Fairy tales collected by the Grimms are full of examples of this: the true mother leaves, and a cruel, unloving mother takes her place; the rightful sister is made a servant, and the ugly, cruel sisters are given the run of the house; a girl is courted by a bear, a frog, or a bird; a common household item, such as a drop spindle or an apple, becomes poisonous or deadly; a girl acts as wife to Dwarves, a gruesome beast, or an old woman. In other Faerie legends, changelings are taken from their place in the mortal world, and given a place in the world of the Fey; valuables such as gold turn to the most base, common materials, such as leaves and twigs; a solid place, such as a hill or mound, becomes a door to another world.

Faeries are constantly drawn to anything with a reflective quality. The way to appease house Faeries is to give them shiny objects; Mermaids always study themselves in a mirror; the evil Queen owns a mirror that predicts the future. This is not vanity, but the attraction of the Kindly Ones to anything waterlike and reflective, revealing the essence of their world, which exists on the other side of the water barrier. As we look at the folkloric record, we'll see the journey across water many more times.

TIME AND THE JOURNEY TO FAERIE

Let's talk about another characteristic of Faerie folklore, one we've already speculated on a bit, the problem of time.

The Ossian myth tells us little about Ossian's stay in Tir N'an Og. Perhaps like the three rabbis or like Bran Mac Febal, Ossian was unable to tell of his adventures in that land to Saint Patrick, who records the hero's stories before Ossian dies of profound old age. He could return, but could not tell what he had seen there. But we do know this: that like Rip Van Winkle, Ossian's seven years in Tir N'an Og lasted three hundred years in our world. Inspired by his knowledge of Faerie stories like Ossian's, C. S. Lewis has the young hero of *The Final Battle*, Eustace, exclaim to his companion upon a trip to Narnia, "It's the usual muddle about times, Pole." To which the sitting Narnian king replies, "That too comes in all the old tales. The time of your strange land is different than ours."

How do Faeries perceive time in our land? Do their journeys here lose time upon their return? Or gain it? We aren't told much about this in the old stories. But the Faeries that come to our world seem at home with time here, and able to come and go at will. If anything, they seem to command time in our world. The Elf Queen, Niamh and the Queen of the Isle of Women all seem to appear to their lovers, Thomas, Ossian and Bran Mac Febal, at the precise moment these mortals will notice them. And while Sadb seems to be simply wandering the forest, vulnerable to hunters, she has fallen quite conveniently into the sights of Ireland's greatest hero, Finn Mac Coul, the one man who can communicate with her in her deer state and save her. Was this by her well-timed design?

The Faerie women in these tales see through the veil of the two worlds, identify their potential lover (or victim), and come at just the right moment. Is this a talent the Fey have developed over their centuries of flitting between our two worlds?

Some Faeries are summoned in "real time" by a single, instantaneous event in our world. Both Tam Lin and the Beast are summoned to our world by the pulling of a rose. Misery is also a call to the Kindly Ones. In the tales collected by the Grimm brothers, sorrow finds an Elfin ear: the Faerie Godmother in the case of the sobbing Cinderella; cobbling Elves in the case of the mournful shoemaker; and when the maid laments that she cannot spin straw into silk, her lamentation summons Rumplestiltskin, starting a guessing game between the two.

Faeries seem to have some innate ability to "read" time as it is perceived in our world. They can appear at just the right moment, and disappear in what to us seems like a night or a day. There is always a brief encounter that turns out to have been years or centuries.

We'll continue to look at water, time and Faerie divination. For now let's agree on these characteristics of the Faerie world:

- It is separated from us by time and water.

- Its denizens may come and go into our world at their will.

- The Faeries know us well enough, and see us as both sexual partners and as sacrificial lambs.

- When we mortals venture there, we may not survive. But if we do, we will be rewarded by both passionate gifts and unnatural abilities.

- But if we make it back, we will be unable to say what we have seen there, and we may go insane out of a desire to return.

The next chapter looks at mortals who have dared to reside in that world, and who travel at will between the worlds. Folklore calls them by several names, but perhaps the most common is changelings.

Chapter 3

CHANGELINGS

It was noon on a Tuesday, but Jamie could not get his wife out of bed. True, the baby had cried all night. All night, and again all morning. But by dawn, Mara had stopped responding, and Jamie had to do the best he could with a cloth dipped in warmed goat's milk.

"Mara, it's the baby again," Jamie said.

"I hear him," she said without expression.

"Will ye nae feed the poor bairn?"

"Poor bairn? Jamie, have you nae seen the child?"

"Aye," the man said. "So I have seen him."

"And he looks nae different to ye?" the woman asked, a deep frown passing over her usually soft face.

"Indeed he does so. He was the prettiest bairn a few days back, I swear, the color o' cream and berries. And now brown he is, like a nutmeg."

"You nae think it strange?" Mara asked her husband.

"I know nae the ways of infant children, Mara. I thought it might be a normal thing."

"Well I' taint," the woman sighed. "It is nae normal, and it is nae right."

Jamie thought for a moment. "I'll get the old woman, that I'll do. She'll know what ought to be done."

Mara heard the door close as Jamie went out. She sighed, and let the bairn shriek.

Changelings are mortals who exchange their human lives for Faerie lives. Whether by design or by chance, they are brought into the Faerie world, and become denizens thereof.

Many changelings are taken as babies by the Kindly Ones. Perhaps the most famous example of this is seen in Shakespeare's *A Midsummer Night's Dream*. Titania, Shakespeare's name for the Faerie Queen, has captured an Indian infant. Oberon, her husband, desires the child as his attendant. This conversation between Puck and a Faerie in Act 2, Scene 1, updates the audience on the situation:

> Puck:
> The king doth keep his revels here to-night:
> Take heed the queen come not within his sight;
> For Oberon is passing fell and wrath,
> Because that she as her attendant hath
> A lovely boy, stolen from an Indian king;
> She never had so sweet a changeling;
> And jealous Oberon would have the child
> Knight of his train, to trace the forests wild;
> But she perforce withholds the loved boy,
> Crowns him with flowers and makes him all her joy:
> And now they never meet in grove or green,
> By fountain clear, or spangled starlight sheen,
> But, they do square, that all their elves for fear
> Creep into acorn-cups and hide them there.
> (Shakespeare, *A Midsummer Night's Dream*, Act II, Scene 1, 18–31)

While Shakespeare never reveals the Faerie King's or Queen's motive for capturing the boy in the first place, we can guess that the child might someday become the tithe to Hell. But as an infant, the child is doted on by the Queen, and given all of her motherly affection.

The Faerie Queen, called Mab, Morgan, Titania, or Aine, is well known for taking human children. In one myth, the Faerie Queen leads the Wild Ride or Wild Hunt through the British forest at Samhain eve, or Hallowe'en. During this ride, she gathers up the spirits of crops killed in the harvest and of animals killed in the hunt. But if children are sleeping nearby, they too are gathered up in the ride through the forest and taken as changelings to the Faerie Lands. (If children sleep uneasily as Mab's train passes by, they are "riding the night mare," a phrase that has stuck with us.)

The notion of Faerie changelings exists in many European cultures, from England to Ireland, Germany to Denmark. Anywhere there are Faeries, in fact. In each culture, we hear of Faerie children left in return for human children. The Fey babies left in our world by the exchange are said to be ugly and yellowish of complexion. They will eat ravenously and leave no food for the rest of the family. In their first year of life, they will have grown a full set of teeth, and have claws for hands. The changeling might also be wiser than a human child. But a changeling will not live long. Though it eats everything in the cupboard, it will never thrive, and it will die in a few years. When buried, the changeling child's body will turn to a pile of leaves or a charred branch, called a stock.

In an example collected by the Grimms, Nixies that came into a certain town were humans who were stolen as children, and now live as Nixies, or water spirits:

> From time to time Nixies would emerge from the Saal River and go into the city of Saalfeld where they would buy fish at the market. They could be recognized by their large, dreadful eyes and by the hems of their skirts that were always dripping wet. It is said that they were mortals who, as children, had been

taken away by nixies, who had then left changelings in their place. (Ashliman 1996, Grimms, no. 60)

The Spanish have the same legend, and call these water Sprites Xana. The Xana exchange their babies for human ones to have their offspring baptized, and return the humans when their own children are properly christened.

Beauty in human children is believed to attract the Faerie exchange. This is why the Irish considered it bad luck to look too long or too fondly at a baby. Blond hair is a trait particularly sought by the Fey, but any beautiful girl or adorable boy might be at risk. One theory goes that the changeling exchange is a memory of an exiled group of people who lived in seclusion, and actually replaced their sick children with healthy, beautiful children from surrounding towns and farms. It is in fact a common folklore that Gypsies will steal non-Gypsy children.

Women who are newly married or new mothers are said to be most at risk. In Ireland, a fear of many a new mother is that her child will be stolen by Faeries, and an ugly demon child left in its place. A folk remedy for a woman who suspects that this has occurred is this: Boil water in an eggshell within proximity of the child's cradle. If the child is truly a Faerie, demon or troll, the creature will sit up in the cradle and speak, saying, "Though I've lived a thousand years, I've never seen water boiled in an eggshell!" Having blown its cover, so to speak, the Faerie will fly up the chimney, and the human child be replaced in the cradle.

In their book *Children's and Household Tales*, the Grimms tell the same story, collected in Germany:

A mother had her child taken from the cradle by elves. In its place they laid a changeling with a thick head and staring eyes who would do nothing but eat and drink. In distress she went to a neighbor and asked for advice. The neighbor told her to carry the changeling into the kitchen, set it on the hearth, make a fire, and boil water in two eggshells. That should make the changeling laugh, and if he laughs it will be all over with him. The woman did everything just as her neighbor said. When she placed the eggshells filled with water over the fire, the blockhead said:

Now I am as old
As the Wester Wood,
But have never seen anyone cooking in shells!

And he began laughing about it. When he laughed, a band of little elves suddenly appeared. They brought the rightful child, set it on the hearth, and took the changeling away. (Hunt 1884, ch. 39, Third Tale)

In another story, the mother brews ale in an acorn. The changeling child sits up in its cradle and proclaims: "Now I am as old as an oak in the woods but I have never seen beer being brewed in an acorn." (*Ibid.*)

Other very lovely courses of action include feeding the decrepit baby foxglove until its intestines burn out, or heating a shovel red hot and using it to lift the ugly child into a hearth fire. In all of the folklore, conventional wisdom says to badly mistreat the Faerie child. This awful treatment of the deformed infant will cause the Fey to return the human child.

Because of this horrendous treatment taught by folklore, cases have been known of women killing human children suspected of being Fey. There was a case in Norway where a mother killed her child by placing him into an oven, thinking the child was a changeling. In 1826 England, Anne Roche killed a boy named Michael Leahy because the boy was thought to be possessed by Faeries. And a famous Irish case involved Brigit Cleary, a grown woman killed by her husband and other men in 1895 after a local storyteller accused Brigit of being a changeling.

Safety is recommended over sorrow. Jacob Grimm offers these tips for preventing an exchange of your human baby for a Faerie child:

Placing a key next to an infant will prevent him from being exchanged.

Women may never be left alone during the first six weeks following childbirth, for the devil then has more power over them.

During the first six weeks following childbirth, mothers may not go to sleep until someone has come to watch the child. If mothers are overcome by sleep, changelings are often laid in the cradle. To prevent this one should lay a pair of men's pants over the cradle.

Whenever the mother leaves the infant's room she should lay an article of the father's clothing on the child, so that it cannot be exchanged. (Grimm 1877, 450–460)

In Grimm's suggestions is the old lore that iron (a key) or clothing can be used to banish the Fey. Other lore advises leaving scissors or an iron coin in the crib.

PRYDERI, THE CHANGELING CHILD

From the *Mabinogion*, that Welsh compendium of myth and folklore, comes a story of a changeling child and his falsely punished mother.

Pwyll, an earthly king who had visited the Otherworld, fell in love with Rhiannon when he saw her from the mound at Arberth. He and this woman of the Otherworld were married, the account tells us, and Rhiannon bears a son.

As night falls, six women are set to watch over Rhiannon and her newborn. But the women fall asleep, and when they wake, the child has vanished. The negligent women are terrified that they will be burnt at the stake for their crime, so they devise a plan. They kill a pup, and smear its blood on Rhiannon's face and hands. They wake the house, and claim that in a raging fit Rhiannon ate her own son, and that she was so violent that they could do nothing to stop her.

Pwyll did not want to punish his beloved wife, but his nobles demanded justice. So Rhiannon was sentenced thus: She must sit at the castle gate all day. Anyone who came to the castle must listen to the story of her crime. Then she must allow them to ride on her back into the castle. In other words, Rhiannon became a horse. She was commanded to do this for seven years.

Now at the same time, the lord of Gwent Ys Coed, whose name was Teirnon Twryv Vliant, saw that every May Eve his prized mare would foal, and the foal would disappear. He vowed to find the culprit, and so on this May Eve he stood watch over the mare. The moment the mare foaled, Teirnon saw a huge clawed hand come through the barn window and grab the foal. The lord drew his sword and hacked off the arm of the Otherworldly creature. Both arm and foal fell at the lord's feet.

At that moment he heard a noise inside his house, and when he looked, there was a baby lying on his floor swaddled in a brocade mantle. Teirnon was puzzled, but he and his wife decided to keep the boy as their own, as they were childless. They baptized the child Gwri Golden Hair, and raised him as their son. When he was old enough to ride, Teirnon gave Gwri the horse that had been born the night of his strange discovery.

But there came a time when Teirnon and his wife heard the story of Rhiannon's crime and her subsequent punishment. Teirnon carefully gathered information and considered what to do with the boy. He finally came to his wife and confided his suspicion that Gwri Golden Hair was actually Pwyll's son by Rhiannon. He even pointed out that the boy looked exactly like Pwyll, and his wife agreed. So they resigned themselves to return the boy to his true father, their king. Teirnon took three men with him, and Gwri rode the horse his father had given him.

They rode to the castle at Arberth, where Rhiannon told them as they approached that she had killed and eaten her son, and that she would ride each of them into the castle on her back. But Teirnon and his party declined to be carried. They rode their horses into the castle and sat at a feast table with Pwyll, where they told their king their story. All present agreed that the boy looked just like Pwyll, and that the women had lied on the night of his disappearance.

So Rhiannon was vindicated, and the boy was returned to his true father. Because of the years Rhiannon had spent in her punishment, and the relief of finding her son alive, the boy was renamed Pryderi, which means "care" or "anxiety." For their loving care of the boy, Teirnon and his wife were granted fostering of the child, and when he was old enough, Pryderi was given to Teirnon to train as a knight. In the end, Pryderi became king of Arberth, and married Kigva as his queen.

This very strange Welsh changeling tale is a mix of myth, tradition and Faerie lore. Let's take a closer look at each element.

Rhiannon is an Otherworldly woman, who appeared to Pwyll on a magical horse while he stood upon an enchanted mound. The two were married and had a child.

When that child disappears right after the birth, there is the false accusation. In order to escape punishment, the six women-in-waiting swear that their mistress has killed and eaten her own son in a violent rage. Violence and psychotic episodes often work their way into stories of Faerie kidnap. In the accounts of changelings, women are killed because they are assumed to be Fey, and women who have just given birth are never to be left alone for fear that the Fey will cause them to do terrible things to their child. In Shakespeare, the changeling child of Oberon and Titania causes the king and queen of Faeries to argue terribly with each other, so much so that their Faerie servants hide from them for fear of their rage. The presence of the Otherworld is felt keenly by a woman made vulnerable after giving birth, and a newborn child, especially a beautiful one, attracts the attention of the Good People and with it a high state of violent emotion.

Faerie presence also creates a reversal of roles (like a mirror reflection in water). In this case the queen becomes a servant, and her servants become the rulers of the grisly situation.

Rhiannon's punishment is to be turned into a horse, her job to mount visitors on her back and ride them into the castle. At the same time, each May Eve (Beltane, a time when the veil between our world and the Otherworld is thin) a foal is being kidnapped by the very Faerie that has taken Rhiannon's son. To further the association between horse and human, the boy is given the rescued foal as his own when he is old enough to ride, and he mounts this horse to return to his true mother. Here again is the Faerie reversal of roles: Gwri rides a changeling horse to his mother, but she must offer to assume the role of a horse and carry him before she can be restored as his true parent.

Horses are an animal associated with kingship among the Celts. In ancient Irish tradition, when a king is crowned, he must have sex with a white mare. The mare is then killed and cooked into a stew, which is eaten by all attending. The white mare is associated with many Celtic Goddesses, such as Rhiannon, Epona, Rigatona and Mari. The seed of the king inside the sacrificed mare represents the union of king and land, and is a symbolic sacrifice of the Seven Year King. The Seven Year King sacrifice is carried out by the Fey as the tithe to Hell. So one element of the strange kingship sex ritual is that it ties the king of Ireland to the Faerie world. In part, the king must derive his right to rule all of Ireland from both humans and the Fey.

The horse is also an animal that appears constantly in Faerie lore. In chapter 4, various Faerie creatures appear as horses, often seducing humans in this guise. Centaurs are a type of Faerie creature that appear as both horse and human, and have sex with humans, horses and other centaurs. Puck can also appear as a horse, causing both harm and good in that guise. Shakespeare alludes to this when he has Puck turn Bottom the actor into an ass, a horse that appears ridiculous to a human audience, yet is lovely and sexually desirable to the Faerie Queen (another Faerie role reversal).

The exchange of horse for heir apparent Pryderi is carried out across three worlds. In the Faerie world, the clawed creature steals both the prince himself and each foal born by Teirnon's prized mare. The Faerie creature intends to leave a changeling for Gwri/Pryderi, and that changeling would have been the snatched foal. But the Fey beast does not have to leave the animal. First a pup is exchanged for the newborn by Rhiannon's women. Then Rhiannon herself takes the foal's place, turned into a horse and mounted by humans visiting Arberth castle. Now the exchange is complete in two worlds, the Faerie world and the mortal world.

Finally, in the world of the Gods, the exchange takes place as well. Teirnon Twryv Vliant means "Man of Thunder" in Welsh, and the *Mabinogion* oddly describes Teirnon as "the best man in the world." (Guest 1877, 354) The thunder-wielding Sky God is a common Father God figure throughout European paganism, and this archetype is seen in such Gods as Zeus, Jupiter, Thor and Beli. It seems that after being stolen by the Fey, Pryderi is fostered by a Sky God, who has also traded the child for a horse, each of the foals stolen every May Eve. Here too is another Faerie role reversal, for the Sky God is subject to a mortal king, Pwyll, and his Underworld queen.

Finally, having been redeemed from being sacrificed as the tithe to Hell by none other than a God, Pryderi can return to the mortal world, where he will vindicate his mother. She can now live fully in the mortal world, and give up her Horse Faerie nature. Returned to the role of mortal mother, and in doing so completing the pact between her husband Pwyll and the Otherworld, she no longer has to show the world her horse Faerie nature. The Faerie role reversal is broken, and the Underworld no longer seems to have power in Rhiannon's life as a mortal woman.

But these things never work out that smoothly. Both Pryderi and Rhiannon are plagued by the Fey for many years to come. In a later

Mabinogion story, both Rhiannon and Kigva, Pryderi's wife, are kidnapped by a different Faerie, Llywd, son of Kil Coed ("the Grey One of the Woods"). Pryderi must capture Llywd's wife for a hostage exchange, which he does when the woman takes the form of a mouse. In the *Mabinogion's* most comic episode, Pryderi builds a tiny gallows and threatens to hang the little woman-mouse-Faerie as her husband disguises himself as a scholar, a king and a bishop to plead for her life and pay her ransom.

I wish I could say Pryderi's trouble with the Otherworld ends on this comical note, but sadly it does not. Later on in the *Mabinogion*, Pryderi is given a pog (herd) of pigs by Otherworldly Arawn, the first pigs ever to exist on earth. The pog of swine are meant to further the covenant between Arawn's world and Pryderi's house. But another enchanted character, Gwydion, covets these critters. First he pulls the oldest Faerie trick in the book: he gives Pryderi a big sack of money for the pigs. Of course, hours later, in the cold light of morning, the bag of gold coins turns out to be a bag of leaves and twigs. So Pryderi chases Gwydion down, and a fight ensues.

Now fights between humans and Otherworldly enchanters never end well for the human involved. So it was that Pryderi was killed, as a direct result of his ties to the Otherworld.

In many ways the story of Pryderi is very similar to the Arthurian legends, and Pryderi is much like Arthur's son Mordred. Arthur himself is born because of an enchantment, when Merlin (a character much like Gwydion) causes Uther Pendragon to shape shift into the nobleman Gorlois, so that Uther can have sex with Gorlois's wife, Ygrain. When Ygrain gives birth to Arthur, like Pryderi, the child is immediately spirited away, this time by Otherworldly Merlin. (Gwydion also spirits away a newborn child, his sister's son Llew Llaw Gyffes). Also like Pryderi, Arthur is fostered, never knowing his true parentage until he is old enough to assume his throne.

But things become even more enchanted when Arthur actually assumes the throne of England. Like all Celtic kings, including Pryderi,

Arthur must seal a covenant with the Faerie world. He does this by having sex with his sister, Morgan Le Fay (Morgan of the Faeries), a title of the Faerie Queen. From this union comes Mordred, who is raised in the Faerie world, and who kills Arthur in the end. This is nothing more than the sacrifice of the Seven Year King, also seen as Morgan Le Fay paying the tithe to Hell. Arthur is the Seven Year King, ruling Britain, and then sacrificed by the son of the Faerie Queen. In this case, neither a horse nor a mouse will do as an exchange for the sacrifice: Arthur himself must die, so that the land may prosper (just as Pryderi dies for his covenant with the Otherworld, killed over a pog of pigs).

CHANGELING ADULTS

Many changelings are not children, but adults. Some are said to resemble the human they replaced, but they are dour of disposition. They will be emotionally distant, and take no interest in family and friends.

Adult women are often the ones taken. In Child's collection of ballads, number 40 is a tune called "The Queen of Elfland's Nourice" [nurse]. In it a mortal woman grieving for her son who has died is told by the Elf Queen that if she nurses an Elf child, her son will be returned to her. The woman's journey to Elfland to carry out her bargain is described very much like True Thomas's journey, through rivers of blood to a three-way crossroads.

In the next song, the Faerie Queen captures an adult man. He is now a changeling, doomed to die in the tithe to Hell.

TAM LIN

You are a beautiful young woman, born into a noble house on the Scots-English border. Your name is Janet, though you go by Rose, for the gorgeous red bloom on your clear, smooth cheek. You are a wiry, tall girl with thick red hair that falls in curls about your shoulders, and a fiery spirit.

Though it was improper, as a child you climbed through trees and bushes and rode your colt across the moors. Any adventure amused you, especially searching for the wild red bloom that was your namesake.

One day, on a patch of your father's land where a ruined castle lay, you found a growth of the loveliest wild roses you'd ever seen. Most were still buds, the spring being young, but you plucked one gorgeous flower and rode home. Your heart sang for joy inside you.

Now you're seventeen. Your skin is peaches and cream, and the red of your cheek is like apples. Your hair is wild and thick, the color of burgundy wine, and you bind it with gold thread. You are courted by many young men of the estates surrounding your father's land, but none pleases you. Your love is to ride and to wander your lands, seeking what adventure and beauty you may find.

It is early summer, and each summer you've come here to the patch of roses by the ruined castle. So you set out on a lovely warm day, the sun growing strong and the May shoots just greening. But this summer is different. The land seems strange to you somehow. You sense some vague danger. Your horse starts, and you have to coax him on. He rides, but sniffs the air.

There is the ruined castle, and there the briar growth. You dismount, and walk over the heather in your high leather boots. You pick a wild rose, and suddenly a cloud seems to cover the afternoon sky.

A young man stands before you, dark and handsome, but with a devilish aura. His eyes are fire, and he wears mail above a green robe. He grabs your wrist.

"My lady, that rose is mine," he says. His voice rings like bells, yet it is eerie and still.

"This land is mine, by right of my father," you say haughtily, pulling your arm away. "All blooms in it, all who live upon it, are mine to command."

"Not I," the young man says. "I am the Faerie Queen's to command, and she has bid me guard her roses."

You turn your head away, turn your back to this insolent man, and mount your horse. But the young man approaches you. "You will meet me here tomorrow," he says. "You owe me a gift now."

You make a sound in your throat, and ride. Suddenly the land again feels familiar. The sky is sunny and clear. You shake your head, and decide you were imagining it all. That young man was nothing, just a stranger, a knight of some noble's guard that had wandered astray. You laugh at the whole conversation.

In your father's hall, as evening falls, you take a servant girl aside. You trust these simple village girls to be honest with you. They are not very smart, but they have an uncanny common sense.

"Do you know the ruined castle?" you ask. "Is there someone living there? A man? A knight, perhaps, who has lost his way while returning from some battle?"

The girl shudders, and makes the sign of the cross. "A Ghost!" she says. "Tam Lin! The place is haunted," she tells you. "The Kindly Ones dwell there. You must not go there, my lady. They say the Mabon, the Young Lord, takes a sacrifice of any young woman he desires. Their mantle. Or," she stops, and looks cautiously about, "their virtue."

"Ridiculous," you say.

"No, my lady." She speaks in hushed, worried tones. "There was a girl of the town that wandered into the place. I hear she was gathering flowers for the May. He came upon her, and knew her. She had a child last winter. A changeling's child." Again the cross. Her eyes were lowered.

You shake your head at the girl. "Silly superstition. That girl loved some acne-scarred artisan on May Eve, and did not want to give her bairn the father's name." You walk away, and when you glance back, the girl is kneeling with hands held to her mouth in frenzied prayer.

Night comes, and you lay on your bed, dreamily. You rub your wrist, still sore from where he grasped you.

All night you can think of nothing but him. His eyes, his ringing voice, the hollowness of his cheek. You toss and turn in your dark red quilts. You feel a stirring in your belly, one you've never felt before. You sit up and pray, but you feel God does not heed you. You vow you will not ride to that place again.

In the morning you mount your horse and ride. You mean to go towards the village, perhaps to the smithy to order your horse newly shod. But you find yourself on the path over the moor. You reach the briar patch, and harvest a double red flower. You set your mouth in defiance.

The young man appears. He wears the brightest green you have ever seen. His eyes are like dark clouds.

"Are you Tam Lin?" you ask him.

"There are some who call me that."

"What do you desire of me, Tam Lin?"

He approaches you, and you dismount. You hold your head high, but he gazes into your eyes without flinching. His hands are upon you. You don't resist. He takes you in his arms, and you let him. He wants you, and you give yourself to him, like the doe who surrenders herself to the autumn stag. His hands are beneath your kirtle, caressing your skin. You close your eyes. No man has ever made you feel this way.

He pushes you down, and you fall into the thicket of roses. A briar cuts your flesh, and you bleed.

※

This is the story of Tam Lin and Janet, a changeling and a landed young woman who becomes his lover. Below is one version of the song as Child collected it (Child 1965, #39). While versions differ in the details, this one has the important elements:

I forbid ye, maidens a',
that wear goud on your gear,
To come and gae by Caterhaugh,
For young Tom Line is there.

There's nane that gaes by Carterhaugh
But they leave him a wad,
Either their mantles o' green,
Or else their maidenhead.

But Janet has kilted her green kirtle
A little above her knee,
And she has broded her yellow hair
a little above her bree,
And she has gaen for Carterhaugh,
As fast as she can hie.

She hadna pu'd a double rose,
A rose but only twae,
Till up then started young Tom Line,
Says, Lady, thou 's pu nae mae.

Why pou's thou the rose, Janet?
Why breaks thou the wand?
Why comest thou to Carterhaugh
Withouthen my command?

Carterhaugh it is my ain,
My daddy gave it me;
I'll come and gae by Carterhaugh,
And ask nae leave at thee.'

Janet has kilted her green kirtle
A little aboon her knee,
And she has snooded her yellow hair
a little aboon her bree,

She is on to her father's ha,
as fast as she can hie.

Four and twenty ladies fair
Were playing at the ba,
And out then came fair Janet,
The flowr amang them a'.

Four and twenty ladies fair
Were playing at the chess,
Out then came fair Janet,
As green as ony glass.

Out spak an auld grey-headed knight,
Lay owre the castle wa,
And says, Alas, fair Janet,
For thee we'll be blam'd a'.

'Had your tongue, you auld grey knight
Some ill dead may ye die!
Father my bairn on whom I will,
I'll father nane on thee.'

Out then spak her father dear,
He spak baith thick and milde;
'And ever alas, sweet Janet,' he says,
'I think ye gae wi childe.'

'If that I gae wi child, father,
Mysell bears a' the blame;
There's not a laird about your ha
Shall get the bairnie's name.

'If my lord were an earthly knight,
As he's an elfish grey,
I wad na gie my ain true-love
For nae lord that ye hae.'

Janet has kilted her green kirtle
A little aboon her knee,
And she has snooded her yellow hair
A little aboon her bree,
And she's away to Carterhaugh,
As fast as she can hie.

She hadna pu'd a double rose,
A rose but only twae,
Till up then started young Tom Line,
Says, Lady, thou 'a pu na mae.

Why pu's thou the rose, Janet,
Out owr yon groves sae green,
And a' to kill your bonny babe,
That we gat us between?

'O tell me, tell me, Tom,' she says,
'For's sake who died on tree,
If eer ye were in holy chapel,
Or christendom did see.'

'Roxburgh he was my Grandfather
Took me with him to bide,
And ance it fell upon a day
That wae did me betide.

'Ance it fell upon a day,
A cauld day and a snell,
When we were frae the hunting come,
That from my horse I fell.

'The Queen of Faeries she came by,
Took me wi her to dwell,
Evn where she has a pleasant land
For those that in it dwell,

But at the end o seven years,
They pay their teind to hell.

The night it is gude Halloween,
The Faerie folk do ride,
And they that wad their true-love win,
At Miles Cross they maun bide.'

But how shall I thee ken, Thomas,
Or how shall I thee knaw,
Amang a pack o uncouth knights
The like I never saw?'

'The first company that passes by,
Say na, and let them gae;
The next company that passes by,
Say na, and do right sae;
The third company that passes by,
Then I'll be ane o thae.

Some ride upon a black, lady,
And some ride on a brown,
But I ride on a milk-white steed,
And ay nearest the town:
Because I was an earthly knight
They gae me that renown.

'My right hand will be glovd, lady,
My left hand will be bare,
And thae's the tokens I gie thee,
Nae doubt I will be there.

'Then hie thee to the milk-white
And pu me quickly down,
Cast thy green kirtle owr me,
And keep me frae the rain.

'They'll turn me in thy arms, lady,
An adder and a snake;
But hold me fast, let me na gae,
To be your warldly mate.

'They'll turn me in your arms, lady,
A grey greyhound to girn;
But hald me fast, let me na gae,
The father o your bairn.

They'll turn me in your arms, lady,
A red het gad o iron;
Then hand me fast, and be na feard,
I'll do to you nae harm.

'They'll turn me in your arms, lady,
A mother-naked man;
Cast your green kirtle owr me,
To keep me frae the rain.

'First dip me in a stand o milk,
And then a stand o water;
Haud me fast, let me na gae,
I'll be your bairnie's father.'

Janet has kilted her green kirtle
A little aboon her knee,
And she has snooded her yellow hair
A little aboon her bree,
And she is on to Miles Cross,
As fast as she can hie.

The first company that passd by,
She said na, and let them gae;
The next company that passed by,
She said na, and did right sae;

The third company that passed by,
Then he was ane o thae.

She hied her to the milk-white steed,
And pu'd him quickly down;
She cast her green kirtle owr him,
To keep him frae the rain
Then she did all was ordered her,
And sae recovered him

Out then spak the Queen o Faeries,
Out o a brush o broom:
"Them that hae gotten young Tom Line
Hae got a stately groom.'

Out then spak the Queen o Faeries,
Out o a bush of rye:
that has gotten young Tom Line
the best knight in my company.

'Had I kend, Thomas,' she says,
A lady wad hae borrowd thee,
I wad has taen out thy twa grey een,
Put in twa een o tree.

'Had I but kend, Thomas,' she says,
Before I came frae hame,
I had taen out that heart o flesh,
Put in a heart o stane.'

At the song's start, we are given a stern warning: that women who
"wear gold in your hair" (or "wear goud on your gear" in this version) may not go near Carter Hall (Carterhaugh). In Saxon English
culture, it was common for unmarried women to weave gold thread
into their hair; married women would cover their hair, or weave silver thread into it. Gold signifies the sun. Unmarried young women
wore their sexuality in the light of day, for any to see. Silver is the

moon. Married women hid their sexuality from the view of any but their husband. So we're immediately clued in that the young woman is single and looking.

The ballad singer warns us that any woman who rides to Carter Hall will be forced to make a sacrifice to Tam Lin. One such sacrifice might be her mantle, a cloak with a particular weave that signified her family's title and prosperity (like the tartan worn by Scots clans). Many of these cloaks may be seen in the archeological finds yielded up by the peat bogs of northern Europe.

But mantles are no great prize compared to a lovely young woman's virginity. At least that's what the song says. (Don't get snarky with me, I'm just telling you what the song says.)

Now we meet Janet, who dresses in her kirtle, and rides to Carter Hall. She pulls a rose, and instantly there appears Tam Lin.

One element of ballads is their subtlety. As with any great story or saga, the listener is required to draw a few conclusions from the information she or he is given. We have no back story up to this point. Some of the back story comes up as the song develops, but I think we can be reasonably sure that Janet and Tam Lin have seen each other before this moment. Janet rides directly to Carter Hall, and picks that rose. She knows what she's doing.

The rose is a common plant, grown in forest, garden and thicket throughout northern England. It is likely that roses grew at Carter Hall, either as a wild plant, or as a once-cultivated prize in the ruined gardens of that decaying castle. Tam Lin is summoned by the pulling of that rose, showing that he is tied to the natural growth of the land.

It is quite common for the Fey to be summoned by the destruction of the natural world. In Norse myth, Elves are summoned by the destruction of the forest. In "Seven Hundred Elves," originally a Danish song, a band of warlike Elves is brought to bear when a farmer begins cutting trees in their woods. The farmer, according to the ballad, fells the "Oak and the Birch," among other trees. The

Elves appear, and challenge the farmer's right to make their woods his home. A fight ensues.

Another fight involves the forest spirit Herne. According to a story told in modern times in central England, Herne punishes a group of "teddy boys," London hipsters, for tampering with artifacts they find in the forests around Windsor. One of the boys is shot dead by Herne with an invisible arrow. Mythically, the Elves and Herne are each incarnations of the Pagan figure of the Green Man.

Throughout Pagan culture we find the Foliate God, or Green Man, a man with leaves for beard and hair, whose power grows with the crop or the forest. Foliate Gods were carved into the walls of Irish churches, perhaps as a sign that while the new God, Jesus, ruled the hearts of the Irish, the Foliate Man still ruled the growth of the crops. Without this growth, the people would starve. The Green Man must be appeased.

Shakespeare knew this, and gave floral attributes to his Faeries in A *Midsummer Night's Dream*: Peaseblossom and Mustardseed. (His other two Faeries also had countryside garden names: Moth and Cobweb.) Almost three hundred years later, illustrators such as Mary Cicely Barker and Kate Greenway had brought the connection between Faerie and foliage well into the public mind. Both artists, and their contemporaries, portrayed the Fey as impish children, wandering playfully through flowerbeds. Each Faerie had a flower name, and wings to match its bloom.

In every village and town of England there is a folkloric Foliate Man referred to as Jack in the Green, Hob, Cobb, and most especially, John Barleycorn. Each English village has a song about John Barleycorn, usually with common lyrics. Every town boasts its own melody to the tune, and often you can tell where a country dweller hails from by the tune he or she sings to "John Barleycorn."

The song tells of the cycle of the harvest, as seen through the eyes of the crop, poor little John. He is planted and grown, allowed to prosper and attain his height and might. Then he is harvested, bound, threshed and ground. In the end, he is exalted: "For the huntsman he can't hunt the fox/nor loudly blow his horn/and the tinker can't mend his kettles or his pots/without John Barleycorn."

Here is a version of the traditional song collected in central England. Various rock bands, including Traffic, Steeleye Span and Jethro Tull, have done modern renditions of the tune, with various sets of traditional lyrics and differing melodies.

There were three men came out of the west,
their fortunes for to try
And these three men made a solemn vow
John Barleycorn must die
John Barleycorn must die

They've plowed, they've sown, they've harrowed him in
Threw clods upon his head
And these three men made a solemn vow
John Barleycorn was dead
John Barleycorn was dead

There's beer all in the barrel and brandy in the glass
And little sir John in his nut brown bowl
Proved the strongest man at last

They've let him lie for a very long time,
'til the rains from heaven did fall
And little Sir John sprung up his head
And did amaze them all

And did amaze them all
They've let him stand 'til Midsummer's Day
'til he looked both pale and wan
And little Sir John's grown a long long beard
And so become a man
And so become a man

There's beer all in the barrel and brandy in the glass
And little sir John in his nut brown bowl
Proved the strongest man at last

They've hired men with their scythes
so sharp to cut him off at the knee
They've rolled him and tied him by the way,
And served him barbarously
And served him barbarously

They've hired men with their sharp pitchforks
who pricked him to the heart
And the loader he has served him worse than that
For he's bound him to the cart
He's bound him to the cart

There's beer all in the barrel and brandy in the glass
And little sir John in his nut brown bowl
Proved the strongest man at last

They've wheeled him around and around a field
'til they came onto a barn
And there they made a solemn oath
On poor John Barleycorn
On poor John Barleycorn

They've hired men with their crab tree sticks to cut him skin
    from bone
And the miller he has served him worse than that
For he's ground him between two stones
For he's ground him between two stones

There's beer all in the barrel and brandy in the glass
And little sir John in his nut brown bowl
Proved the strongest man at last

For the huntsman he can't hunt the fox
Nor loudly to blow his horn
And the tinker he can't mend his kettles or his pots
Without John Barleycorn
(Traditional; arr. Klein 1995)

With his vigilant guard over the foliage of his domain, Carter Hall, Tam Lin acts as the Green Man. He seems instantly aware of Janet's desecration of the growing things, and he arrives in a flash, demanding to know why the maiden has pulled the rose. His blood is the land, his heart the flowers. Janet has galloped through, seeing some nice-looking roses. A little sniff, a little sigh, a little pluck, and when Tam Lin appears, there's Janet, caught red-handed with her rose.

The rose in the language of flowers is love, female beauty, and passion. This is why we give roses as a sign of love and commitment. Janet's rose with its unfolding blossom looks like a woman's labia, and its bloom is the bright red of excited flesh in the cheeks and the vulva. Janet's choice of flower is sexually alluring to our changeling, Tam Lin.

The rose as a sexual symbol, and as the domain of Faerie, becomes apparent in several of the stories collected by Jacob and Wilhelm Grimm. In *Beauty and the Beast* (a French tale the Grimms collected as *The Summer and Winter Garden*), Beauty, the youngest daughter of a once-wealthy merchant, wants nothing more than a beautiful rose. Too poor now to purchase the delicate flower, her father sneaks into a forbidden garden (recalling both Janet's intrusion into Carter Hall, and the story of Eden). He picks a rose, which he has been warned he is not meant to pick (like the warnings issued of both Carter Hall and of Eden). The Beast appears, in the same fashion as Tam Lin, and claims his life. The man offers his virgin daughter instead, who must now live with the Beast until she falls in love with him, and takes him as her husband. When this happens, she discovers that the Beast is a changeling, and that his true identity is that of a prince: Just as Tam Lin is a knight, not a true Faerie. (In the Grimms' version, she returns from her father's funeral after a long absence, and finds the Beast dying beneath a cabbage patch. Cabbage is another petal-rich plant, and once again reminiscent of the labia).

Another Grimm story that features the rose is that of *Snow White and Rose Red*. In this tale, twin sisters were named for white and red roses that grow in their family's garden, marking one as chaste (white) and the other as sensual (red). True to her namesake, Rose Red is the bolder of the sisters, independent and confident of her ability to survive in the forests and the fields. Rose Red befriends a bear, who comes to be close with both sisters. In fact, both girls sleep with the bear each night. When a Dwarf threatens the girls, the bear saves them, finally revealing that it he is a prince under enchantment (a changeling). Rose Red marries the reformed beast.

That this fragrant, feminine blossom has immense power over the Faerie world is clear from these stories. Tam Lin is obviously excited by the picking of the flower. He appears instantly in this excited state, and we can deduce that some hanky-panky ensues. In fact, Janet is left in a family way by their tryst.

Why does Janet allow herself to be taken by this strange changeling creature? A changeling she hardly knows, for we later see Janet questioning Tam Lin about his origins. Janet offers us the explanation that she is the true owner of Carter Hall, the heiress of the place by right of her birth:

> Carterhaugh it is my ain,
> My daddy gave it me;
> I'll come and gae by Carterhaugh,
> And ask nae leave at thee.

She is steward of the land, a position hotly contested by Tam Lin. Perhaps it is this antagonistic relationship that causes Janet to fall for Tam Lin, a basic psychology in many teen or twenty-something relationships. For young women, it is often the "bad boy" who excites them, especially when that young man usurps a domain they see as their own. They are spurred on by antagonism, and often young lovers punch and tease each other as romantic play. That Tam Lin claims Carter Hall as his own, that he is tied to the land, and that he is young, "fair and full of flesh," and as one version of the song states, attracts the maiden. I might even imagine that as she grew up around the ruined castle, Janet caught glimpses of the Faerie, observed him, and tried to engage in conversation, until one day she was old enough to desire him sexually. Well, the time has come: she gives herself to him, forsaking mortal (common) men.

If Janet is owner of Carter Hall, and Tam Lin is guardian of the land, the young lovers are placed in the position of Priestess and Priest, representatives of the Goddess and God of this land (ancient Pagans did not believe in one great Goddess and one great God, as modern Pagans might: they believed that a set of local Gods and Goddesses ruled over each area of forest, field and stream). In their claims to stewardship of the land, they join, and make the land fruitful. In fact, their union has started a child within Janet.

In many of the tales of Faerie and human sexual union, a child is produced. While Tam Lin was once human, and will be again, other Faeries produce children with mortals as well. In many tales of the Selkie, a Scottish Faerie half-seal and half-human in form, a seduction produces offspring. We've also seen that Elves, Nymphs, Nixies and enchanted animals spawn half-human children.

Janet may very well want to produce an heir to Carter Hall that is half-human and half-Fey. This ground may have been contested for long ages, and Janet may see it as her place to end the spat between human and Faerie by producing an heir who is both. This would settle the dispute, and create an ownership of the land that would bring the two races together. Maybe this was Janet's plan all along.

Janet returns home in a family way from her trysts with the changeling, and breaks the news to Dad. Dad is ready to blame one of his knights, but Janet lets him know, defiantly, that no mortal husband interests her; only Tam Lin will do:

'If my lord were an earthly knight,
As he's an elfish grey,
I wad na gie my ain true-love
For nae lord that ye hae.'

Janet returns to Carter Hall to throw down with Tam Lin, and get the scoop on his origins.

Tam Lin tells Janet his story: He was an earthly knight who fell from his horse. In some versions of the song he falls in battle. Here, he falls while hunting; we've seen humans fall prey to Faeries while hunting before. Remember Pwyll and the white stag? In Tam Lin's case, the Queen of Faerie catches him and steals him away to Faerie. Now he fears he will be the tithe to Hell, because he is "faire and full of flesh," according to some versions.

The tithe to Hell. We have discussed the cover-up story that country people used to validate their belief in the Kindly Ones after Christianity took hold. Faeries were angels that did not take sides during the war in Heaven. Because they were not on God's side, they could not stay in Paradise. But for not siding with the Devil, they were not doomed to Hell. They were cast into a "between" world, a place within the plane of Earth, called the Faerie Land.

But to avoid being damned, the Queen of the Fey must pay a tithe to Hell every seven years; a mortal, who is fair and "full of flesh."

Where did this notion come from? I believe it comes from the memory of the Seven Year King.

Throughout Pagan Europe, a tradition existed of the Seven Year King, or the Oak King. In each town, at every seventh Summer Solstice, games of skill would be held. The strongest, fastest, most skillful young men would compete. The Greek Olympics was part of this tradition.

Through grueling competition, a "King" would be chosen who would reign for seven years. During that time, the lucky king would eat the first food of the harvest, would have sex with young women who had come into sexual readiness, and would be offered the best of everything in the village he "ruled." Finally, at the end of seven years, he'd be led into the fields by the village's elder women. A rope would be placed around his neck, a ritual knife brought from behind the back, and he'd be both cut at the throat and hanged or suspended as he died. His blood would flow into the field, assuring a bountiful harvest for seven more years.

In northern Europe, the Seven Year King would be buried in the peat bog surrounded by scared objects such as ritual hunting horns (called lurs), sacred knives and sealed jars of grain. Many of these bodies were mummified by the peat, and are displayed in museums today. One sacrifice found was a sixteen-year-old girl, so perhaps men were not the only sacrifices made. (In the 1973 movie *The Wicker Man*, Rowan Morrison, the Queen of the May, is slated to be the sacrifice. Unable to part with this Nymph-like beauty, the town lures a police officer into becoming a substitute sacrifice.)

The story of Hercules (or Heracles, "Chosen of Hera") is another memory of the Seven Year King. Heracles endures various trials, reminiscent of the trials of skill in the competition. He is finally chosen by the Goddess Hera to rule the Greek world. When he dies, he ensures the fertility of the land.

In British myth, the circle of male death and rebirth is played out in the Oak King–Holly King cycle. The Oak King, or the Robin, is born in the spring, from the winter union of Goddess and God. He comes as a youth into the physical reality of our world, growing with the grain in the fields and the young animals of the forest. Gaining strength, the crops grow high and the hunted animals prosper.

Then at Summer Solstice, or Lithia, the young God is given the scythe, the tool of his own death. (In the *Mabinogion* tale of Llew Llaw Gyffes, one trial is to trick his mother, Arianrhod, into arming him). He is cut down at the harvest and killed at the hunt, becoming the Holly King or the Old God. At Samhain, or Hallowe'en, he is brought by the Wild Ride into the Underworld, or the Faerie world, where he rules as the Lord of Death. There he makes love to the God-

dess (as in the story of Hades and Persephone), and their progeny is
born as the new Oak King. (For more on this, see *The Flowering Rod:
Men and their Role in Paganism* by Kenny Klein.)

Just as British myth in the time of Christianity made Faeries into
fallen angels, it has made the Seven Year King a tithe to Hell, given
over by the Faerie Queen. "Fair and full of flesh," as Tam Lin describes
himself, the tithe is enticing to Satan, and greedily taken. His sacrifice saves the Fey from an existence of damnation.

So sweet, pregnant Janet has to save her lover from this horrific
fate. Great. And not so easy . . . Tam Lin explains to her that this
night, Hallowe'en (the Irish Samhain, traditionally the night of the
sacrifice of the Seven Year King), there will be a procession of the
Faeries over water—Miles Cross, a ford in a river. Janet is to let several companies of Elves pass, then find Tam Lin on a white horse, his
to ride because he was once a mortal knight. When Janet takes Tam
Lin from his horse, she must cover him with her kirtle (her riding
cloak). He tells her the Fey will turn him into a series of ferocious
animals. First he will be turned into a snake or serpent: the symbol of
Eden and of the Goddess.

The Faerie Queen is Mab, the Goddess of the dark world. She is
Morgan Le Fay in the Arthurian myth and L'Annawnshee (Underworld Faerie) in British lore. Her symbol is the snake, which has
represented the divine female since ancient Babylon. Janet will be
confronted by the true identity of the Faerie Queen when she first
takes Tam Lin as her mortal lover. But she is told she must keep him
cloaked in her clothing (which has the weave or design of her family
crest on it, representing her ownership of this land: it's Janet's way of
insisting that she now owns Tam Lin, too).

Then he will be turned into a greyhound, the hound of Hell, or the
vicious demon dog. The dog represents, among many other things,
the deepest urges in humans. In the Tarot card The Moon is a stream,
the unconscious mind, with a dog on one bank and a wolf on the
other: symbols representing a person's socialized, acceptable persona

(dog) and her primal, animal urges (wolf). Janet is to be faced by the raging terror of her deepest urges, her own sexuality, which got her into this mess in the first place. In some versions of the song, this transformation is into a lion, also a symbol of earthly lust. Janet must face the fact that her passions are violent and capable of destroying her. Only her self-control can save her from being ripped to pieces by these beasts. She again wraps her transformed lover in her cloak, and keeps him out of the Queen's sight.

This stage of the sequence calls to mind stories like *Beauty and the Beast*. Janet, like Beauty, must face her lover as a hideous beast. She cannot love him in this form, but by remembering his inner essence, that he is her true love beneath this ghastly exterior, she may transform him back to a handsome or desirable shape. In the water-mirrored Faerie world, that which we find most desirable may be mirror imaged by that which we find most horrible and deadly.

Next, in the version here, Tam Lin will be turned into "a red het gad o iron." Ouch! If the serpent and the lion did not drive home the point that Janet's sexual desire could kill her, how about a nice red-hot iron poker? Do I need to spell out the sexual symbolism here?

Finally Tam Lin is turned into a naked man. This is a sign that the Queen has returned Tam Lin into our world with nothing from her world; he is reborn as a human. Also, it is a sign that Janet now owns her lover's sexuality. He is given back to her as she desires him: naked, sexual, hiding nothing, keeping no secrets.

Now Janet must complete one final, odd task. Janet must douse Tam Lin with liquid:

'First dip me in a stand o milk,
And then a stand o water;
Haud me fast, let me na gae,
I'll be your bairnie's father.'

It seems that to fully return to our world, Tam Lin must pass through liquid as he did to get to Faerie in the first place. The barrier of liquid or mist must be traversed back again, so that Tam Lin will be emotionally present in our world, and free to fully engage in his child's life. The water-mirror of Faerie is banished, and Tam Lin may be human again (very like the horse exchange Rhiannon had to endure to live as a human in the *Mabinogion*).

Finally the Queen speaks angrily, saying that if she had foreseen this, she would have taken out Tam Lin's eyes, and put in "twa een o' tree." Mab does not want her former lover to return to Earth with the Faerie sight, and wishes that she could give him wooden eyes to prevent this. She also states, in this version, that she would have replaced his heart with a stone. Sweet.

The Queen in "Tam Lin" is not the loving, generous Elf Queen of "True Thomas". Nor is she the motherly, nurturing Titania. She is vengeful and jealous. She wishes to punish Janet for stealing her lover, and she wants to punish Tam Lin both for his betrayal of her affections, and for leaving before she could sacrifice him. She is a Black Widow, loving mortal men and then sacrificing them, and angry when the men do not play along. She is the seducer-murderer Faerie.

In talking about changelings, we've run into a few Faeries in animal form: Rhiannon the horse, Rose Red's bear, and Tam Lin shape-shifting into a snake and a dog. The next chapter looks at some of the folklore concerning Faerie animals. Who knows, maybe one of them will be sweet and cute?

Chapter 4

FAERIE BEASTS

Faeries often appear in animal forms, and just as often animals accompany them. The Glastig often have the hindquarters of a goat, which they keep hidden beneath their long hair. Reynardine is a fox when he is not in human form, and the Selkies become seals when in the water. There's a story of Puck in which he takes the form of a horse, allowing an old miser to ride on his back until he reaches an impressive speed, then disappearing altogether from beneath the curmudgeon. Sadb, the wife of Finn Mac Coul, was in the form of a deer when Finn first encountered her, and their child was Ossian, "Little Deer." Not the first animal/human Finn would run into and not the last: Finn's hunting hounds, Bran and Sceolan, were actually his own nephews under an enchantment. And let us not forget Tam Lin. When he is pulled from his horse by his mortal lover Janet, he is changed into a serpent, a dog, and in some versions, a lion.

The realm of Faerie stories can involve witches, a memory perhaps of the healers and herbalists who came to know the Faerie magic. Witches have always been associated with animals, in ways both good and bad, and this comes from the real-life practice of Witches in ancient communities. Witches have animal familiars, which popular tales characterize as black cats. But *Witchcraft Today* author Gerald Gardner's research showed that Witches were more concerned with wild animals, and that the words *witch* and *Wicca* may come from a Saxon word meaning "to foretell the future by the actions of animals." (Gardner unpublished) We still see this in the tradition of Groundhog Day on February 2.

It was common practice for Witches or shamans of the community to have a close relationship with animals, especially hunted animals. I had a dear friend from Iceland who told me that her grandfather would spend six months each year "living in the mountains with the reindeer." In Siberian, Lapp, and Icelandic cultures, the shamans would dress in the skins of an animal, rub themselves with the fat of the creatures to take on their scent, and live among the beasts. In their trance work, they would communicate with animals in the "dream time" or whatever their own culture called the trance state. To the people of their community, they would become the animal. These rites, still done in places like Iceland, are remembered in dances like the Abbots Bromley Horn Dance, an English Morris dance performed with huge antlers, depicting the rutting of Irish deer (which have been extinct for a few thousand years. The antlers are that old!).

Stories of Faeries part-human and part-animal are probably the basis of werewolf stories. They are also behind the popular notion of a Witch turning a person into a frog or newt, as seen often in the Grimms' stories (the Frog Prince, for instance). These tales may come not only from Faerie, but also from mythology, where Goddesses and Gods are often seen in animal form. Zeus turned himself into both a swan (to seduce Leda) and a bull (to seduce Europa); Bran and Branwen, God and Goddess of Wales, were ravens; Odin commanded ravens and dogs; Egyptian deities were always depicted with the bodies of humans and the heads of animals. These images, blended with Faerie lore, crept into popular consciousness, and became the basis of many folk tales.

When Faeries appear as animals, they may act in ways both helpful and harmful. The Glas Gaivlen is a Faerie cow, white with green mottle. Its appearance in a farmer's field on May Day brings good harvest for the coming year. The Dun Cow of Kirkham and the Gwartheg Y Lyn of Wales are similarly beneficial. But beware a speckled, hornless cow in your herd. These Faerie cattle will lead the entire herd to disappear into a rock or a hill, never to be seen again. And the Cro Sith are believed to be cows that live under the sea, eating meillich (seaweed) until they come ashore to live among their mortal sisters.

In the Child ballad "The Queen of Elfland's Nourice" (Child #40, if you're keeping track), a mortal woman whose son dies asks the Queen of Elfland to return the son in exchange for the woman nursing a changeling. The Elf Queen answers the mortal woman in the voice of a Faerie cow:

I heard a cow low, a bonnie cow low,
And a cow low down in yon glen:
Long, long will my young son greet
Or his mother bid him come hence!

You'll be pleased to know that the Elf Queen agrees to this bargain and brings the woman to Elfland on her magical white horse; and that noble beast begins our discussion of Faerie animals.

HORSES

Horses are common in the lore of the Fey, and Faeries are often seen riding very fine mounts. In the songs "Tam Lin" and "Thomas the Rhymer," the Faerie or Elf Queen is riding a horse (in the case of Tam Lin, she catches him when he falls from his own horse; in Thomas's case, he must mount her horse to reach Elfland). Ossian is connected to mortal Ireland by riding a magical white horse that can run upon water. Pwyll meets his Otherworldly wife Rhiannon while she is riding a mare that cannot be caught by any mortal horse. Rhiannon herself must become a horse in the story, and her changeling son Pryderi is traded for a horse. In British mythology, lots of Goddesses are associated with horses: Epona, Rigatona, Regina and Mab are just a few. One reason for this might be that horses leave a crescent-shaped hoof print, which might have been associated with the moon, and therefore with moon Goddesses. In fact, a moon-shaped canyon in Iceland is named Asbyrgi, said to have been created by the footfall of Odin's horse Sleipnir.

Like any other Faerie animal, horses of the Fey can be good or bad. The Kelpie is a Faerie horse that (like the Cro Sith) is equally at home in water or on land. Called the Shoopiltee in the Shetlands and the Nokken in Norway, the horse appears mortal, but on closer inspection one notices water constantly dripping from the animal's mane. The beast is usually harmless, and can be seen eating water plants in streams and rivers.

But beware the Each Uisge, a nasty Faerie horse that lives in saltwater. This creature appears as a fine pony, and many a human has been tempted to mount the creature and ride. This is great while inland, but as soon as the Each Uisge senses water of any kind, it will carry the rider to his death from drowning, and eat the rider's body. This Faerie may also take the form of a handsome man, and seduce young women. In its manly form, the creature can only be spotted by water weeds in its hair. In the Scottish Highlands, young women are taught to avoid strangers who are seen near water.

Here is a Highlands story of this unpleasant animal:

A blacksmith lost his daughter to the Each Uisge, who seduced the girl and then drowned her. He and his son plotted their revenge. They tempted the creature to appear in horse form by roasting a sheep close to the water. When the Faerie emerged in horse form, the men speared it with red hot hooks. Once dead, the creature turned to jelly.

Charlotte Bronte mentions a similar Faerie horse, the Gytrash, in *Jane Eyre*:

As this horse approached, and as I watched for it to appear
through the dusk, I remembered certain of Bessie's tales,
   wherein
figured a North-of-England spirit, called a 'Gytrash'; which, in
the form of horse, mule, or large dog, haunted solitary ways,
   and
sometimes came upon belated travellers, as this horse was now
coming upon me. (Bronte 1897, chapter xii, 211)

Jane realizes she is not in the presence of the Gytrash when she
sees a gentleman on the horse, for she states: "Nothing ever rode the
Gytrash: it was always alone."

Horses often show up in Fairy tales as enchanted creatures. In the
strangely named Turkish story *The Horse-Dew and the Witch*, a shah
(lord) asks his three daughters to personally feed his prize horse
while he is away for a time, as he does not want any stranger near
the animal. The two older daughters try to feed the horse, but he will
not accept food from them. The youngest daughter feeds the horse
with no difficulty. Upon his return, the shah learns of this, and marries his youngest daughter to the horse. But each night, the stable is
transformed to a rose garden, and the horse to a handsome young
man. The couple lives happily (and during the day, we assume the
girl gets in a good deal of riding).

Otherworldly horses turn up constantly in folklore. Take for instance Odin's horse Sleipnir, an eight-legged creature with runes
carved on his teeth. The story of Sleipnir's birth is a strange one:
the Gods of Asgard accepted an offer from a stonemason to repair
the walls of Asgard, in return for the sun, the moon and the hand
of Freya. The Gods accepted, assuming the stonemason would never
finish the job in the agreed amount of time. But the mason turned
out to be an enchanted being called a *hrímthurs*, a Faerie creature
made of ice that inhabits a frozen Faerie world. The hrímthurs rode
a Faerie steed named Svadilfari, capable of riding fast enough for the
Faerie to finish his work under the deadline. To prevent this, Loki

transformed himself into a mare, and distracted Svadilfari by mating with him. The resulting colt was Sleipnir, given as a gift to Odin.

Sleipnir carried Odin on the Wild Ride or Wild Hunt, the same Wild Ride or Faerie Ride said to be led by Mab in English folklore. In Sweden, the legend is called Odin's Hunt, and Odin rides his eight-legged horse "no higher above the ground than an ox wears its yoke." So if one sees Odin riding, it is safest to throw oneself on the ground. In many of these legends, Odin is not seen as a God, but as a Faerie or spirit, consigned to the Wild Ride for the misdeed of having hunted on Sunday during his human life. In these stories, Odin is very similar to the British Herne, especially in Shakespeare's account of him as a forester turned into a Faerie and now haunting Windsor Forest.

Faerie or God, Odin always hunted with his hounds at his side. Swedes say that one may not see Odin's Hunt, but one will hear his two hounds, one baying loudly and the other baying softly. One legend says a person can only protect himself by throwing iron between him and the dogs. Throughout the Faerie record, these sorts of canines appear as huge, menacing creatures called Hell Hounds.

HELL HOUNDS

You're walking through a dusky forest road on a dark evening. The light has waned from deep azure at twilight into a dark starry night. An owl cries off to your left, and the crunch of pine needles creates a calming rhythm beneath your feet.

Suddenly the air seems very still. Sound is muffled, and the owl has stopped calling. You sense something and your hair stands on end. You stop, feeling your heart pound, and stand alert, listening.

Then it happens. You hear baying behind you, so close it's almost upon you. You jump back, into the sheltering trees. An enormous vision gallops by, black as midnight, and you smell the horse sweat and sense the hoof beats. You look for the rider, but see nothing except a black space. Like a hole, empty, impenetrable. A long dark cloak streams out behind the apparition.

Suddenly they are beside you! A pack of hounds, as huge as Shetland ponies, baying and screeching. They sniff you as they run by, glaring at you with red eyes as huge as saucers. Your heart thumps; you feel a terrified tingling in your hands and feet. You can't run, and you fear standing still. Their breath is foul, like stagnant water. They trail spittle from serrated lips and panting jaws.

Now in a moment they're gone. The hounds and the frightful mounted figure have galloped off along this lonesome road, leaving the forest night in dark, freezing quiet. Then, in a few moments, the owl resumes hooting, the air becomes tranquil. You stand perfectly still, shaking, wondering. You feel your chest and torso. You're unharmed, still alive. The night cloaks you.

Perhaps you have met with the Hell Hounds of Wales, the same white hounds that drew Pwyll to his fateful meeting with Arawn, and the same sort of white hound that crossed Ossian's path on his journey to Tir N'an Og. White hounds with red ears, baying frightfully, as large as horses, following Herne the Hunter, or Odin, or Mab on her wild ride through the Samhain night. Perhaps it was Black Shuck that crossed your path, chilling your blood to ice. A huge black mongrel with red eyes as big as saucers. Or maybe it was the devil dogs of the old South.

Dogs as guardians of the Underworld are seen in the oldest of myths. In Greek legend, Cerberus guards the Death World, preventing the dead from returning to our lands. And in Turkish myth, Hecate, stern Goddess of the Underworld, has the triple heads of a horse, a serpent and a dog. A jackal-headed God guards the Egyptian Underworld. Hounds are often guardians and hunters of the borders between our world and the elusive land of the Fey.

British folklore and Faerie myth is full of Hell Hounds and demon dogs. In East Anglia, a part of England still named for its Viking ancestry, there is a story of Black Shuck, or the Doom Dog. This ghastly creature is said to be the size of a horse, with flaming red eyes like saucers. His name comes from a Viking word *scucca*, meaning "demon." And there are those who swear he is real, and that they've seen him. Here is a sixteenth-century account:

On August 4, 1577, during a thunder storm, Black Shuck stormed through a country church in Blythburgh near the Suffolk border. According to accounts: "He ran up the nave, past a large congregation, killing a man and boy and causing the church tower to collapse through the roof. As the dog left, he left scorch marks on the north door which can be seen at the church to this day." (Ellis 1924, 304)

The encounter is remembered in a verse recited by East Anglia locals:

All down the church in midst of fire, the hellish monster flew And, passing onward to the quire, he many people slew. (Traditional, East Anglian song.)

In stories throughout the Isles, these dogs are known by other local names: Moddey Dhoo of the Isle of Man, said to haunt Peel Castle; Gwyllgi of Wales; in Yorkshire, the Barghest, whose name might come from the Northern English pronunciation of *ghost* as "guest," haunts the countryside and terrorizes the night. Anyone who meets the Barghest will soon die. Sir Walter Scott alludes to this belief in *The Lay of the Last Minstrel*, placing the Barghest on the Isle of Man:

For he was speechless, ghastly, wan Like him of whom the Story ran Who spoke the spectre hound in Man. (Scott 1899, Canto VI, v. 26)

Herne, the eerie deer-headed spirit of Windsor Great Park, is said to travel with his pack of baying white dogs with their red ears. Herne is known to some as God of the Forest, a deer-headed Green Man figure, much like Arawn. But in Windsor Great Park, Herne is said to be a Faerie or spirit. He is mentioned in Shakespeare's *The Merry Wives of Windsor* as the ghost of a forester, in Act IV, Scene 4:

There is an old tale goes that Herne the Hunter
Sometime a keeper here in Windsor Forest,
Doth all the winter-time, at still midnight,
Walk round about an oak, with great ragg'd horns;
And there he blasts the tree, and takes the cattle,
And makes milch-kine yield blood, and shakes a chain
In a most hideous and dreadful manner.
You have heard of such a spirit, and well you know
The superstitious idle-headed eld
Receiv'd, and did deliver to our age,
This tale of Herne the Hunter for a truth.
(Shakespeare, *The Merry Wives of Windsor*, Act IV,
Scene 4, 27–37)

Notice that in Shakespeare's account, Herne is antlered or horned, associated with the deer and with deer-headed Underworld kings like Arawn and Cernunnos. He is also associated with an ancient oak tree, Herne's Oak, in Windsor Great Park. It has been local legend there for centuries that Herne's Oak was a huge tree in the Home Park near Frogmore House, an area adjoining Windsor Great Park. This tree was destroyed in 1796, and King Edward VII replanted an oak on that spot in 1906. We've seen with Tam Lin and other Fairies that certain enchanted beings haunt a particular tree or plant, and are excited by anything disturbing that bush. This seems to be the case with Herne.

One theory of Herne is that he is Wodin or Odin, not the God but the Swedish Faerie that leads Odin's Hunt. Another Saxon name for Odin is Herian, and from that came Herne. Odin hung himself inverted in an ash tree (the World Tree of Norse myth). This could be true of Herne and his oak. In some legends Herne the forester was hanged from Herne's Oak.

Herne may also be connected with the Celtic God Cernunnos, associated with animals like the deer and the hound, and a protector of the forest. But whether God or Faerie, Herne is said to ride a great black horse through the forest, leading the Wild Ride. He summons demon dogs by blowing a hunting horn, and they run baying behind him. Windsor is home to the castle of England's Royalty, and legend says that the baying of Herne's hounds is an ill omen for the Royal Family.

Herne's legacy seems to have been applied to a local figure, Henry of Poitou, a twelfth-century abbot of Peterborough. This abbot must have been rather unpleasant: he was hated by the people of the area, and was accused of plurality (which I assume means that he took several wives, rather than that he cast several votes). It seems he was also a relation of Henry I. The *Anglo-Saxon Chronicle* for 1127 states that abbot Henry was in league with the Devil, and that he was seen in the company of "huge and hideous" shadowy huntsmen on "black horses and goats" (Satanic beasts according to the Church of that time), accompanied by dark hounds "with eyes like saucers and horrible." Numbering about twenty or thirty (this according to what were deemed reliable witnesses), the riders traveled on wooded roads from Peterborough to Stamford, Lincolnshire, "winding their horns as they went." The sightings lasted from Lent to Easter.

Herne's name may actually be linguistically tied to another Underworld figure, that of Arawn. It's quite possible that Herne is simply a pronunciation of that Otherworld king's name, applied over time to an apparition of Windsor.

Like Herne, Arawn is an antlered God or Fey of the English and Welsh forests, spoken of in the *Mabinogion*. The human hunter Pwyll chases a pack of Arawn's white hounds of Annwn (the Underworld) away from a white stag, and sets his own mortal dogs on the animal. This episode causes Arawn to feel that Pwyll owes him a debt of honor, and sends the human hunter into his own dark world. The dogs, then, are guardians of the way to the Underworld, or Faerie world. *Mabinogion* translator Lady Charlotte Guest has this to say about the legend: "The Dogs of Annwn are the subject of an ancient Welsh superstition, which was once universally believed in throughout the Principality, and which it would seem is not yet quite extinct. It is said that they are sometimes heard at night passing through the air overhead, as if in full cry in pursuit of some object." (Guest 1877, note 340b to Pwyll Prince of Dyved, 340)

The Hounds of Hell may also be spoken of as riding through the night with Mab, the Faerie Queen, in the forests of England. Often she is said to be chasing a stag, sometimes identified with Herne himself. Her white dogs with red ears lead the Wild Ride, baying and barking as they go.

These legends of hounds are remembered in modern literature. Perhaps the best known instance is Arthur Conan Doyle's novel-length Sherlock Holmes story *The Hound of the Baskervilles*, in which criminals use a local superstition of the Hell Hound to terrorize the village. In the story, Holmes appears to be familiar with the Devil Dog legend, and realizes that the suspects are using this long-standing terror to achieve their criminal goals.

Hell Hounds are known in stories and songs throughout the English-speaking world, including the United States. The great Blues musician Robert Johnson sang often of devils haunting him or possessing him. In 1937, he recorded these lyrics:

Gotta keep on movin' gotta keep on movin'
Blues falling down like hail
Gotta keep on movin' gotta keep on movin'
Blues falling down like hail
And these days keeps on worrying me
Hell hound on my trail
(Traditional, sung by Robert Johnson, RCA, 1937)

In Southern Black culture, the Hell Hound became a common image. Preachers often spoke from the pulpit of Hell Hounds carrying off sinners to the eternal flame. Johnson used this terrifying image in this song and several others, often referring to his own sin and damnation: Blues folklore has it that Johnson had sold his soul to the Devil to become a great Bluesman.

From the great brute strength of dogs and horses, let's go to the tiniest of Faerie creatures. No, sorry, not Tinker Bell. Tinker mouse!

GALLOWS FOR A MOUSE

One of the strangest stories in the Welsh *Mabinogion*, "Gallows for a Mouse," is about Pryderi's father-in-law and his confrontation with Faerie mice, resulting in a changeling ransom.

After the death of Pwyll and a great battle in the Otherworld, Pryderi returns to his mother, Rhiannon, and his wife, Kigva. With him rides his battle companion Manawydan. During the feast honoring their return, Rhiannon falls for Manawydan, and with Pryderi's blessings the two are married.

But Otherworld trouble follows Pryderi like flies follow the garbage truck. In a very short time, all the people of Wales disappear completely, leaving the two couples the only occupants of that country. Not a soul is to be found in any field or house. Puzzled, the four debate what to do. Finally Pryderi, Kigva, Manawydan and Rhiannon set out for England, where they try their hand quite successfully at several trades.

But each time they ply their craft successfully, the tradesman of that town grow jealous of the skill of Pryderi and Manawydan, and vow to kill them. Each time the two Welshmen learn of the plot and flee, to try a new trade in another town. In each town the same thing happens, and finally they decide to return home.

Back in Wales, the men decide to feed themselves and their wives as hunters. One day Pryderi is hunting, and loses his dogs when they chase a boar into a strange castle. (Remember that Pryderi's father, Pwyll, began his strange Otherworld adventures by following his hunting dogs. Pryderi's apple did not fall far from the tree.) The young king pursues his dogs into the castle, and never comes out.

When Manawydan tells Rhiannon of her son's fate, the horse Faerie ventures into the strange fortress and also disappears.

Manawydan and Kigva are now alone in Wales, and decide to farm the land. They grow fields of grain, and each time a field is ready to be harvested, Manawydan makes a plan to reap the next day. But each morning he is to begin harvesting, he finds the field has been eaten bare when he arrives. After this happens several times, Manawydan vows to watch the field all night. (Remember the lord Teirnon who found his foal missing each May Eve, and vowed to watch his mare all night, resulting in the return of the changeling child Pryderi himself?)

At midnight, Manawydan heard "the greatest uproar in the world," and beheld a large host of mice! So many he could not count them. The rodents ate his field of grain to the ground in minutes, and began to run off. But one mouse seemed fatter and slower than the rest, and Manawydan was able to catch the thief and place her in his glove.

Manawydan returns home, and Kigva asks him what he has in his glove. He answers, "A thief I caught stealing from me," and tells his daughter-in-law the strange story. He explains that he plans to hang the culprit the next day. Kigva tells Manawydan it is beneath his station to hang a mouse, but he will not relent.

The very next day, the last man in Wales rides to Gorsedd Arberth, a Faerie mound, and prepares a gallows upon which to hang the rodent.

Strangely, at that moment a scholar approaches. Since there have been no people other than himself, Rhiannon, Pryderi and Kigva in Wales for seven years now, Manawydan questions the scholar. The scholar says he has been studying abroad, and when he asks Manawydan what he is up to, the man tells the scholar, "Hanging a thief I caught stealing from me." The scholar tells Manawydan it is beneath his station to touch the creature, and offers Manawydan a pound for the mouse. But Manawydan refuses his offer, and the scholar leaves.

In moments, as Manawydan is finishing his gallows, a Druid approaches. The conversation is repeated: When asked what he is doing, Manawydan replies, "Hanging a thief I caught stealing from me," and the Druid offers Manawydan three pounds for the rodent. Again Manawydan refuses, and continues readying for the execution.

Now a bishop approaches, and goes through the same conversation with Manawydan. "Hanging a thief I caught stealing from me," Manawydan says once again. The bishop offers seven pounds for the mouse. Again the offer is refused.

The bishop asks Manawydan what he will accept for the mouse, and the man answers that he wishes to have Pryderi and Rhiannon returned, and Wales put back to normal. For the scholar, Druid and bishop are none other than Llywd, son of Kil Coed, a grey one of the woods, or Faerie king. Because of an old grudge against Pryderi, the Grey King has enchanted Wales, hiding its population in the mists of the Otherworld. His retinue asked to be turned to mice so they could harrow Manawydan by devouring his grain, but Llywd's own wife was pregnant, and could not run as fast as the other mice. So Manawydan was able to capture her, and force Llywd to ransom her and break the enchantment. Wales is put back to rights, and Pryderi and Rhiannon are returned to their spouses.

The mouse seems a strange animal for a Faerie to appear as, but it's more common than you may think. In France, Italy and Spain, the Tooth Faerie is actually a mouse, La Petite Souris. The creature burrows beneath the bedclothes to take a tooth and leave a coin. In one French tale, the little mouse helps a good queen by hiding under the pillow of her evil rival and knocking his teeth out while he sleeps. (I know, you were hoping the mice Faeries would be sweet and cute.)

The idea of Faerie mice stealing teeth is not so far removed from these Faerie mice that steal grain. When one is caught, it is the one mouse to which the Underworld King is sexually linked. In a sense she is like a Nymph, an animal woman whose seductive hold on the king forces him to ransom her back. His need for her outweighs his desire for revenge on Pryderi.

Mice are burrowing creatures, and creatures that burrow and hibernate are often seen as sleeping in the Faerie world (more about this in chapter 7).

While this synopsis of "Gallows for a Mouse" may be odd and humorous reading, the *Mabinogion* tale in its original is highly recommended. Most of the stories in this Welsh collection are beautiful and sad, but this one is outrageous and funny. It is not to be missed by anyone interested in the lighter side of Faerie.

SEALS

The two women sat in late afternoon, sewing tirelessly. The good clear light of noon was failing now, and the older woman rubbed her eyes and looked up toward the window and out at the sea.

"Mother," the younger woman said, "let us take a rest. The light is failing. It's not good for your eyes."

"My eyes are not what they once were," the older of the two said. "More's the pity."

"I was wondering something, Mother," the younger woman said. She was just barely out of her teens, and still had the blush of youth on her red cheeks. "Perhaps now is a good time to ask of it. I saw Uncle Jamie just yester eve, brought him a soup I did. Why is he always so sad? It seems worse since me cousins have grown and married, and don't they get sad sometimes too, and stare out to sea? What is the curse I've heard tell of on them? All the villagers speak of it. But they hush when I come near, and don't say a word."

"Aye, that's a sad story," the older woman commented. "Well, you're old enough now, I suppose. You ought to know.

"Years ago Jamie was a happy lad, as right as any of us. He loved the sea, and would fish every day. Good he was at it too, and would bring in baskets of fish for the market.

"One day he was raving when he got home. A seal had followed his wee boat for miles, and he said naught but that it was enchanted, a Selkie, that had followed him. He had made up his mind it was a seal maiden, and he fancied himself in love. We all thought him a bit daft, but the stories ran round the island that such things be, seals that may turn to women in the night. So we bit our tongues and bided our time, and let poor Jamie rant. Perhaps we should have stopped him then, poor dear, but we knew so little of these things.

"Well, it was but a few short weeks later that Jamie brings a young woman home to meet our mother. Dark she was, with hair as black as a raven and eyes to match. He called her Celia, and don't you think he told Mother they were to be married, and that very Sunday. A sweet girl she was, but strange. She was a bit cold, distant. You couldn't put your finger on it, but sure you could feel it.

"So Sunday came and went, and Jamie and Celia were married. But the rumors spread about the island that this girl, Celia, odd as she was, had come from the sea. That Jamie had found her swimming as a seal, and had made some pact with her, that she'd marry and bear his children. Many days me sisters and I would catch the girl staring off to sea, and when we followed her gaze we'd see a pack of seals on a dark speck of rock, staring back. 'My other family,' Celia would say. 'I'd like you to meet them someday.'

"We were polite girls, your aunts and I, so 'we'd be delighted to meet them' was all we'd say.

"Time went by, and your cousins were born, Brigit and James. Such adorable babies. And dark they were, like their mother, and with the look of the sea about them like their dad. Good children they were, well behaved and polite, Celia saw to that.

"It was seven years later that we noticed a sadness about the girl, and she stopped speaking, and went so quietly about her work. The seals came closer to the shore then, and she would stand for hours and stare at them. Strange it was, and make no mistake.

"And then one day she was gone. Brigit always said it was her own fault. She said she'd found an old leather coat in the attic, and asked her mother what it was. And when Celia saw it, she put it on straight-away, and off to the sea she was. Well, don't you know it was her own seal skin? Jamie had hidden it from her all those years, and now she had it back, and gone she was to join her kin in the sea.

"Well, that's the story, strange as it may sound. And now all of these years have gone by, and all Jamie can do is stare at the sea, and see the seals off on the rock, and think of the woman who he brought home from the sea on that day. And your cousins long for their mother, but don't you think they go to the sea on full moon nights, and can speak to the seals, and they know their ways? And that's the end, and the truth of it."

The younger woman looked out the window, and considered. "I feel it's true, Mother. I feel it's true."

~·~

With their huge eyes and childlike faces, seals evoke a special tenderness in us. Seals are also fierce hunters, and very sexual creatures. During mating season, female seals will entertain dozens of lovers, and males fight for the favor of a particularly attractive female. In these ways seals are very much like humans.

Faeries that can take the form of both seal and human are called Selkies. Selkies seem to take great delight in courting human lovers, producing human/seal offspring, and just generally being involved with human lives. But in the end, Selkies always prefer the life of the seal, returning to the sea and breaking the heart of their human lover. Selkie/human children struggle with the decision to live in our world or the seal world, and this is a terrible decision for them to have to make.

The coasts of Ireland, Scotland, Iceland and Norway abound with stories of Selkies. Also called Silkies or Selchies in Scotland and Ireland, the name seems to come from the Orkney Islands, a group of Scottish coastal islands. There the name for a seal is *selch*. In Norway, the enchanted creatures are called Finfolk.

Selkies enjoy human companionship, especially the sex and romance. Both male and female Selkies court human lovers, and plenty of tales involve either gender. They often either seduce a human or allow themselves to be seduced by one. But it seems that Selkies can only spend short amounts of time in human form, even when they've created a happy family with a human.

A traditional Scottish song called "The Great Selkie" concerns the King of the Selkies who seduces a mortal woman. After she's had a son by him, he returns to land to claim the child. We find that, as in many Selkie tales, humans who hunt seals kill both father and son are while they are in seal form. Here is the song as Child collected it (Child #113):

An earthly nurse sits and sings,
And aye she sings, Ba, lily wean!
Little ken I my bairn's father,
Far less the land that he sleeps in.

Then one arose at her bed-side,
An a grumbly guest I'm sure was he:
'Here am I, thy bairn's father,
Although that I be not comely.

'I am a man, upon the land,
And I am a silkie in the sea;
And when I'm far and far from land,
My dwelling is in Sule Skerrie.'

'It was not weel,' quo the maiden fair,
'It was not weel, indeed,' quo she,
'That the Great Silkie of Sule Skerrie
Should have come and gi'en a bairn to me.'

Now he has taken a purse of gold,
And he has put it upon her knee,
Saying, 'Give to me my little young son,
And take thee up thy nurse's fee.

'And it shall come to pass on a summer's day,
When the sun shines heat on every stone,

That I will take my little young son,
And teach him for to swim the foam.

'And thee shall marry a proud gunner,
And a proud gunner I'm sure he'll be,
An the very first shot that ere he shoots,
He'll shoot both my young son and me.'

When the song begins, we find an "earthly nurse" (a mortal woman nursing a child), lamenting that she does not know where the child's father has gone off to. The Selkie, a great king of the Land of Seals (in Scottish, Sule Skerrie), appears in her home (and her bed), saying, "Here I am, your baby's father, a Selkie." The woman laments that she was unaware that her lover was a Selkie. She appears to be aware that bearing a child with a Selkie is never good.

The Selkie gives the woman a bag of money, and takes the child to teach him the ways of the seals. But he predicts that the woman will marry a gunner (a seal hunter), and that her new husband will kill both father and son.

In one sense, this story is a reverse of the Snow White scenario, the evil stepmother. In most Faerie stories involving an evil stepparent, like "Willie's Lady" (see chapter 6), *Snow White* or *Cinderella*, the malicious parent is a replacement mother, intent upon killing her daughter whom she sees as competition for her lover's affection, or for her own children's resources (like the Prince, whom Cinderella's stepsisters seek to marry in place of the true daughter).

In this song, the evil replacement parent is a stepfather. After living a life with his human mother on land, the child of the Great Selkie will return with his true father to the sea. The Selkie predicts that his lover will marry a human seal hunter. The new father will kill both the Selkie and his son. We might see this as a simple error: the human seal hunter does not realize that the pair of seals he harpoons is his wife's lover and child. But in light of all of the other Faerie stories about the usurping parent, we might see the actions of the stepfather as a move to rid his wife of her former lover and her son by him; the human destroys his Otherworldly competition, making himself the only object of his wife's affection.

FINFOLK AND MERMAIDS

While most seal Faeries are benevolent and sweet to their human lovers, there seems to be another type of enchanted sea creatures: Finfolk, who are malicious and dour. Throughout Scotland and Ireland there are tales of good Selkies and bad Finfolk who harm humans after seducing them.

The Finfolk live beneath the sea, in a castle called Finfolkaheem ("Home of the Finfolk" in Norwegian). They also inhabited a disappearing island in the Orkneys called Hildaland, a legendary place very similar to Tir N'an Og or Avalon. The Finfolk would come ashore in various disguises: human, animal, or even as floating clothing. They would approach an unsuspecting human, and capture her or him, dragging the unfortunate captive to Hildaland. There the mortal would be forced to marry the enchanted creature and spend his or her days performing drudgery in the Faerie's service. One reason for the capture of humans is rumored to be the fate of Finwives who do not marry a mortal: they lose their beauty, becoming Finhags. In this way, Finfolk seem to be like vampires, leeching the energy of humans to retain their youthful beauty.

Farther north, among the Saami of Norway, there seems to be no distinction between the two races. To these ancient fishermen, Selkies and Finfolk are the same, and are also seen as Merfolk. These Saami beliefs have come as far south as the Orkneys, where Saami fishermen are occasionally observed. Sightings of the Finfolk have been reported as recently as the eighteenth century. Here is an account by one John Brand, who visited the Orkneys around 1700 on a mission from the Church:

> About five years hence, a boat at the Fishing drew her lines, and one of them, as the Fishers thought, having some great fish

upon it, was with greater difficulty than the rest raised from the Ground, but when raised it came more easily to the surface of the water upon which a creature like a woman presented itself at the side of the boat, it had the face, Arms, breasts, shoulders etc. of a woman, and long hair hanging down the back, but the nether part from below the breasts, was beneath the water, so that they could not understand the shape thereof.

The two fishers who were in the boat being surprised at this strange sight, one of them unadvisedly drew a knife, and thrust it into her breast, whereupon she cried, as they judged, Alas, and the hook giving way she fell backwards and was no more seen: The hook being big went in at her chin and out at the upper lip. The man who thrust the knife into her is now dead, and, as was observed, never prospered after this, but was still haunted by an evil spirit, in the appearance of an old man, who, as he thought, used to say to him, "Will ye do such a thing who killed the Woman." (Brand 1905, 171)

One favorite disguise among Finwives was the Mermaid. The female Finfolk would take on the appearance of a mer-girl to seduce fishermen in their boats, carrying them off to Hildaland. In British, Scottish and Irish lore even seeing a Mermaid means certain death. This verse from the song "Sir Patrick Spens" (Child #58) describes what happens when the crew of a ship piloted by an inexperienced sailor sees a Mermaid and fears the worst:

Up there came a mermaid then,
A comb and glass all in her hand,
"Here's a health to you, my merry young men,
For you'll not see dry land again!"

Similar lore is related in Homer's *Odyssey*, of the Mermaid-like Sirens. Ulysses says:

At sea once more we had to pass the Sirens, whose sweet singing lures sailors to their doom. I had stopped up the ears of my crew with wax, and I alone listened while lashed to the mast, powerless to steer toward shipwreck. (Butler, Book 12, Verse 1)

SELKIES AGAIN . . . THE FEMALE ONES

Completely different than Mermaids or Sirens, female Selkies are sweet and gentle to humans, only hurting us by their difficult choices between love and family. The most common tales of female Selkies go like this: A young man is fishing and sees a seal. Watching the seal, he sees her shed her seal skin and become a beautiful nude woman, dark and sad. The young fisherman waits until the beautiful Faerie wanders away and then hides the seal-maiden's skin. He waits until she returns, and asks her to marry him. He tells her that at the end of seven years of marriage, he'll return her seal skin. They have children and live happily, until someone (usually one of the children) finds the skin. With her skin returned to her, the Selkie wife returns to the sea, often never seeing her husband again.

The Irish and Scots, generally a people of fair complexion, believe that children born of the love between Selkies and mortals are dark, with black hair and dark brown or black eyes, and that these traits are passed down through the generations. These children are drawn to the sea, and often understand the speech of seals. Sometimes the child can communicate with his or her mother in her seal form. Very often these children feel a sense of loss. They long for the sea when they are human, but long for their human family when they are seals. Their stories never end well.

Getting involved with a Selkie is just not a relationship with a stable future, and I would advise against it.

DEER

Deer are a presence in every mythology and all through Faerie lore, probably because deer are a major food group. "What's for dinner, honey?" "Venison!" was probably a conversation that went on throughout history from the days of the caves to the era of castles, from cottages to log cabins. "Venison? Mmm mm good!"

The deer has a nice rack, and by that I mean the deer is antlered. Antlers hold a mythic and iconic appeal throughout the world. People in parts of Asia believe that consuming ground deer antler will enhance a man's virility. This is called sympathetic magic: the antlers represent a stag's sexual prowess, so it will help a man's prowess in that department. (Again, this is not something I recommend trying. There are very good herbal supplements on the market today to enhance male performance.)

In the Lapp and Norse countries, the antlered reindeer is associated with speed and swift movement. These deerlike animals are part of the legend of Wodin, and ghastly reindeer flew through the night in that spirit's train. In fact, it's likely that Wodin himself was depicted with antlers. Antlered Wodin and his Wild Hunt inspired many of our images of Santa Claus, so Father Christmas may very likely be antlered as well (see chapter 9). Time and disbelief made the great deer tiny, as they did with many Faerie creatures.

Herne and Arawn are mythic hunting creatures who seem human enough except for their imposing rack of antlers. This is true of Cernunnos as well, a mainland Celtic God of the hunt. Cernunnos is a title meaning "Antlered One" rather than a proper name. The title was probably applied to several Celtic antlered Gods. The famous Gundestrup cauldron, dug up from the peat bogs of western Europe, depicts an antlered God holding a torc, symbol of power, and surrounded by animals. This figure, with his mighty rack of antlers, is usually referred to as Cernunnos.

There are females with impressive racks too. Fliadais, an Irish Goddess, was either seen as a deer herself, or as a woman whose

chariot was drawn by deer. She was much like the figure of Cernunnos on the Gundestrup cauldron, a mistress of animals and the wild
creatures: she was said to have a cow whose milk could feed thirty
people a day, and she called her worshippers her "herds." She also
had a daughter, Fland, who was something of a Siren, luring men to
their deaths by singing to them from the water.

The Greek Artemis is similar in myth to Fliadais. She is also a deer
goddess, and like her Celtic counterpart, is seen as protector of animals and of the wild places. Young women in the service of Artemis
were called *arktoi*, "bear-girls," and were charged with the job of "acting like bears." (This is an interesting title: later, in Romanized Britain. a young man would take the same title when he became king:
Arthur, "the Bear." It's also interesting to wonder what these girls
did when acting like bears.) Artemis is further associated with the
deer by her actions, such as turning the hunter Actaeon into a deer
for spying on her while she was bathing. In deer form, Actaeon was
eaten by his own hounds (recalling the legend of Pwyll and Arawn).

The most interesting aspect of Artemis is that Artemis is attended
by many maidens, some of whom are mortal (or dead mortals), and
many of whom are Faerie Nymphs. In *The Odyssey*, Homer tells of
these Nymphs, mentioning the association with deer:

> Artemis far-shooting ranges the mountainside . . . taking her
> pleasure among the boars and the running deer; Nymphs of the
> countryside, daughters of Zeus . . . are all around her and share
> her pastime; Leto her mother is glad at heart. With head and
> forehead Artemis overtops the rest, and though all are lovely,
> there is no mistaking which is she. (Butler, ch. 6, verse 102)

The Nymphs Homer describes include the Okeanides, who appear as nine-year-old girls. These Nymphs, of whom there are exactly three thousand, are something like our modern eco-warriors,
guarding Earth's freshwater sources, including streams, rain clouds
and underground wells (Artemis bathes in freshwater streams often,

so sixty of the Okeanides are sort of on permanent assignment to her). The Okeanides' various Nymphs include: Naiads (Spring and Fountain Nymphs), Leimonides (Pasture Nymphs), Nepheli (Cloud Nymphs), Aurai (Breeze Nymphs) and Anthousai (Flower Nymphs).

From Crete, there are the maiden Nymphs who are daughters of a river God named Amninos. Again, these Nymphs, the Amnisiades, are associated with freshwater and with the animals of the forest. In fact, some of the Nymphs who attend Artemis have bird legs.

A few of Artemis's crew are mortals who have been given Nymph-like characteristics and immortality; changelings, in other words. One is Britomartis, a girl from Crete who hunts deer and was said to have invented the hunting net. Here is what the Greek poet Callimachus said of her in his "Hymn to Artemis":

> Which of the nymphs dost thou love above the rest, and what heroines hast thou taken for thy companions? . . . And beyond others thou lovest the nymph of Gortyn, Britomartis, slayer of stags, the goodly archer . . . . (Mair and Loeb, Hymn III: to Artemis. Verse 183)

Three other changelings are the maidens Oupis, Loxo and Hekaerge. These three were from Hyperboreiai, a mythical northern land named for Boreas, God of the North Wind. This land seems very like Britain or Saxony, and the three maids may well have been a folkloric record of British Faeries that came to be associated by the Greeks with their huntress Artemis. Their names all refer to shooting the bow (Hekaerge, for instance, means "hitting from a distance"). Each is an expert deer hunter, and each maiden fought to her death in defense of her chastity when threatened with rape or molestation. For this act, each was enchanted and brought back to life.

As well as being in Artemis' retinue, these Hyperborean maids are worshipped as deities in their own right, and young maidens' rituals to them involve leaving offerings of hair:

It is customary for the girls to . . . offer a lock of their hair before their wedding, just as the daughters of the Delians once
cut their hair for Hekaerge and Oupis. (Jones 1.43.4)

BACK TO DEER

Everyone knows the Banshee howls when a death is to occur. But
the Bean Sidhe was once known as a Faerie woman who drove herds
of red deer, milking the creatures for drink and cheese. The mainland Celts referred to deer as "Faerie cattle" and their Banshee herds-
woman was able to shape shift into deer form. This tradition was
seen in County Cork in stories of the An Chailleach Bhéarach, the
Old Woman of the isle of Beare, who could transform into a deer and
commune with the dead.

The deer as guardian of the dead is seen in the myths we've discussed, of Herne, Cernunnos and Arawn. The deer as a God or Goddess of the land of death is common to Norse myth as well, where a
stag is said to stand upon the highest hill of Valhalla. The *Poetic Edda*
also refers to four stags who feed upon Ygdrassil, the World Tree. It
was a deer that brought Pwyll to his bargain with the Underworld,
and a deer that bore Ossian. Later a deer would cross Ossian's path
as he and Niamh rode the magical white horse from our world to Tir
N'an Og. In each story, antlered creatures stand guard at the gates of
Faerie, and draw humans in.

In the Grimms' tale of *Brother and Sister* (or *Little Sister and Little
Brother*), a sister and brother are forced to hide in the forest from a
wicked stepmother, very like Hansel and Gretel, except this story
comes complete with deer and changelings. The boy drinks from a
magic stream and becomes a deer. The sister vows to remain in the
forest and care for him. One day a king happens on the deer while
hunting. Following the animal, the king spies the sister, with whom
he falls in love. The king and Little Sister are married, but in time
the evil stepmother finds out. She kills Little Sister and replaces the
girl with her own child (i.e., the stepsister, making her a changeling

wife). In time the king discovers the treachery and kills the change-ling and her mother. The boy is returned to human form.

AND FINALLY, BIRDS

In speaking of Artemis's maidens, we mentioned birds, especially the Amnisiades who sometimes appear with bird legs. Also present among the Nymphs attending Artemis are the Flower Faeries, the Anthousai. The presence of these Nymphs recalls a tale from the Welsh *Mabinogion*, of Blodeuedd.

Somewhere between a changeling, a Faerie and a Goddess, de-pending on who you speak to, Blodeuedd (you'll also see her name spelled Bleudwedd and Blodwedd) is a woman made of flowers by Gwydion, the great Welsh god of magic and music. Gwydion's son/nephew, Llew Llaw Gyffes ("the Lion with the Steady Hand," a title of the Welsh Sun God) needed a wife, but could not marry a mortal woman due to a curse his mother had placed upon him. So his father (or uncle; different versions of the tale give different information) makes him a hot babe from nine flowers of the forest.

Blodeuedd and Llew Llaw Gyffes do fine for a while, until the Flower Girl falls for the antlered God of Winter, Gronw (in some ver-sions, Goronwy). Gronw kills Llew Llaw Gyffes, but of course being the Sun God, Llew comes back to life and kills Gronw (the cycle of summer and winter). In the midst of all this seasonal bloodshed, Blodeuedd is transformed into an owl.

Now the name Blodeuedd means "Flower Face" in Welsh, and sure enough, the people of that country consider the owl to be a Faerie creature, and call it Flower Face, Blodeuedd.

Also from the *Mabinogion* comes the story of Branwen. Branwen, which means "White Raven," is a princess/Goddess held hostage by the king of an underworld set in Ireland. Though she was prom-ised to the Underworld ruler as a bride, she is held hostage in the king's kitchen, and the cook boxes her ears daily. Branwen befriends a small wren (the wren, a tiny British bird that represents winter, bears the full name raven's sparrow, or bran's (wren's) sparrow; Bran ["Raven"] is Branwen's brother). Branwen teaches the wren to speak, and sends it across the Irish Sea to Wales, where it finds her giant brother Bran. The tiny bird tells Bran that his sister is held captive, and Bran mounts an army of enchanted ones, including Pryderi and Manawydan, to cross the waters to the Underworld and rescue her. To cross the seas between the worlds, Bran lays himself across the waters, spanning the two banks, and allows his army to walk over his back. This is an image of the raven, Bran, bridging the human world with the Otherworld. In the course of the ensuing battle, a magical cauldron is used that can bring slain warriors alive, again allowing the dead to cross the river back into our world. No good comes of this.

A constant theme here is that birds, especially ravens and sparrows, can get back and forth between worlds easily, and bring information from one shore to the other. The idea of a Faerie bird that can speak and impart useful information is a pretty common one in folklore. Many French, German and Persian stories tell of these enchanted birds. In fact, the story is so common that we have a phrase in English that "a little bird told me," meaning "that information just came to me from a magical source." Many Faeries take on the form of birds to prophesy or to give extrasensory information to humans, including the Sirin of eastern Europe, the Vilas of Russia, and the owl of wisdom sacred to Greek Athena.

Below is an odd British song in which enchanted birds offer advice to humans about love and loss. (Notice that the bat, a mammal, is considered a bird here. Bats are more like mice, and we've already discussed those little rodents.)

> Aye said the little leather wing bat
> I'll tell to you the reason that
> The reason that I fly by night
> It's because I've lost my heart's delight

Aye said the blackbird sitting on a chair
Once I courted a lady fair
She grew fickle and turned her back
And ever since then I'm dressed in black

Aye said the woodpecker sitting on a fence
Once I courted a handsome wench
She grew scared and from me fled
And ever since then my head's been red

Aye said the little turtledove
I'll tell you how to win her love
Court her night and court her day
Never give her time to say oh, nay

Aye said the blue jay away he flew
If I were a young man I'd have two
If one were faithless and chanced to go
I'd add the other string to my bow
(Traditional)

Winged ones like these advice-giving birds appear constantly in folk stories, and the Grimms collected many tales involving just such enchanted birds. In *Fitcher's Bird*, a fairly complex Fairy tale, a wizard disguised as a beggar beguiles three sisters (very similar to the tale of Blodeuedd, in which Gwydion disguises himself and his son as itinerant minstrels to win the right for Llew Llaw Gyffes to marry). The first two sisters are killed by the wizard, but the youngest sister manages to bring the older two back to life and escape by disguising herself as a bird (the title character).

Another Grimms' tale, *The Singing Springing Lark*, is very similar to *Beauty and the Beast*. In this tale, the father seeks not a rose for his daughter but a singing springing lark. Finding the lark, he attempts to capture it, but once he has it, he is approached by a lion. The lion tells him that he must either forfeit his life or give the lion the first person he meets on his journey home. Of course that first person is his daughter, who must now marry the lion. And as you might have guessed, the lion is a prince under a wicked spell.

But the bird element does not end there. The lion prince is transformed into a dove, and the girl must follow him around the earth for seven years. He is finally transformed back to handsome prince form, but has forgotten the faithful girl and is about to marry a princess. The girl rescues him, and the two fly away together on the prince's giant bird. The elements of spending seven years in the Otherworld, and of forgetting what one has experienced there (or not being able to tell of what was experienced there) are common Faerie elements. (If you didn't see that right away, you just haven't been paying attention.) The Singing Springing Lark, besides its Beauty and the Beast beginning, seems to be an adaptation of the Ossian story or The Voyage of Bran Mac Febal with the genders simply reversed.

CERRIDWEN

One of the most ancient Welsh myths involves several animal transformations, ending in that oddest of birds, the chicken.

Cerridwen (pronounced KER-id-wen. The Celts have no soft "c" in their language groups) is believed to be everything from an Underworld Goddess to a Faerie to a witch. In the story below, she has many characteristics of a Faerie Queen, similar to Mab, L'Annawnshee or Morgan Le Fay. Cerridwen controls a cauldron of rebirth (similar to Morgan Le Fay's association with the Holy Grail). She rules an Underworld, but can transform herself into an animal to enter various other worlds. She has a changeling child whom she forces to work for her, and later tries to kill. Her chase of this changeling in various animal guises may be seen as the Wild Ride across the sky and the fields, ending in the gathering of grain. In this way she is very much like Mab.

Here is the story:

Cerridwen had a magical cauldron of rebirth, which she kept in her castle. She also had a son, Afagddu, who was hideously ugly. She wanted to make him wise. It seems that Cerridwen had devised a brew that could grant all knowledge. This elixir must be stirred in the cauldron for one full year. Only the first drops would bestow all knowledge; the rest would be deadly poison. Cerridwen mixed the ingredients, and then set her servant Gwion Bach to stir it for a year and a day.

At the end of that time, Gwion Bach was excited to end his long servitude of mixing the brew. But as he put his ladle down, the first drops of the boiling concoction flew out of the cauldron and onto his finger. He instinctively nursed the burnt finger in his mouth, and so tasted the magical first drops. Now Gwion Bach had all the wisdom the brew could imbue and Afagddu would have only the deadly poison left in the cauldron.

Fearing Cerridwen's reaction, Gwion Bach acted quickly. He became a hare, and jumped out of the castle window. But Cerridwen quickly figured out what had happened, and she turned herself into a hound and raced after him.

Gwion the rabbit ran through a green field, but Cerridwen the dog gave speedy chase. Coming to a river, Gwion became a fish. But Cerridwen became an otter and chased him again. So Gwion rose from the water and became a sparrow, with the Underworld Queen close behind him in the form of a falcon.

Finally from the air Gwion Bach spied a barn. He threw himself to the floor of the threshing room, and became a grain of corn on the floor among the thousands of grains there. Cerridwen became a hen, and ate the grains.

Once she had eaten him, Cerridwen grew pregnant with Gwion Bach. She vowed to kill him the instant he was born. But the newborn was so beautiful she could not bring herself to do it. She threw the babe into a river.

An Elfin king happened to be passing by as the child floated downstream. The Elf took the babe from the water, and named him Taliesin, Welsh for "The Shining Brow." Taliesin grew up to be an enchanted bard, and is known as the greatest Celtic singer that ever lived.

This weird story of a changeling eaten by a bird and rescued by an Elf (in some versions, the rescuing king is said to be a Celtic king named Elffin. You can probably do the math on that one) and then destined to be a great bard is in keeping with a lot of British bird lore. In the course of their chase, Cerridwen becomes a bird twice; first a falcon and then a hen. This gives a glimpse into Cerridwen's true nature as an Underworld Bird Faerie, similar to Blodeuedd or Branwen. Like many enchanted birds, Cerridwen can gift the gift of song and prophesy to humans.

Cerridwen is also the quintessential evil stepmother, the origin of that character in the tales of *Snow White* and *Cinderella*. First, like the stepmother of Cinderella, she places her stepson in charge of toil and drudgery, while her own child is meant to reap the rewards of that work. Like Snow White, the boy ingests a food, the magical brew, that changes the roles they are in (Snow White ate the apple, or tomato in the French version). Like Snow White, Gwion Bach is chased by his evil stepmother; like Cinderella, there is a magical transformation involving animals, which helps put the boy in his proper station; like Snow White, the boy is doomed to die, but is spared because of his beauty; and like Snow White, the child is fostered by Otherworld creatures (Elves, rather than Dwarves). Gwion Bach also crosses between worlds in his animal forms: from Cerridwen's Underworld to our fields and farms, and into the Faerie world with the Elf king. All of these trials are an initiation that puts Gwion Bach in his rightful place as Taliesin, the great bard who is given song and prophesy by Cerridwen the Underworld bird creature. (Compare Gwion Bach's initiatory trials to those of Pryderi.)

We are never told what became of hideous Afagddu, but we assume he remains in the Underworld, a lurking danger in that enchanted place. He is like the stepsisters in *Cinderella*, unable to reap the reward that must be bestowed upon the true child. Like that story too, Afagddu is simply a catalyst, providing motive for the stepmother's hatred of her changeling ward. The real action, and the transformation, exclude the stepsiblings and involve only Gwion Bach or Cinderella. The stepsiblings are unable to change, and so are left behind or destroyed.

Child collected a ballad that I believe is based on the tale of Cerridwen, though it's similar to many songs known throughout Europe and the Middle East. In it a magical blacksmith transforms himself into the various animals in pursuit of the object of his love, a woman who wishes to remain chaste. He may be the very first stalker in history. Remember that blacksmiths are known in lore to be enchanted, as their skin becomes black from their work, making them lucky or Faerie blessed; blacksmith lore always places them at the side of the most beautiful female creatures, such as Venus and Freya, both married to hideous Dwarf smiths. Versions of this song exist in French and Italian, and there is a Persian treatment as well. The basic story is told by Scheherazade in the *Arabian Nights* tales. A similar story is given in Hindu scriptures: The first woman transforms into a cow to escape the first man's advances. He becomes a bull, which is how cattle were first created. In some earlier versions of the song seen here, the two lovers are running from a wizard or sorceress (such as Cerridwen), or from ogres.

Here it is as Child #44, "The Two Magicians":

The lady stands in her bower door,
As straight as willow wand;
The blacksmith stood a little forebye,
Wi hammer in his hand.
'Weel may ye dress ye, lady fair,
Into your robes o red;

Before the morn at this same time,
I'll gain your maidenhead.'

'Awa, awa, ye coal-black smith,
Woud ye do me the wrang
To think to gain my maidenhead,
That I hae kept sae lang!'

Then she has hadden up her hand,
And she sware by the mold,
'I wudna be a blacksmith's wife
For the full o a chest o gold.
'I'd rather I were dead and gone,
And my body laid in grave,
Ere a rusty stock o coal-black smith
My maidenhead shoud have.'
But he has hadden up his hand,
And he sware by the mass,
'I'll cause ye be my light leman
For the hauf o that and less.'
O bide, lady, bide,
And aye he bade her bide;
The rusty smith your leman shall be,
For a' your muckle pride.

Then she became a turtle dow,
To fly up in the air,
And he became another dow,
And they flew pair and pair.
O bide, lady, bide,

She turnd hersell into an eel,
To swim into yon burn,
And he became a speckled trout,
To gie the eel a turn.
O bide, lady, bide,

Then she became a duck, a duck,
To puddle in a peel,
And he became a rose-kaimd drake,
To gie the duck a dreel.
O bide, lady, bide,

She turnd hersell into a hare,
To rin upon yon hill,
And he became a gude grey-hound,
And boldly he did fill.

Then she became a gay grey mare,
And stood in yonder slack,
And he became a gilt saddle,
And sat upon her back.
Was she wae, he held her sae,
And still he bade her bide;
The rusty smith her leman was,
For a' her muckle pride.

Then she became a het girdle,
And he became a cake,
And a' the ways she turnd hersell,
The blacksmith was her make.

She turnd hersell into a ship,
To sail out ower the flood;
He ca'ed a nail intill her tail,
And syne the ship she stood.

Then she became a silken plaid,
And stretchd upon a bed,
And he became a green covering,
And gaind her maidenhead.

While the smith has his way with the maid in this version, there
are other versions where he does not. The chase across various

worlds, mundane and enchanted, is carried out throughout each version of the song, and always harkens us back to the tale of the bird creature Cerridwen, the Wild Ride, and other Faerie chase legends.

Chapter 5

FAERIE MUSIC

She was dead. The Nymph, the most beautiful creature he had ever seen. Her alabaster skin, her lips redder than red, the funny front tooth imperfect in that face of perfection—she lay motionless now, not breathing, not moving. It had been seconds since the serpent had lashed out from its lair, bitten, left behind two cruel pinprick marks. She just looked at him and closed her eyes. She fell into his arms and didn't move.

He expected her to wake up. He expected her to open her eyes. He expected that it was all a dream, that his senses were fooling him, that he'd realize this wasn't really happening. That his father would come down from the sky and reverse time, so that he could pull her from the snake's sting seconds before.

But she lay dead.

He couldn't stand it. This could not happen. He shivered, holding her, feeling her grow colder.

Days passed. He could not eat. He could not sleep. His lyre offered no comfort.

Or did it?

He woke with a start one night from a troubled sleep. He had seen her, pale and sad, in that other place, the world of dream. The world below. That dreary, cheerless place, silent as a stone.

That was it, wasn't it? Silent as stone. Without the comfort of laughter, bird song, music.

He took his best lyre, the one Hermes had given him. He began the long journey below. Through thorny paths, roads red with clay that looked like it had been mixed with blood. Long days he slogged along, singing lightly to himself, making up his mind on which song would be just right.

The ferryman was somber and austere during the silent river crossing. Several others were on the ferry, all dead of course. A man who had been crushed by a cart. A woman old and feeble. A young slave girl, pretty, with deeply tanned skin, beaten to death by her mistress. There was still pus oozing from the gashes left by the whip that had struck her chest and arms. She alone seemed happy to be here, riding the still waters between the worlds.

Now the ferry docked. He was the last off, giving his coins to the ferryman, smiling and then checking the smile. No smiles here, he thought.

Now the dusty path to the great hall, where the two of them sat; his Uncle Hades and the beautiful woman from the sunlit lands. His uncle agreed to see him, asked his servants to let the lad in. He came before the stately God, humble, serene.

"Uncle, I would play my lyre for all assembled here." The God of the Dead nodded, hardly perceptible, but there it was, a slight movement of the head. He began. He played the saddest song he knew, a lay written by his aunt Melpomene. The God bowed his head, and Persephone let a single tear fall.

In time the beautiful Goddess of Green Things whispered to her husband, who lifted his hand in a command to stop. "My wife would hear a cheery song," he commanded. The lad began at once, a song of the Fey, who dance in circles of mushrooms at deep midnight. All in the hall began to sway, or tap their shoeless feet.

Finally the tune was ended.

"What shall we give you as reward?" the great God asked his nephew.

"One who dwells here. A Nymph: Eurydice."

The Green Goddess whispered again, and the God of Death nodded.

"Your wife," he said gravely.

"Yes," said the young man.

"Take her," the God said after a pause. "But you must leave, and never look back. Do you understand this condition of our bargain?"

"I do," the lad said.

She stood at the door to the hall, as silent as earth, as transparent as mist. He took her hand, sighed to see her, and they began the walk up the long dusty road.

***

The Faeries are great makers of things. Anything made by humans can be made by our Otherworldly counterparts, from clothes, shoes and hats, to saddles and bridles, from thrones and courtly robes, to instruments of all kinds. And as well as we are able to play music upon our instruments, the Fey can play better, sweeter, brighter and sadder. But there is a good deal of danger in the music of the Kindly Ones, as there is in all things Faerie.

Faeries are known to play a wide variety of instruments, especially the fiddle (a common name for the violin, for anyone who wonders at the difference between those two instruments), the viol (an older type of violin), the tin whistle (a small Irish flute), and especially the harp. In *The Fairy Mythology*, Thomas Keightly states:

> The Norwegians call the Elves Huldrafolk, and their music Huldraslaat: It is in the minor key, and of a dull and mournful sound. The mountaineers sometimes play it . . . . There is also a

tune called The Elf King's Tune, which several of the good fiddlers know right well, but never venture to play, for as soon as
it begins both old and young, and even inanimate objects, are
impelled to dance, and the player cannot stop unless he can
play the air backwards, or that someone comes behind him and
cuts the strings of his fiddle. (Keightly 1860, 79)

Like the Norwegians, the Irish have a rich musical tradition with
many tunes said to be taught to humans by the Fey. One tune called
"Sidhe Beg Sidhe Mor" ("The Little Faerie Mound and the Big Faerie
Mound") was known to be taught to the great Irish harper Turlough
O'Carolan by the Faeries. The tune tells of a war between the queen
of Sidhe Beg and the queen of Sidhe Mor. O'Carolan played this
tune in the great halls of Ireland, and it is still played today, considered one of the loveliest Irish tunes ever. Another very lively tune is
called "The Fairy Reel," and is quite popular among Irish fiddlers.

The magic of Faerie music can be seen in several Grimms' tales. In
The Wonderful Musician, a fiddler traveling alone in the forest calls to
himself the company of animals and humans simply by playing his
fiddle. A wolf, a fox, a rabbit and finally a woodsman respond to his
playing, the woodsman protecting the fiddler from the beasts who
have assembled.

In the folk tale of *The Pied Piper of Hamlin*, it is a magical piper who
lures first rats and then the children of Hamlin into a subterranean
land (the Faerie world). The pipe is another name for the tin whistle,
or fipple flute, and the piper's pied clothing, made of multicolored
squares, is a sign that he is of the Fey or the spirit world. Being called
off to the Otherworld by music is a common element of Faerie lore.
In the story of Ossian, we saw that Ossian himself was lured away to
Tir N'an Og by Niamh when she sat playing her harp on a hillside.
As soon as he heard the sound of her playing and singing, he was
captivated, and could no longer stay in Ireland. Only homesickness
broke the spell seven years later, with disastrous results.

Enchantment by Faerie music can have disastrous results. In one tale, said to be a true story, a gentleman wrote of his encounter with a young woman in County Clare who just sat by her fire each day, singing a plaintive, wordless tune. When he asked about her, he was told that she had once heard the Faerie harp. Afterwards she had no memory of love or hate, or indeed, of anything but the beautiful Faerie song she had heard. The gentleman was also told that when the spell was broken, the girl would die. Keightly concurs, citing a story he has heard of a Danish town called Garun, in the parish of Tanum. The people of the town would hear music coming out of a Faerie mound, played by "the very best musicians. Anyone there who had a fiddle, and wished to play, was taught in an instant. But whoever did not do so might hear them within, under the hill, breaking their violins to pieces and weeping bitterly." (Keightly 1860, 79)

The danger of Faerie music is in the tales of Mermaids and Sirens. In each story, the singing of these Faeries lures sailors and other unfortunates to their death by drowning or sinking. It never seems to be the intention of the beautiful magical creatures in these tales to kill. They usually sing because it's simply what they do. It is human frailty, the inability to resist the music and the incredible beauty of Mermaids and Sirens that cause the listener's death. This is probably true of Faerie harp playing as well: the Faerie probably has no intention of beguiling the casual listener. Although it seems apparent that Niamh did, indeed, know the effect that her playing would have upon Ossian, and used that effect to her advantage. The same with the Elf Queen that sang to the nurse as a cow in "The Queen of Elfland's Nourice." But apart from these few stories of intentional beguiling, it seems we humans are just pretty weak when it comes to the temptations of Fey music.

These stories of temptation and death at the singing of the Fey have become cautionary tales, often meant to warn men about the evils brought on by sexual temptation. "If you get too close to this kind of beauty, it's gonna do you in" is the moral here. Through the

Middle Ages and Renaissance, and into the Puritan Age and the Victorian era, these tales took on this cautionary air, and were told to discourage sexuality and lust (more about that in chapter 6).

The notion that our threshold for pain and control is much lower than that of the Fey is seen in so many stories. It seems that the Fey can withstand music, nights of dancing and general roughhousing that we humans cannot. The Wild Ride is an annual party for the Fey, but if we are caught in it, we will suffer and die. A night of Faerie drinking can cause a human to sleep for a century. And the music the Good People constantly listen to will rob us of our will, and leave us without a soul. Some may see this as intentional. The Faeries play their music, give us drink or lure us into their dances to trap us and harm us. But I disagree. I think that the Faeries simply do not understand our frailties. They want us to have fun with them, to do the things they do for amusement, but when we do these things, we are injured by them. The Faeries are like a child playing rough with a favorite toy, and crying when the toy becomes broken.

But Faerie music can be healing and protective as well. In the *Mabinogion* story of Bran, the birds of Rhiannon sing to the survivors of the Irish war, and their singing heals the men from what we would today call post-traumatic stress disorder. And remember that the music of the tromb, or Jew's harp, saved a young man from the wiles of the Glastig.

Brian Froud relates an Irish tale of two young men, both crippled in some way, one good and bright, the other dense and lazy. The bright young lad is resting one evening from a journey home from the fields made difficult by his infirmity, when he hears the singing of Faeries. The song lingers on these words: "Monday Tuesday Monday Tuesday." The lad listens for a time, then chimes in with the words "Wednesday Thursday." The Faeries, excited by the young man's improvement of their song, cures the lad's hunchback and sends him home hale and sound.

The story goes on to say that the other boy, who is not as quick on the uptake, hears of the cure and is bidden by his mother to seek the Faeries so they can heal him too. He finally hears the song, "Monday Tuesday Wednesday Thursday . . ." but bungles the melody so horribly when he tries to add "Friday Saturday" that the singers curse him, adding the first boy's hunch to his own hunchback. The boy hobbles home dying. The Faerie-taught song is still sung today in Ireland as "Dia Luain, Dia Mairt" ("Monday Tuesday").

The music of the Fey is above all magical. As with Ossian, it bewitches, heals or beguiles. In the *Mabinogion* story of Math, son of Mathonwy, when the young Sun God Llew Llaw Gyffes is pierced with a spear by Gronw and becomes an eagle, his uncle Gwydion sings an enchantment to lure Llew down from a tree, so that he can be healed of his wound. The song Gwydion sings is translated by Lady Charlotte Guest as:

Oak that grows between the two banks;
Darkened is the sky and hill!
Shall I not tell him by his wounds,
That this is Llew?

Oak that grows in upland ground,
Is it not wetted by the rain? Has it not been drenched
By nine score tempests?
It bears in its branches Llew Llaw Gyffes!

Oak that grows beneath the steep;
Stately and majestic is its aspect!
Shall I not speak it?
That Llew will come to my lap?
(Guest 1877, 430)

Each verse of this spell-song relates to a factor in Llew's condition: Oak is one of the flowers from which Llew's wife Blodeuedd was created; Llew's rotting eagle flesh is soaking the oak tree like rain; and Llew is a majestic prince, being the nephew of Math, king of the Welsh gods. Gwydion's song does indeed coax Llew into Gwydion's lap, where through his harp playing Gwydion heals his nephew. Gwydion had used his harp earlier in the story to beguile Arianrhod and her maids into believing they were being attacked by an enemy fleet. This enchantment was used to trick Llew's mother into arming him, against the curse she had put on the boy that he should not bear arms unless she armed him.

In one other instance in this story, Gwydion forms Llew's wife, Blodeuedd, out of nine flowers of the forest. Though no spell is recounted in the *Mabinogion* as we have it now, preeminent Scottish singer and storyteller Robin Williamson conjectures that this too was done through a song, and he wrote a song after the type of enchantment piece Gwydion might have used. (For the full story of Llew Llaw Gyffes, read the *Mabinogion*, a must for all serious students of Faerie, Welsh folklore and mythology.)

KING ORFEO

The ballad "King Orfeo" describes a battle between the Lord of the Faeries and the titular king over the king's wife, who has been abducted by the Faerie leader. King Orfeo wins his lady back "Devil Went Down to Georgia" style, though on the harp, rather than the fiddle. Here is one version of the song:

> There was a King lived in the West,
> Green the woods so early,
> Of all the harpers he was the best,
> Where the hart goes yearly.
>
> The King he has a-hunting gone,
> Green the woods so early,
> And left his lady all alone,
> Where the hart goes yearly.
>
> The King of Fairy with his dart,
> Green the woods so early,

Has pierced the lady to the heart,
Where the hart goes yearly.

So after them the King has gone,
Green the woods so early,
Until he came to a large grey stone,
Where the hart goes yearly.

And he took out his harp to play.
First he played the notes of pain,
And all their hearts were weary,
Then he played the Fairy reel,
And all their hearts were cheery.

The King of Fairy, with his rout,
Green the woods so early,
Has gone to hunt him all about,
Where the hart goes yearly.

"Come ye into the Fairy hall,
Green the woods so early,
And play your harp amongst us all,"
Where the hart goes yearly.

And he pulled out his harp to play.
First he played the notes of pain,
And all their hearts were weary,
Then he played the Fairy reel,
And all their hearts were cheery.

"Oh what shall I give you for your play?"
Green the woods so early,
"Oh let me take my lady away."
Where the hart goes yearly.

The Fairy King said "Be it so"
Green the woods so early,

"Take her by the hand and go."
Where the hart goes yearly.
(Traditional)

Apparently the Fairy King is so enchanted by King Orfeo's harp that he allows his prize to leave the Faerie domain without a fight.

It has been suggested that this song from the Shetlands is based on the Greek tale of Orpheus and Eurydice, in which Orpheus wins his woman back from Hades's world by playing the lyre, an early form of the harp.

The association of King Orfeo and the god Orpheus is strengthened by the refrain that runs through the song. Orpheus is the brother of Artemis, the virgin Goddess whose domain is the green woods ("Green the woods so early") and whose companion is the hart who was once Actaeon ("Where the hart goes yearly").

Since Orpheus is an immortal, the son of the Sun God Apollo and the Muse Calliope, we can assume that King Orfeo is also of the Otherworld, and that his power over the Faerie King comes from his own Faerie abilities with the harp. Referring back to the Greek tale, Orpheus is magically skilled in all things musical (his mother taught him to sing, and his father to play the lyre). Orpheus perfected the lyre's design, and was said to be able to charm any person or animal; even trees would succumb to his playing and singing. He did something no creature had ever done before, which was to convince Hades, by playing music, to allow a resident of the Hotel Hades to check out. Of course, there was one condition, that neither Orpheus nor Eurydice look back. Orpheus blew it by looking back at his wife. She became a resident of Chez Hades once more, and poor Orpheus went home empty-handed.

This element of loss didn't seem to make it into the Shetland telling of the tale, in which we simply learn that King Orfeo gets his wife back.

FINVARRA

The Fairy King of "King Orfeo" is quite similar to the Irish king of the Sidhe, Finvarra. Finvarra would often kidnap mortal brides, and then keep them in his feasting hall, entertaining them with music and drink. The tale states that when these mortal women hear Faerie music, they forget the world they have come from, and know only their life in the Faerie hall.

There is an Irish tale similar to that of "King Orfeo," in which Finvarra kidnaps a woman named Ethna. Her husband, a rich lord, hires workers to dig deeply into the earth until they have dug down so deeply that they can put their ears to the soil and hear the Faerie music. They litter the earth with salt, so that the song they hear will not affect them.

Afraid that the mortal diggings will reach Knockma, his feasting hall, Finvarra orders the humans to stop digging, and states that he in turn will release Ethna.

This he does, but upon her return the woman never smiles or speaks, listening always for the Faerie music that beguiled her. She wastes away, always longing for that sound.

Finally her husband has a dream in which he is told to unlace his lady's girdle and burn it. He does this, and her spirit is returned to our world. The lord's wife is the same happy woman he married.

MAGIC AND THE EFFECTS OF FAERIE MUSIC

Why would Faerie music have these effects on us? What is it about the music of the Otherworld that beguiles us, that drives us to lose our senses, our very identity? What magical powers can these fiddlers and harpers conjure?

For my conjecture on this, we need to look at a very old idea, revived by cutting-edge science.

In Kabalah, ancient Jewish mysticism, there is a belief about the creation of the universe, based upon the letters of the Torah. The Hebrew

Torah, known in Christianity as the Old Testament of the Bible, begins
with this phrase:

בראשית, ברא אלהים את השמים ואת הארץ.

Which is pronounced: Bereshit bara Elohim et hashamayim ve'et
ha'arets.

In the King James Bible, this phrase is translated as "In the beginning, God (Elohim, literally the Gods) created the heavens and
the Earth." But to Kabalists, this phrase means something very different. Bereshit (pronounced, roughly, BER-a-sheet) is a cipher, a series of letters that do not represent a word, but an idea. Bear in mind
that unlike English letters, Hebrew letters each have deep layers of
meaning. Like English letter characters, each Hebrew character represents a sound. But unlike English characters, each also represents a
number, a word, a phrase, a musical note, a mode of thought, a color,
and many other associations. Kabalists study each letter for these layers of meaning, then piece together the series of letters in a Torah
statement, and attempt to decipher deeper meanings than simply
the stated phrase. This area of specialized Kabalistic study is called
Gematria.

Since Bereshit has no literal meaning, Kabalists who study Gematria see it as a formula, a series of letters that represent the way in
which Jehovah God created the universe. (Jehovah, the name of the
Hebrew God, is itself a cipher, composed of the letters yod heh vav
heh. There is no literal meaning to these letters, and Jews often inter-
pret the name of their god to mean "I am as I am," or simply put, "you
cannot understand what I am, so don't bother trying.") According to
the idea of Bereshit, the Gods (Elohim, which is plural) created the
universe by vocalizing the words of the Torah. As each word was intoned, the thing the word represented came into manifestation.

If you ask many Kabalists, they'll tell you that the way Elohim/Je-
hovah accomplished this was to sing the words of the Torah, thereby
singing the universe into being. If this belief has foundation, then
music, or the intoning of particular tones accompanied by particular

words or letter sounds, is the basis of universal energy—what we call Magic. For this reason, modern Jews sing when they pray. In synagogue, a singing rabbi called a cantor sings the liturgy, to place it into the form in which Jehovah first intoned it. In private prayer, Jews *daven* (a form of rhythmic body movement) and sing or chant their prayers. In other words, Jews chant and dance in order to make their prayers meaningful.

Chanted prayer is a very old device, occurring in almost all ancient Pagan religions, in early Christianity, in Hinduism, in Islam, and in many other spiritual paths. Each believes that sung prayer connects us more deeply to the spiritual source. Native American nations each had special sung prayers, accompanied by dancing and drumming. One of the best known is the Ghost Dance. First created by a Paiute religious leader named Wovoka, the Ghost Dance movement taught Plains Indian followers that if they lived righteously and performed the Ghost Dance, the white man would flee the plains and the buffalo would return. The movement spread furiously across the prairie, catching the imagination of many Native Americans. Dance camps sprang up, and many dancers flocked to these places to dance, drum, sing and pray. A slaughter of Ghost Dancers at Wounded Knee camp in Pine Ridge, South Dakota helped put an end to the movement, which whites increasingly feared would unite tribes and accomplish its goal.

Another example is the dancing of both historical and present-day Witches. In history, Witches were reported to dance at the sabbat, often nude, chanting a "rune" or song. In modern Craft, there are two songs, spoken of in the Wiccan Rede: the "Witches' Rune" and the "Baneful Rune." The Rede tells Witches to dance deosil (clockwise, or sunwise) on the waxing moon, chanting out the "Witches' Rune"; and to dance widdershins (counterclockwise, or against the direction of the sun) on the waning moon, chanting out the "Baneful Rune." Most people today associate the "Witches' Rune" with an ancient French chant, which Gerald Gardner collected and included in his *Book of Shadows*:

Eko, eko, Azarak
Eko, eko, Zomelak
Bazabi lacha bachabe
Lamac cahi achababe
Karrellyos
Lamac lamac Bachalyas
Cabahagy sabalyos
Baryolos
Lagoz atha cabyolas
Samahac atha famolas
Hurrahya!
(Gardner, unpublished)

The chant may be based on Old French, though there are words that may be from Ceremonial Magician, John Dee's Enochian language. Lady Sheba's *Book of Shadows* states that the Rune may be used to call the Witches' deities Aradia and Cernunnos.

I know of very few people today who know the "Baneful Rune." It is one of the lost secrets of Wicca.

At the root of all of these sung and danced prayer movements is the idea that music and song creates a stronger tie with the spirit world than speech alone. In each movement, we learn that spoken prayer alone does not hold divine power: only danced, chanted prayer, often with the accompaniment of instruments such as the drum, can cause true transformative magic. The deepest, most primordial sounds touch the being and the psyche, which is why music affects us so deeply in our world.

In modern science, an idea is emerging that the sound of the "Big Bang," the explosive burst that created the Universe, is still resonating throughout space. Scientists have recently begun attempting to record and measure this sound to further understand the creation of all things. University of Virginia astronomy professor Mark Whittle presented a paper to the American Astronomical Society in Denver in 2004 in which he described the primordial sound as a "descending scream, building into a deep, rasping roar, and ending in a deafening hiss." (Whittle 2004) Whittle's work followed research begun at Bell Labs in 1963, when researchers Arno Penzias and Robert Wilson came up with a theory of a lingering sound and a fog of microwaves representing the afterglow of the creation of the universe. Here is an example of science and religion stating the same idea in slightly different terms. Each discipline agrees that a powerful sound created, or accompanied the creation of, the universe. To science it is the sound of the Big Bang. In religious or spiritual terms, this is the echo of the Elohim's song as the Universe was sung into existence.

Sound waves are a source of energy, like light waves or heat waves, and have a profound effect on our physical being. Kabalists, Witches and other spiritualists have seen musical tones as a healing spiritual element for centuries. In the Tarot, which is thought by many occultists to be based on the Hebrew or Egyptian alphabet, each Major Arcana card represents a musical tone in conjunction with its dozens of other layers of meaning. When attempting to bring a force into one's life, prosperity for instance, one might meditate upon a particular card (perhaps the Magician, he who creates his own reality), intone the character (*beth*) using the musical tone associated with the card, the note E natural. This is thought to bring the energy of the card into manifestation, as Elohim/Jehovah brought the universe into being. Native American healers also use sound, especially the sound of a whistle made of a bird's leg bone. This whistle is believed to restore energy to the human body and cure illness.

Now let's say that our world was indeed created by a combination of tones and phrases, a song analogous to the scientific "Big Bang." It is possible that the Kindly Ones, with their much greater understanding of the natural world, have a deep knowledge of these tones and their relationship to our psyches and our physical beings. Their music can cause profound psychological or physiological responses in mortals, changing our perception of the world and of ourselves. Once touched by this process, we may no longer have power to re-integrate our more mundane, less magical reality. Like the maid in the gentleman's story, or like Ethna, having heard this music that is so poignant, so deeply touching the soul, we may no longer have the psychological tools to deal with reality in our mundane world. That is why each of those maids began to waste away, touched by this impossibly beautiful sound, their psyche scarred by the jarring return to the mortal world. Each lost their sense of their surroundings, their loves and hates, their identities, longing to re-experience this deeply transformative sound.

Again, the Kabalah speaks of this, in the story of the three rabbis who, through prayer (intoned characters), enter the Garden of Eden. The story tells us that one dies, one goes mad, and one returns but cannot tell what he has seen there.

Tam Lin fears he will suffer the fate of the first rabbi, dying before he can return to our lands; True Thomas shares his destiny with the third rabbi, unable to convey what he has seen in the Faerie Land, able to see that lovely world but never re-enter, living forever as a stranger to both worlds. And the maid who hears the Faerie music is like rabbi number two. She has lost her sensibilities of our world, present in body, but no longer able to speak or reason, to hate or love. She longs to be back in the world that the music opened in her, touching that part of her psyche and physiology that connected her to the very essence, the magic, of the universe.

One wonders how much psychological illness, like schizophrenia and multiple personality disorder, can be attributed to some connection to an Otherworld that is drawing the afflicted person into its reality, stealing them like a changeling child from our world. How might the behavior of Ethna or the gentleman's maid be explained by modern medicine? Deep depression? PTSD? Was the wisdom of ancient people deeper, understanding that some glimpse of the worlds hidden from our mundane senses caused these rifts in these women's perception of reality? That the Faeries have some unfathomable understanding of how sound affects our fragile psyches? And perhaps a lack of understanding of just how fragile we are, that we cannot withstand the effects of these poignant, capricious sounds the way the Fey can?

I am not the first to wonder this. Excellent novels have been written on this idea. *Woman on the Edge of Time* by Marge Piercy is a story of a woman deemed insane because she was in touch with another reality; and much more recently Jennifer McMahon's *Promise Not To Tell*, a sort of haunted murder mystery, in which a woman with dementia can communicate with the spirit world. In each of these stories a person who seems to be on shaky ground psychologically is in touch with a different reality (though in neither is it the world of the Fey). C. S. Lewis comes closest perhaps to creating a universe wherein humans may come and go between our world and an enchanted world, but his glaringly Christian analogy destroys any notion that his land is based on a true vision of Faerie.

But the stories of Tam Lin and True Thomas show us that humans have believed for many centuries that the Faerie Lands can be entered, though at the cost of sanity and reason. We see from these cautionary ballads that once you hear the music of the Fey, there is no return to the mundane world. Whether because the music of the Fair Ones has captured that essence that is the primordial psyche, or whether because the journey between worlds exacts too much from our fragile constitutions, few of us can travel the worlds without deadly consequences. In fact, just hearing the soundtrack to that trip robs us of sanity. It's a sad world, the mundane, that is so close to the beauty of the Otherworld and its creatures, yet so far.

Chapter 6

FAERIE SEXUALITY

So let's get to the good stuff—Faerie sexuality.

What is the hold these creatures have on us through their beauty, their seduction, their strangeness and their mystique? The way they lure us in, tantalizing us, teasing us. "Touch me," they seem to say. "I'm just over here. Am I not beautiful? Do I not tempt you? Is my music not lovely? Is my song not the sweetest you've ever heard?"

Your brain knows. Your brain says, "Get out of here as quick as you can!" Because you've heard all the stories, you've seen the movies, you've pored over the books. Don't eat the food, you've been warned. Don't speak, don't come too close, and whatever you do, don't dance in a circle of toadstools! Oh, there's so much to remember, as your mind makes checklists of those red flags.

But your body says something different. "Go," it coaxes, "just a little nearer. Smell that delicious scent. Maybe just a quick brush of the hand against that alabaster skin would be safe." You look at the slight blush on this creature's soft, pale cheek. "What must those long, thin fingers feel like when stroking my arm? What must those full lips feel like on mine?" And the song tempts you, beyond the pitiful reason of your tiny little brain. So beautiful. You've never heard anything like it. Yet it sounds so familiar, so like everything you've ever heard.

And that's the end, isn't it? I mean, once you've thought those thoughts, the little temptress (or tempter) has you. There's no turning back, no return, no salvation. Oh, you'll have such pleasure. For an hour, or an evening, or for seven years. But you know what's bound to happen, don't you? Even as you're being caressed, kissed, wrapped in her velvet mantle, you know. Seven years turns to centuries. Or you become the tithe to Hell. Or worse, she leaves you forever, and you are left alone to wander the sea strand yearning, wanting, weeping. Then there's always the possibility of sudden death; your ship hits the rocks, you fall into her sweet arms, and in that all-satisfying caress you are pulled down into the murky depths. But maybe that would be better than living without her?

And don't give me that look of sad surprise. After all, you've heard the stories, you've read the books. You knew it was coming. Don't say, with your last, gasping breath, you weren't warned.

In all of the stories, over and over, the Faeries tempt us with their sexuality. Janet and Tam Lin, Thomas and the Elf Queen, the poor young lad who courted a Selkie; all of them were seduced by these impossibly beautiful creatures, and fell prey to their sexual wiles.

Let us look now at Faerie sexuality and seduction. Sometimes, everything turns out all right in the end. Usually it does not. Let's examine the good, the bad and, of course, the ugly aspects of Faerie sex.

THE GOOD

Enchanted F seeking Mortal M for LTR

Impossibly beautiful human-sized Faerie woman seeking special human man for LTR. Must enjoy long walks on the beach, horseback rides over rivers of blood and nights spent listening to eerie canine howling on lonely moors. Poets and rhymers a big plus. Blacksmiths need not respond.

It doesn't happen often, but every once in a while, a human and a Faerie have a happily-ever-after type ending. Let's look at a few instances where humans and Faeries end up in the sack, and maybe strike up the rare LTR.

Let's start with enchanted animal lovers. Yick, you might say. But give this a chance. The idea of satisfying sex between humans and enchanted animals is nothing new in Faerie folklore. It happens all the time. Women seem especially drawn to animal lovers: Rose Red loved a bear, Beauty fell for the Beast and the Frog Prince was loved by the girl of his dreams. And it's not just the girls; it happens to guys too. Here is an English song in which a human hunter encounters a hare-woman, and the two work out a very agreeable arrangement. It's called, logically enough, "The Bonny Black Hare":

On the fourteenth of May at the dawn of the day
With my gun on my shoulder to the woods I did stray
In search of some game if the weather proved fair
To see could I get a shot at the bonny black hare

Oh, I met a young girl there with her face as a rose
And her skin was as fair as the lily that grows
I says "My fair maiden, why ramble you so?
Can you tell me where the bonny black hare does go?"

Oh, the answer she gave me, her answer was "No
But it's under me apron they say it do go
And if you'll not deceive me I vow and declare
We'll both go together to hunt the bonny black hare"

Well, I laid this girl down with her face to the sky
And I took out my ramrod and my bullets likewise
I says "Lock your legs round me and dig in with your heels
For the closer we get, oh, the better it feels"

The birds they were singing in the bushes and trees
And the song that they sang was "Oh, she's easy to please"

I felt her heart quiver and I knew what I'd done
Says I "Have you had enough of my old sporting gun?"

Oh, the answer she gave me, her answer was "Nay
It's not often young sportsmen like you come this way
And if your powder is willing and your bullets play fair
Why don't you keep firing at the bonny black hare?"

"Oh, my powder is wasted and my bullets all gone
My ramrod is limp and I cannot fire on
But I'll be back in the morning and if you are still here
We'll both go together to hunt the bonny black hare"
(Traditional)

In this tune the woman shifts, in the hunter's focus, between the role of human female and hare doe. The hare has always been an animal associated with sexuality, both because it is observed copulating early in the spring, and because it is strongly linked with such goddesses as Brigit and Oestara. In many English songs the hare is compared to sexually appealing young women. Here is a well-known example:

Young women they run like hares on the mountain
Young women they run like hares on the mountain
And if I were a young man I'd soon go a-hunting
To me right fol-a-diddle-dare-oh
To me right fol-a-diddle-day
(Traditional)

The association between the hare and the fertility of spring is so strong that the Catholic Church could not stop the Pagan practice of hare veneration in the spring celebration. To this day it is customary at Easter for children to receive a hare, or rabbit, as a pet, a veiled celebration of sexuality and fertility. This custom has been observed throughout Europe since the dawn of time. In Scotland and England, the hare is called a *coney*, and a pet hare (like our pet kitty cat) referred to as *pussy*. While some people associate certain slang words with cats, it's actually these terms for a hare that give rise to our slang names for the female genitals (*coney* transforming to *cunny*, and then on to the current term).

In the above song, the enchanted young hare-woman is unflinchingly sexual, pulling the hunter's focus away from killing (which is antithetical to spring and growth) and redirecting him towards her own voluptuous appetites, pointing out to him the garden of delights beneath her apron. She tells him that the hare he is seeking is to be found in her own nether regions ("It's under me apron they say it do go"). She then offers to take him on a guided tour. What this human hunter has run into is one very frisky Faerie girl. In fact, our hare-girl appears to be a Nymph.

Nymphs are Greek Faeries of various types; water Faeries like Naiads (freshwater), Hyades (rain and clouds), Oceanids (duh), forests and glades (Alseids, Dryads, Hamadryads, Leimakids), animals (our hare girl, Fauns, and Centaurs), the Underworld (Lampades) and inspiration (the Muses). The Greek word Nymph (μ) seems to mean marriageable girl or beautiful girl, but it may also mean rose-bud, and may refer to a comparison between a rose-bud swelling or blooming and a woman's vulva swelling during sexual passion. While Nymphs, like most other Faeries, can be harmful and mischievous, they are primarily sexual and alluring. In *Modern Greek Folklore and Ancient Greek Religion*, John Cuthbert Lawson speaks of Nymphs called Nereids:

> There is probably no nook or hamlet in all Greece where the womenfolk at least do not scrupulously take precautions against the thefts and malice of the nereids, while many a man may still be found to recount in all good faith stories of their beauty, passion and caprice. Nor is it a matter of faith only; more than once I have been in villages where certain Nereids were known by sight to several persons (so at least they averred); and there was a wonderful agreement among the witnesses in the description of their appearance and dress. (Lawson 1910, 131)

Nymphs are extremely sexual, mating at will with men, beasts, Centaurs and Fauns. In fact, Nymphs are so hypersexual that many modern terms for a sexually overactive female come from Nymph mythology: in Freudian terms, a hypersexual woman is said to be a nymphomaniac; and in the novel *Lolita*, Vladimir Nabokov coined the term *nymphet*, used by his character Humbert Humbert to describe his attraction to certain pubescent girls, such as Lolita (the nickname of Dolores Haze), a sexually precocious teen who in every way fits the nature and behavior of a mythic Nymph.

When mating with human men Nymphs assume a very human, youthful appearance. While Artemis's retinue of Nymphs was said to appear as nine-year-old girls, we can assume that when mating with human males, the Nymph would favor the appearance of a woman of age to be sexually active and provocative. However, Nymphs often do appear to be what we modern people might consider quite young. In stories, Nymph girls often go through a transformation from girl to woman, like Rose Red as she went from childhood love of the bear to adult marriage. The same goes for Beauty, who was the merchant's youngest daughter, which stressed her immaturity, yet she ended by being a wife for the enchanted Beast. In many of these tales, it's almost confusing that the girl who seems childlike becomes romantic and sexual with a male savior. Snow White is depicted in one version as seven years old, yet she falls for the rescuing prince.

The Lolita-esque element in Nymphs, straddling the line between girl and young adult, may seem creepy and perverse to our modern sensibility. But remember that one aspect of the Nymph is the marriageable young woman. Marriage came early for the ancient Greeks. In our culture where marriage may not occur until people are in their thirties or later, we may forget that only half a century ago, girls of fifteen or sixteen were considered desirable brides. We still observe the customs of the "sweet sixteen" and the quinceañera, both of which were originally rituals to announce a young girl's eligibility to be courted at the age of fifteen or sixteen. In older cultures, the rite of adulthood comes even earlier; in Judaism, it is still celebrated at thirteen (the Bar/Bat Mitzvah). Hopi girls also come of age at thirteen in a ritual called the Kinaalda; and in Amazon and Central American rainforest cultures, like the Kuna of Panama, girls come of age at twelve, in a rite called the Inna Suid. So it is only natural that Faeries that appear to humans as the most beautiful and desirable girls of marrying age would take the form of girls in their teen years, the time of adulthood and marriage in ancient European cultures. Also remember that as young as Nymphs seem, they're likely to be hundreds of years old. And face it; if you could be a hundred and ten but look fifteen—you'd do it.

Nymph lovers are often insatiable, desiring many sexual encounters in a day. This is seen of the hare-girl, who finishes with the hunter and immediately asks when he will return to satisfy her again. Nymphs take sex seriously, so to speak, and their sexuality ties them to the Gods and to spirit. Sex is a sacred act to many Nymphs, as evidenced by their role in such fertility rites as the Bacchanalia. This feast held in ancient Italy on March 16 and 17, originally attended only by women (with men invited later on), celebrated the divine sexuality of the Nymphs who attended Bacchus. Rites like these were the origin of the Witches' sabbats, and when the Roman senate outlawed them, they were practiced secretly. The rite celebrated the myth of Bacchus (called Dionysus by the Greeks), a God of music and wine, who lived on Mount Nysa where he was attended by Nymphs called the Nysiads. Bacchus would drink wine and cavort with his Nymphs, inducing a state of ecstatic madness. Nymph sex was essential for Bacchus to achieve this divine state. Human participants in the Bacchanalia would endeavor to fall into this same condition.

While Nymphs are sexual and live completely in the moment, their sexual relationships change them from girl to woman, and create in them an awareness of responsibility and mortality. In chapter 5, when Orpheus and the Nymph Eurydice married, the Nymph became aware of her own mortality (through her death from being bitten by snakes). The myth says that when Eurydice died, Orpheus sang and played his harp so mournfully that all of the Nymphs wept (also learning of the sadness of death). Orpheus managed to convince Hades and Persephone (who herself had a retinue of Nymphs) to allow Eurydice to return to the world of the living.

In Fairy tales where Nymph-like girls marry, we see the growth process. In *Snow White and Rose Red*, even though the girls love the bear and sleep with him nightly, it is only after they are married to the bear-prince and his brother that they leave their mother's home and take on the role of wives. And while Snow White lives a childish life with the seven Dwarves, sleeping with them nightly, it is only the prince that she will marry who causes her to take the adult role of wife.

Even in male versions of the Nymph myth, the male can act childish and pesky until marriage and sex transform him to an adult. This is seen in *The Frog Prince*, where the frog is a bit of a nuisance to his intended before he reverts to his human form (and she is very little-girlish in her treatment of him until the transformation; it's as if the immature girl sees a frog, but upon her sexual maturity she suddenly notices that he is a prince). The relationship is also begun over a gift exchange (or so it seems to the frog): the girl loses her ball in the pond, and the frog returns it. One element of this exchange is the crossing of water between the worlds: the ball enters the water, and the enchanted creature must carry it back into our world to return it to the girl.

Another aspect of the Nymph marriage is the taking on of human form by the Nymph for the entire period she is sexually active with a mortal lover. While a Nymph may take on many forms—trees, animals, water, wind—she must remain human while she is intimate with her human. In *Snow White and Rose Red*, even though Rose Red has been sleeping with the bear for a full year, the creature must take on his human form before the two can be married. And our hare-girl must be human before she can have sex with the hunter and tempt him into returning to the forest. This is also the case with the Selkies, who must leave their seal skin and take a fully human form before they marry fishermen. If they recover their seal skin, they can no longer maintain their human appearance, and they return to seal form forever.

So Nymphs and other Faeries that want the LTR with a human must follow the rules, give in a bit, and refrain from murdering the object of their desire. Then we just might have the happily-ever-after ending.

Unless you're Orpheus. Let's look at what happens when Fairies live by a whole different set of rules.

THE BAD

Enchanted F seeking Mortal M for one amazing date!

Impossibly beautiful human-sized Faerie female seeks human male for casual encounter. Me: very sensual, excellent singing voice. You: stud without any long-term plans. Tromb players need not respond.

Not all Faeries are quite that serious. For some, the first date is really all they need. And that date can be disastrous.

Remember the Glastig? We spoke of the story of *The Four Hunters and the Four Glastigs*. Out of four young men, only one hunter survived that encounter by playing a Jew's harp or "tromb." The Faerie taunted him with a blow to his sexual prowess:

Good is the music of the tromb
Saving the one note in its train
Its owner likes it in his mouth
In preference to any maid

The Glastig mocks the man by declaring essentially that he prefers music to sex, that he would rather have the tromb in his mouth than a woman's (insert word derived from hare). Of course, the man's control of his yearnings saved his life, as it has many a storied human who runs across this type of seducing-murderer Faerie. It didn't work out so well for his more easily tempted companions.

The Glastig, like many other seductress Faeries, is not in it for the long term. She, in the words of Cyndi Lauper, just wants to have fun. And for the Glastig, the Lorelie, the Siren and a few others, fun involves a brief sensual encounter ending in death and despair. Not your idea of fun? Let's look at some Faeries for whom it's the perfect first date.

REYNARDINE, OR MR. FOX

In the song "Reynardine," a fair maid is wandering the mountains when she meets Reynardine, an enchanted fox-man. In various Scottish stories he is described as a cross between a fox and a human, with red whiskers and beady fox eyes (in these stories he is often called "Mr. Fox"). He seduces the girl, even though she keeps saying that she knows better than to fall for his wiles. Here is the song, a Scottish ballad:

> One evening as I rambled
> Among the leaves and thyme,
> I overheard a young woman
> Converse with Reynardine.
>
> Her hair was black, her eyes were blue,
> Her lips as red as wine,
> And he smiled to gaze upon her,
> Did that sly, bold Reynardine.
>
> She said, "Kind sir, be civil
> My company forsake
> For in my own opinion
> I fear you are some rake."
>
> "And if my parents should come to know
> My life they would destroy

For seeking of your company
All on these mountains high."

"Oh no," he said, "no rake am I
Cast out of Venus' train
But I'm seeking for concealment
All from the judge's men."

"Your beauty so enticed me,
I could not pass it by
So it's with my gun I'll guard you
All on the mountains high."

Her cherry cheeks, her ruby lips
They lost their former dye
And she fell into his arms then
That sly, bold Reynardine

He kissed her once and he kissed her twice
Till she came to again
And modestly she begged him
"Pray tell to me your name."

"Oh if by chance you should look for me
Perhaps you'll not me find
For I'll be in my castle
Inquire for Reynardine."

Sun and dark she followed him
His teeth did brightly shine
And he led her over the mountains
Did that sly, bold Reynardine.
(Traditional)

"Reynardine" is a story-song told in a very old format: the third person narrative of a casual observer. We are told that the singer just happened to wander by the scene, when he "overheard" the maid talking to Reynardine, the fox-man. Many traditional songs use this convention, and there is no emotional involvement on the part of the singer who simply observes the situation.

One thing this song does present us with is a young human woman driven by romantic desires, yet trying to appear modest. The very first thing one wonders is why this maiden was roaming the mountains in the first place. Was she actually hoping to run into this bad boy, the dangerous Mr. Fox? We saw this with Janet in her liaisons with Tam Lin, when she starts picking roses to summon the object of her desire. Perhaps this unnamed lass has seen the beast from afar, and fancies herself in love? We saw this in the *Mabinogion* story of Blodeuedd, who fell in love with Gronw after seeing him while he was hunting outside her castle walls. Perhaps like Blodeuedd the girl has combed the mountain roads to learn more about this mysterious fox-man?

She is certainly something of a moth before a flame. When they meet, she is defensive, but not dismissive. She begs him to leave her alone, saying she fears he is a "rake," meaning a seducer, and that her parents will "destroy" her if they learn of this liaison. But just in the few lines of the song, we can see that she is flirting while saying this. It would have been proper for a young woman of this period to act guarded, to refute a young man's advances, while scarcely hiding her delight in the attention. In fact, in that verse, she goes as far as to admit that she was looking for him ("If my parents should come to know/My life they would destroy/For seeking of your company/All on these mountains high").

His smile disarms her, and he gently assures her that he is not a rake, but a criminal hiding from the police (the "judge's men"). Young women love a bad boy, and this girl is no exception. She faints from the shock of this confession, the anonymous narrator says, right into the beast's arms. He "kissed her once and kissed her twice," until she is revived. We can assume more than just kissing has gone on (just like with Tam Lin and knocked-up Janet).

She finally begs his name, making it seem, at least in the narrator's eyes, that she has just had casual sex with a total stranger. He explains that, should she call at his castle, she need only ask for Reynardine. He then carries her off to his home.

In many cases of a young woman discovering her sexuality and her power over men, she will pick a bad boy, or perhaps a mature charmer, to flirt with and try to tame. How many young women have done this? And how many have fallen prey to the seducer, allowing themselves to be charmed into overstepping whatever boundaries they may have set for themselves? The history of this period is full of them: Picasso was forty-six when he became involved with seventeen-year-old Marie-Thérèse Walter; Ellen Ternan was less than eighteen when a forty-five-year-old Charles Dickens left his wife to marry her; and Benjamin Franklin carried on decades-long flirtations with several women half his age or younger. He even joked provocatively with them about the age difference. The young woman here seems just such a one—riding the mountains to seek the company of this mature, charming outlaw, flirting with him as she protests his advances, then finding herself trapped in her own game, seduced and doomed to become Reynardine's thrall.

We've all met this young woman and her seducer before. Most of us met her when we were quite young. We were too young to understand the sexual element, but we understood the danger the girl's naïveté had caused for her. The girl wore a red cap in the Grimms' version, and in the American version, a red riding hood. The canine seducer was not a fox, but something very close: a wolf.

I have no doubt that the tale of Little Red Riding Hood is a sanitized version of "Reynardine": it has all of the elements of the Reynardine tale. A lovely young woman roams the wilderness, seemingly innocent but also flaunting a veiled sexuality (as Bettelheim points out in The Uses of Enchantment, the red cap or riding hood that the girl wears is of a color that suggests sex and passion [Bettelheim 1976, 173]). She is approached by an older seducer, and rather than protecting her modesty, she tells him where she is going and makes no secret about her agenda. The seducer rushes ahead, destroying the guardian who should be protecting the girl. When the girl arrives, the wolf asks Little Red Cap (as she is known in the Grimms' version) to get into bed with him. She does so, and after a little pillow talk ("What big eyes you have . . ."), she is seduced and devoured.

We are not told in the song what Reynardine does with his beauty after he seduces her. To a Victorian audience, the very thought that the maid was seduced by this Otherworldly beast was punishment enough for her wanton sexuality, and would have served as a lesson in modesty and chastity for maids who sat listening. But other Scottish stories of Mr. Fox delve into a great deal more gory detail, for those young ladies who may not quite have gotten the song's message. These stories have all the same elements: a beautiful young woman falls for an enchanted scoundrel, she rides through the mountains to find him, very bad things happen. One version goes like this:

> A young woman lived in her castle with her seven brothers, all the family she had left after her parents' death. Her brothers cared well for her, and agreed to help her choose a husband. To that end she began to welcome young men from throughout the countryside for dinners in her home.
>
> One day a very handsome man came calling. He had red hair and sharp eyes, and was dressed in rust-colored suits of fine tailoring. He introduced himself as Mr. Fox, and told the maid that he had recently taken residence in his family's castle, not very far away. He was welcomed to a feast, and entertained his eight hosts with tales of his extensive travel. The maid was quite taken with this Mr. Fox and felt perhaps she had found her husband.
>
> "We know nothing of his people, his origins," her brothers warned. "You get to know this Mr. Fox a bit better before choosing him as a mate," they told her.

Mr. Fox called often, and each time the maid felt warmer towards him. But she knew her brothers were right. She began asking after his people, but he evaded her questions and changed the subject when she persisted.

One day the maid hatched a plan. She waited for Mr. Fox to leave after a dinner, and dressing in her dark riding cloak, she quietly followed him over the mountains to his castle. It was a huge, sinister building forged into the side of a mountain. The door to the great hall stood at the mountain's foot. The maid marked the spot and crept home.

The next morning she rode to Mr. Fox's castle. She tied her horse a ways away, and took the mountain paths on foot, arriving at his great hall as morning grew late. Above the feast hall was a wooden arch, which she had not noticed in the dark the night before. On it were carved these words:

Be bold, be bold.

Now she wandered into the hall, a long room with tall support beams and an old oaken table that ran the length of the chamber. At the end was a staircase of white marble. Over this was another arch, which stated in carved letters:

Be bold, be bold, but not too bold.

Now she climbed the stairs, to a wide space filled with barrels and crates. She found this place odd and crossed through it. At the end, over a door to what she imagined to be Mr. Fox's bedchamber, the arch had these words inscribed:

Be bold, be bold, but not too bold
Else your heart's blood will run cold!

Now the young woman heard a terrible noise. She quickly hid herself behind a barrel, and when she looked back she saw Mr. Fox coming up the stairs. He was not alone. He held the ankle of a young maid of the local village who was beaten horribly and shrieking for her life. At one point the screaming maid tried to hold the rail of the stair to stop herself from being dragged upward, but Mr. Fox pulled his great ax from his belt and cut the girl's fingers off! The fingers flew about the room, two of them landing at the foot of the stairs with a horrible thudding sound.

In the end Mr. Fox had the young woman in his upper chamber, very near to where the noblewoman was hiding. After cruelly having his way with the village girl, Mr. Fox placed his jaws around her neck, and rended, until he had ripped her throat open. He feasted on her blood as her terrified eyes glazed over. He then placed the body in one of the barrels that lined the chamber, and walked under the arch and into his private rooms, licking his lips.

That evening, Mr. Fox called at the castle of the noblewoman and her brothers, composed and acting as if he'd had a leisurely day. The maid and her seven brothers set a feast and sat down to eat. But as they were about to dine, the maid said, "Mr. Fox, I dreamed the strangest dream last night."

"Tell us of your dream," Mr. Fox coaxed.

"Well," said the maid, "I dreamed I came upon a great hall, built into the side of a mountain. And over the arch of the door was written the words Be Bold, Be Bold."

"It never was, nor ever shall be!" said Mr. Fox, looking a bit awkward.

"And as I wandered into the great hall, I came upon a stairway. And over this was written, Be Bold, Be Bold, But Not Too Bold!"

"It never was, nor ever shall be!" insisted Mr. Fox, whose cheeks looked quite red now.

"And when I climbed those stairs, I came upon a room full of barrels and containers, and on the arch over this room was written: Be Bold, Be Bold, But Not Too Bold, Else Your Heart's Blood Will Run Cold!"

"It never was, nor ever shall be!" declared Mr. Fox. He was now crimson, and his eyes narrowed to dark beads.

"And into this room came a man, dragging a poor young maid of the village! The maid tried to hold on to the staircase, but the man cut her fingers off! The man treated her in a horrible way, molesting her and beating her. He murdered the unfortunate woman, Mr. Fox, and drank her blood! Then he placed her in a barrel."

"This never was, nor shall it ever be!" Mr. Fox loudly cried, jumping up from his seat.

"It was, indeed, Mr. Fox. And the man I saw was you. And here are the dead girl's fingers to prove it."

Upon the dining table, the woman threw two hideous fingers, cut from the hand of the dead girl, which she had collected as she raced from Mr. Fox's castle. Upon seeing these, Mr. Fox reached for his sword.

But the maid's seven brothers were prepared. They drew upon Mr. Fox, and hacked him to pieces. And thus ended the life of the cruel Mr. Fox!

Compared to the song, this story tells us quite a bit more about the Fox Man: that he has the appearance of a gentleman; that he moves from one castle to another to mask his serial killings; and that he courts noble maids, but kills at random from among the peasantry. Also in both accounts, Mr. Fox is a charmer, skilled at seducing noble young women. We presume he has been doing this a long time, and has grown quite good at it.

Reynardine, or Mr. Fox, is a typical seducing-murdering Faerie. Like the Glastig or the Lorelie, this Faerie lures his victims with his charm, looks and nobility, and then murders them after enjoying them sexually. While Mr. Fox is male, he has the same strategies as his female counterparts: mate and destroy.

The story of Mr. Fox has many similarities to various vampire tales, including the most well known, Bram Stoker's account of Count Dracula. These two tales may have common roots; after all, Stoker culled his vampire legends from the Eastern European countryside, while Mr. Fox is the stuff of Scots-English folklore. These are similar pools, and often contain many common stories.

Both Dracula and the Fox Man present themselves as gentlemen, and both seem to have their own code of honor concerning the process of killing women. In both *Dracula* and *Mr. Fox*, the villain disposes quickly of peasant maids (in *Dracula*, Lucy Westenra, who is sexually precocious and fickle, peasantlike qualities for a Victorian woman), but spends long periods of time courting noblewomen (in *Dracula*, Mina Harker). Other similarities include assuming canine identities: Mr. Fox is, of course, a shape-shifting Faerie who can take the form of a fox; Dracula assumes the identity of a huge dog when he springs from the wrecked ship, the *Demeter*, and he attacks Lucy and her mother as a wolf. Both villains also have the ability to draw women to them in their remote, eerie locations: The woman in the song "Reynardine" is riding around the mountains, drawn to the fox-man; Lucy begins long bouts of sleepwalking that carry her to the Whitby graveyard where Dracula waits for her. Finally, we are told by Van Helsing that Dracula must be killed by having a stake driven through his heart, and then being decapitated (having his body cut apart); Mr. Fox is hacked into pieces by the vigilant brothers. While a vampire is a very different breed than a Faerie, Count Dracula in his myth-derived, novelized form has all of the qualities of a seducer-murderer Faerie. Stoker probably used a good deal of Faerie folklore in creating the character of the Blood Count.

One more story to consider is the Grimms' story of *The Robber Bridegroom*, which is nearly identical to *Mr. Fox*.

In this story, a beautiful woman is betrothed by her father to a man who appears to be a wealthy gentleman. But she is suspicious, especially when her fiancé tells her he lives in a lonely house deep in

the forest. Like the woman in *Mr. Fox* and sleepwalking Lucy Westenra, the maid travels into the forest, drawn by a trail of ashes the
fiancé has left on the path for her. However, this girl is smart. Real-
izing that ashes will blow away in a wind, she leaves her own trail of
lentils and peas.

Arriving at the house in the gloomy forest, the maid hears a caged
bird warn:

> Turn back, turn back, my pretty young bride
> In a house of murderers you've arrived!

The warning is repeated several times (like the "Be Bold" warning). The maid finally finds an old woman in the basement, preparing a pot of boiling water. The hag explains that the men of the house
are cannibals, and are preparing to eat the maid, rather than marry
her. Sure enough, the robbers return with a local peasant girl and
strip her naked. They cut her into pieces, and her finger flies out and
falls onto our heroine's lap as she is hiding behind a barrel.

With the old woman's help, the maid escapes when the robbers
have fallen asleep. The next night, the robber fiancé arrives for dinner. The maid tells of a dream she's had, in which she of course relates the entire story, and shows the dead girl's finger as proof. The
robber bridegroom is killed by the girl's dinner guests.

In every way this story is identical to *Mr. Fox*, except that the robber bridegroom appears mortal, rather than Otherworldly. However,
Maria Tatar, writing in *The Annotated Brothers Grimm*, points out that
the robbers "resemble the cannibalistic ogres and giants of folklore,
and like the giant in 'Jack and the Beanstalk' they devour intruders."
(Tatar 2004, 189) So we can infer that these robbers are not mortal
but some type of Otherworldly seducer-murderer just like our Mr.
Fox.

Again, all of these stories also resemble the sanitized *Little Red Cap*,
or *Little Red Riding Hood*: the young woman whose innocence belies
a budding sexuality; the house in a remote and dangerous location;

the journey through the wilderness; the lure of the canine seducer-murderer; and finally the seduction and devouring of the girl.

Sometimes this kind of dismal first date has a happy ending. In *The Robber Bridegroom* and in *Mr. Fox*, the girl's protectors save her from death; in these stories her brothers. In *Little Red Cap*, the girl is seduced and devoured, but the woodcutter rescues her in the end. This character is never really mentioned in the story until he arrives to save the girl, but his attraction to Little Red Cap tells us that despite our perception of the wandering girl as a juvenile, she is sexually alluring. *Little Red Cap* shares a common ending with *Dracula*; Mina is seduced and killed, but Van Helsing and Harker redeem her soul; in the song "Reynardine," the girl is simply forsaken. Poor thing . . .

THE DEMON LOVER

Another Otherworldly seducer-murderer to watch out for on your long trips across lonely wilderness areas is "The Demon Lover." Also called "The House Carpenter" (Child #243), this song is not about a dismal first date as much as a romantic reunion. It's a Scots-English border song about a married woman who is called away by a former lover whom she presumed was dead. Well, he sort of is. He's apparently become a changeling, and wants to take the woman with him to the Otherworld. Unlike Janet, who is called upon to rescue her lover, this woman is destined to go with him to a fairly unpleasant Underworld.

"Well met, well met, my own true love
Long time I have been absent from thee
I am lately come from the salt sea
And it's all for the sake, my love, of thee"

"I have three ships all on the sea
And one of them has brought me to land.
I've four and twenty seamen on board
And you shall have music at your command"

She says, "I am now wed to a house carpenter
To a house carpenter I am bound.
And I wouldn't leave my husband dear
For twice the sum of ten hundred pound"

"Well I might have a king's daughter
And fain she would have married me
But I forsook her crown of gold
And it was all for the sake, my love, of thee"

"So I pray you leave your husband, dear
And sail away with me
And I'll take you where the white lilies grow
All on the banks of Italy"

"And this ship wherein my love shall sail
Is wondrous to behold
The sails shall be of shining silk
And the mast shall be of red beaten gold"

So she dressed herself in her gay clothing
Most glorious to behold
And as she trod the salt water's side
Oh she shone like glittering gold

They hadn't sailed a day and a day
And a day but barely three
She cast herself down on the deck
And she wept and wailed most bitterly

"Oh hold your tongue, my dearest dear
Let all your sorrows be
I'll take you where the white lilies grow
All on the bottom of the sea"

And as she turned herself roundabout
So tall and tall he seemed to be

Until the tops of that gallant ship
No taller were than he

And he struck the topmast with his hand
The main mast with his knee
And he broke that shining ship in two
And he dashed it into the bottom of the sea

In one variant of the song, when the woman gets aboard the ship she notices that her demon lover has a cloven hoof for a foot:

They had not sailed a league, a league
A league but barely three
Until she espied his cloven foot
And she wept right bitterly

This is very similar to the appearance of the Glastig or the Each Uisge, Faeries who appear human but who retain some animal characteristic that they try to keep hidden while doing their dirty work. Remember how the Glastig appears human, but might have the hindquarters of a goat beneath her skirt? Yeah, it's like that.

The woman in this song is a bit unsympathetic, because she leaves her husband (and in many versions, her children) for this one-time now-enchanted lover. She must still have strong feelings for him, and she's delighted to have him back, cloven hoof and all. But we know when she gets on that ship that she's bound for troubled waters.

Like the young woman in "Reynardine," the house carpenter's wife knows this full well. Each young woman goes despite her own rational objections. You can't really blame them. That's the lure the Faeries have over us. They confuse our rational thoughts and leave us yearning for their love, their sex, their food, their music. Notice, by the way, that the demon lover promises Faerie music as part of the great life the house carpenter's wife will have: "I've four and twenty seamen on board/And you shall have music at your command." Once she's been subjected to that darn Faerie music, how can she refuse?

Really, she can't. And then, the demon lover exacts his revenge on his one-time beloved for moving on with her life in our world while he is a changeling in the land of the Sidhe.

THE UGLY

Enchanted F seeks Human M for love and utter devotion

Enchanted Plain Jane type seeks handsome Human male for love and devotion. I've been hurt before, please go gently: I get a little nasty when angered. Must be willing to commit utterly! Must love my mother. Those familiar with knot and cord magic need not respond.

Faerie music, charm, Faerie food, wine . . . it can really sweep a girl off her feet, especially when the guy/fox/dog/bunny is a handsome devil. But that giddy, alluring Faerie charm can even turn the ugliest suitor into the love of some lucky girl's life. Put on your enchanted beer goggles, and let's take a look.

BEAUTY, BEAST, CUPID, PSYCHE

Probably the best-known instance of ugly Faerie sexuality in Grimms is *Beauty and the Beast*. In this story, a merchant who has three lovely daughters asks each daughter what gift she would like when he returns from a business voyage. Two daughters ask for expensive trinkets, but the youngest, Beauty, simply asks for a lovely rose.

As the merchant returns from market, he is caught in a violent storm. He seeks shelter in a castle but cannot find the castle's owner no matter how he calls out. He is given a nice meal by unseen hands and in the morning prepares to leave. But as he leaves the grounds, he sees a garden full of roses. He remembers his youngest daughter's request and picks a rose. At the very moment he does, a hideous beast appears. The monster says he will kill the man, but the man pleads for his life. Finally the Beast proposes that the man will be spared if he brings his youngest daughter to live in the castle.

The daughter bravely sets off to save her father by moving to the Beast's home. At first she is horrified by the creature, but later she finds herself enjoying his company. In time she grows quite fond of him.

After being in the castle for quite a while, she learns that her father is dying. Beauty pleads with the Beast to allow her to return home to nurse the man, promising she will come back to the castle when her father is well. The Beast agrees, but as time passes, the maid does not return. The Beast grows heartsick.

When Beauty finally returns, she finds the Beast nearly dead in a cabbage patch in his garden. She realizes her love for him and says aloud that if he would only live, she will marry him. At that moment, a spell is broken and the beast becomes a handsome prince. He and Beauty marry, and he commands that roses always grow in his gardens.

Beauty and the Beast owes its origins to the Greek myth of Cupid and Psyche. In that tale, the god Cupid falls in love with Psyche, a beautiful mortal. Venus opposes the union, so Cupid secretly houses Psyche in a beautiful castle to protect her from the disapproving Goddess. Cupid visits his lover at night, but warns her she must keep the lamps unlit so she cannot see him. Psyche assumes he is a horrible monster, and makes love with him but is also frightened of him. In the end she discovers Cupid's identity and must visit Hades before she can marry him. Finally Zeus gives Psyche immortality; she marries Cupid and gives birth to Voluptas, from whose name we get the description "voluptuous." We tend to use this description for a curvy woman, but the Victorians used it for anything sexually alluring; a girl might have been described as having voluptuous lips. An underground English digest of erotica, *The Pearl*, published from 1879 to 1880, bore the subtitle A *Journal of Voluptuous Reading*.

While I have filed both of these stories under the heading of *The Ugly*, they are both those rare tales where a mortal falls in love with an Otherworldly creature and lives to tell about it. In both stories, in fact, the beauty lives happily ever after (in Psyche's case, literally ever after). In fact, Beauty is almost like a mortal seducer-murderer: she allows the Beast to fall in love with her, then like a Selkie leaves him, breaking his heart. We only like her because she returns, and because we, with our horrible bourgeois ethic, feel that because the Beast is ugly, Beauty has every right to reject him. But there may be even more to Beauty's rejection of the Beast than meets the eye.

When girls are first developing sexually, they may focus their newly emerging adoration on a particular boy or man, idolizing his looks and charm. But his sexual organ seems like a horrible monster. In time, because of their developing sexual urges, girls are forced to accept their lover's apparatus, and its involvement in their sexual activities, in order to have a relationship with their lover. Almost as if the man and his organ are two different entities. In time, the young woman learns to love the organ in question and welcomes its pleasurable effects on her. At last, the newly sexual girl integrates the handsome man she loves with the monstrous appendage and sees them as one being, whom she can love and accept.

This is the evolution of Beauty's thought. At first she is forced by her father to leave her childhood role of youngest daughter and take on the role of an adult woman, running a household and taking a lover who appears to be a horrible beast. Yet he is gentlemanly, charming and thoughtful; all the things Beauty might consider attractive in a man. Finally, as she matures a little sexually, she can view him as a handsome prince, whose sexual functions give her as much pleasure as his charm and conversation. Her acceptance of physical love transforms the Beast not in reality, but in Beauty's perception.

At least that's the psychological explanation. But all Faerie stories have that element, a view into the human psyche, because Faeries have that lure to us: They seem to know us, our vulnerabilities, our yearnings, our passions. They can reach out to us through their impossible beauty, their deep lust, their passionate music, in a way that shows us our own deepest, sometimes dreadful thoughts and desires.

We become helpless, eating the food, caressing the voluptuous bodies, responding to touch or song, even though our rational mind screams, "Don't give in! Don't do it!" The Faerie world is like a mirror that forces us to see those things within ourselves that we keep most hidden, even from our own sight. In *Beauty and the Beast*, the perfect, dutiful daughter must obey her father, but in doing so, the Beast forces her to face her own lust and sexual desire, despite her unwillingness to do so.

In this tale we also once again see the "bad boy" motif, which we saw in "Reynardine." The good girl is attracted to her polar opposite, the bad boy. This occurs constantly in life. How many sweet, studious girls yearn for the local bully, the biker, the gangsta', decrying that he has a heart of gold that she will bring out? Faeries know this weakness in young women, and the seducer Faerie takes full advantage of it! Fortunately for Beauty, the Beast actually loves her and would never do her harm. Phwew! She's doing a lot better than that girl roaming the Scottish mountains. The Beast also represents the charming older man, the experienced seducer. He loves Beauty, but preys on her youth and innocence.

A few other elements of *Beauty and the Beast* worth mentioning: Beauty is a changeling, exchanged for her father's life (the Seven Year King sacrifice). Like Janet, Dad summons the Beast by pulling up a rose, a symbol of nature and of sexuality. Beauty is a child, but is cast into the role of adult woman; we have seen this in *Snow White and Rose Red*, in the tale of *Snow White* and in *Sleeping Beauty*. As we saw in *Little Red Cap*, each of these Nymph-girls appears childlike, but their lovers respond to them as adult women. This is even more poignant in the case of Beauty when the story insists that she is the youngest of three daughters. Beauty responds to the Beast's charm, though she sees him as a monster. Finally she matures, and sees him as a handsome prince. She finds him near death (about to leave our world and enter the Underworld) in a cabbage patch (cabbage is another sexual plant, representing the folds of a woman's sexual organs). The Beast can only find rescue from death in the embrace of his lover, so he attempts to find a substitute for Beauty's sex in the symbolic cabbage plants. The plant summons Beauty (just as the rose first summoned the Beast) who returns to the Beast just in time to save him. This is a reversal of other Nymph-girl stories: it is usually the prince who must rescue the Nymph-girl.

KING HENRY

Folklore gives us a few other beast-lover tales, in the form of two traditional ballads. This first one is a tale that involves one King Henry. In this case, the beast is an Otherworldly female, and King Henry is the innocent mortal trapped in a great hall, or castle, by her. The song is a Scottish-English border ballad, Child #32:

Let never a man a-wooing wend that lacketh things three:
A store of gold, an open heart, and full of charity
And this was said of King Henry, as he lay quite alone
For he's taken him to a haunted hall, seven miles from the
   town

O, he has driven him the deer before, and the doe down by the
   glen
'til the fattest buck in all the flock, King Henry he has slain
His huntsmen followed him to the hall, to make them burly
   cheer
When loud the wind was heard to howl, and an earthquake
rocked the floor

As darkness covered all the hall where they sat at their meat
The greyhounds, yowling, left their food and crept to Henry's
   feet
And louder howled the rising wind that burst the fastened
   door
And in there came a grisly ghost, stamping across the floor

Her head hit the rooftop of the house, her middle you could
   not span
Each frightened huntsman fled the hall, and left the king
   alone
Her teeth were like the tether-stakes, her nose like club or
   mell
And nothing less she seemed to be than a fiend that comes
   from hell

Some meat, some meat, you King Henry, some meat you bring to
   me
Go kill your horse, you King Henry, and bring some meat to
   me
He has slain his berry-brown steed, it made his heart full sore
For she's eaten it up, both skin and bone, left nothing but hide
   and hair

More meat, more meat, you King Henry, more meat you bring to
   me
Go kill your greyhounds, King Henry, and bring some meat to
   me
He has slain his good greyhounds, it made his heart full sore
For she's eaten them up, both skin and bone, left nothing but
   hide and hair

More meat, more meat, you King Henry, more meat you bring to
   me
Go kill your goshawks, King Henry, and bring some meat to
   me
He has slain his good goshawks, it made his heart full sore
For she's eaten them up, both skin and bone, left nothing but
   feathers bare

A drink, a drink, you King Henry, a drink you bring to me
Sew up your horse hide, King Henry, and bring some drink to me

He has sewn the bloody hide, a pipe of wine put in
And she's drank it down all in one drop, left never a drop
  therein

A bed, a bed, you King Henry, a bed you'll make for me!
Oh you must pull the heather green, and make it soft for me!
He has pulled the heather green, and made for her a bed
And taken has he his good mantle, and over it he has spread.

Take off your clothes, now King Henry, and lay down by my
  side
O swear, O swear, you King Henry, to take me as your bride
God forbid, said King Henry, that ever the like betide;
That ever a fiend that comes from hell should stretch down by
  my side

When the dark had gone and the day had come and the sun
  shone through the hall
The fairest Lady that ever was seen lay between him and the
  wall
I've laid for many a gentle knight that gave me such a thrill.
But never before with a courteous knight, that gave me all my
  will!

Martin Carthy, perhaps the greatest living English folk singer, says in his liner notes for King Henry:

"King Henry" is a heavily Anglicized Scottish way of telling the Beauty and the Beast story, the only difference being that the sexes are reversed . . . this ballad originated in the Gawain strand of the Arthurian legend. The King Henry in the ballad probably never existed, since the point of the tale is that chivalry has its own rewards. (Carthy 1974)

So according to Carthy, this was a fictitious Henry. But is it? King Henry I of England (1100–1135) was rumored to have had several dealings with Faeries.

According to Walter Map, writing in or about 1190, a historical English aristocrat around the time of William the Conqueror by the name of Wild Edric caught a Faerie woman in a forest; she consented to be his wife on one condition: he would never taunt her about her Otherworldly origins. Years later he said something cruel about her Faerie nature, and she vanished. She had given him a cup, and later Edric gave the Faerie cup to King Henry I. In another story, related by Gervase of Tilbury (c.1150–c. 1228), there's a Faerie cup from Gloucester. This cup, decorated with precious jewels, could be had by any worthy knight who would simply go into the forest, to a certain hill, and call out loudly for it. The knight could drink from the vessel to gain strength, provided he return it to the Kindly Ones. The cup one day fell into the hands of an aged knight, who, "contrary to Custom and good manners," kept it. But the Earl of Gloucester heard about it, sentenced the robber to death and gave the horn to King Henry I.

In the same era, William of Newbury relates a similar story, but says it happened in Yorkshire. He says that a peasant coming home late one night and passing by a Faerie hill heard singing and shouting. Seeing a door open in the side of the barrow, he looked in and beheld a great banquet. One of the attendants offered him a cup, which he took, but would not drink from (apparently he'd heard all the stories). Instead, he poured out the drink and kept the vessel. He managed to escape the Fey, apparently, because of his swift horse. The story goes on to say that the cup, described as "of unknown material, of unusual color and of extraordinary form," was presented to Henry I. (Hartland 1891, chapter VI)

Henry seems to have a good deal of Faerie lore centered on him, and that usually happens when a well-known person has dealings that are suspected of being Otherworldly. The warning given to Edric not to taunt his lover for her Faerie origins seemed to be a common element of stories such as those told of Henry and his nobles. Gardner, in *Witchcraft Today*, says:

The Fairy mistress was a recognized type called the Leannan Sidhe [L'Annawnshee]. She was good and beautiful, but dangerous, but you must not beat her or she would run back to her people taking her children and her dowry of Fairy cattle with her. Usually she exacted a promise not to tell of her Fairy origin ... (Gardner 2004, 57)

In the Irish tale of the Earl of Desmond, he is said to have married the Faerie Aine Queen of Knockaine (Anne's Hill). She married the earl on the condition he would never comment on the odd behavior of her children. Desmond one day commented on the fact that Aine's son was jumping in and out of a bottle, and the Faerie immediately left him and returned to her Faerie mound. Shortly afterwards, the earl was turned into a wild goose.

If some Faerie lore is based on an ancient race such as the Picts, Henry I may have had contact with these hill dwellers and even took one as a mistress. Word got out, and people spoke of Henry's Faerie involvement. Another hypothesis is that Henry had dealings with the Otherworld, a supposition of several royal figures.

So in the song Henry, a real or imagined king, goes hunting, and catches a great buck. Very like Pwyll, there is a price for his catch. As he is making a feast in his hunting hall (presumably deep in the forest, the domain of the seducer-murderer Fey) a giantess appears. She is hideous, described as a demon, a fiend from Hell, with teeth like tethering stakes and a nose like a club. The other hunters flee the hall in her presence, but brave Henry stands firm and asks the giantess what she desires. Meat, she tells Henry.

This giant stature of the Faerie is not new. In "The Demon Lover," just before the Demon Lover sank the ship, he became giant in stature, reaching the top of the main mast. We also saw in "Reynardine" type stories that the house in the remote forest (or mountains) was sometimes peopled by giants. The Demon Lover and this Faerie giantess can change their stature at will, resuming their human size when desired.

The giantess asks Henry for food and drink, and specifies that she wants to eat his animals. She begins asking for greater and greater sacrifices from Henry: the slaughter of his prized hawks, his well-trained hunting dogs and his thoroughbred horses (just like the merchant father, who must give the Beast the sacrifice of his most precious daughter). Henry gives her each of these things, perhaps recognizing (like Pwyll) that the buck he killed was indeed hers by right, and there is a debt owed. If the king is actually Henry I, it makes a good deal of sense: Henry was the son of William the Conqueror, the first in a line of Norman kings who took from the Saxons such rights as the hunting of the deer. The Normans usurped the ownership of the lands and forests of England, and perhaps Henry felt that a Faerie creature was coming now to avenge that deed. In any case, Henry probably realizes that the giantess can eat him just as easily as she can eat his horses and hounds. This reminds us of the cannibals in the *Mr. Fox* stories.

Finally the giantess commands Henry to lay down with her, which he balks at. "Oh God forbid," he says, "that ever a fiend that comes from Hell should stretch down by my side!"

But this is not a fiend from Hell, but a denizen of Faerie, which Henry must have recognized, because in the morning he is sleeping contentedly beside her. She has now become "the fairest lady that ever was seen." She is apparently a shape-shifter who can show herself to Henry as she wishes him to see her: as an ugly demon when it suits her; then as a total hottie when it's time to get their groove thing on. She has not devoured Henry in a cannibalistic sense, but she has devoured him sexually. Henry is probably counting his lucky stars at that point that the fair Faerie stopped there.

One element of this beast-to-beauty motif is that of personality integration. In each story, *Beauty and the Beast*, *King Henry*, *Cupid and Psyche*, the beastly characters' basic personalities do not change: what changes is their lover's perception of them. I have said that Faeries provide us with a mirror of truth. In this case, we understand that people or creatures may have many facets, sides they show in one situation but not in another. We all have this shape-changing ability: one person (and you know who you are) might be a perfect student in the classroom, a perfect wife or daughter, husband or son in the family, and an absolute terror in a bar or in heavy traffic. In a more extreme example, a mob hit man may be a dutiful father; a white collar criminal might be a loving son. We often choose to see people as we wish to see them, rather than as they really might be. Or perhaps it is fair to say, we see people as our cultural and social mirror allows us to see them; and as we change our outlook, by maturing, by becoming more educated, or by being dealt with lovingly, kindly, unjustly or harshly, our views of others are transformed.

Here the Faerie creatures allow us to experience just this sort of perceptive transformation (as Faeries often do). In each story, the creature is an abject nightmare to their prospective lover, but upon slightly closer inspection, has certain wonderful qualities. The Beast, while hideous, is kind and gentle. The giantess, while also not a looker, is, like Henry, voracious and lascivious, qualities a man like Henry would admire in a woman. And while Psyche may have dreaded Cupid's looks, we can only imagine how great that sex in the dark must have been. If the mortal can just look past the superficial, they will get what their heart most desires. And unlike most dealings between mortals and the Fey, have the storybook ending. Who can ask for more?

And in each of these stories, the human is forced to shift their perception, accepting the good qualities of their lover over the whole looks thing. Which, each human learns, the creature can fix. How about that? So a beast becomes a prince, and a demon becomes a hottie. The Faeries here mirror changes in perception that we mortals experience in our human world as well.

ALLISON GROSS

We have seen this motif of looking beneath the surface again and
again in Faerie. The surface we must look beneath is the water, the
mirror that must be crossed to reach the world of the Sidhe, be it
Tir N'an Og, Carter Hall or Avalon. In that reflective surface, what
we perceive in our world may appear very different. Gold coins may
appear as leaves; a delicious meal may be poison fruit; a bear, a frog, a
beast or a demon may be a beauty or a handsome prince. Faeries have
the ability to disguise the things we most want in order to test our
loyalties or to probe our psyches. These initiatory experiences may
kill us, drive us insane or bring us to our rightful place.

But this part of our discussion is called *The Ugly*, and sometimes,
our perception just doesn't shift. In the beast song "Allison Gross,"
the human does not see the charming qualities of his hideous lover
and is turned into a worm (which might mean dragon, or might just
be an icky worm) for his troubles. Don't get too worried: the Faerie
Queen turns him back again. For a price, of course. Child collected
it as #35.

Allison Gross that lives in yon tower,
The ugliest witch in the north country
Has trysted me up into her bower
And many a fair speech she made to me

She stroked my head and she combed my hair
She set me down softly on her knee
Says "if you will be my lover so true
So many fine things as I would you give"

She showed me a mantle of red scarlet
With golden flowers and fringes fine
Says "if you will be my lover so true
This goodly gift it shall be thine"

"Away, away, you ugly witch
Go far away, and let me be
I never will be your lover so true
And I wish I were out of your company"

She brought me a scarf o the softest silk
Well wrought with pearls about the band
Says "if you will be my lover so true
This goodly gift you shall command"

She showed me a cup of the good red gold
Well set with jewels so fair to see
Says "if you will be my lover so true
This goodly gift I will you give"

"Away, away, you ugly witch
Go far away, and let me be
I never will be your lover so true
And I wish I were out of your company"

She's turned her right and round about
And thrice she blew on a grass-green horn
And she swore by the moon and the stars above
That she'd make me rue the day I was born

Then out has she taken a silver wand
And she's turned her three times round and round
She's muttered such words till my strength it failed
And I fell down senseless upon the ground

She's turned me into an ugly worm
And then she tied about the tree
An ay, on every Saturday night
My sister Maisry came to me

With silver basin and silver comb
To comb my head upon her knee

But or I had kissed her ugly mouth
I'd rather be tied about the tree

But as it fell out on last Hallow-even
When the seely court was riding by
The queen lighted down on a river bank
Not far from the tree where I was tied

She took me up in her milk-white hand
And she's stroked me three times over her knee
She changed me again to my own proper shape
And I never more will be tied about the tree

This song may not be especially noteworthy in our discussion—the less than lovely Ms. Gross may not be a Faerie or enchanted being at all, but a witch or sorceress, complete with a silver wand—but check out the ending. The human, after rebuking Ms. Gross' advances, is turned to a worm (in the original, wyrm). He is then chained to a tree.

While he is tied to his tree, the Seely Court rides by. The Seely Court is an Irish term for the Wild Ride, led by the Faerie Queen. The Queen seems to take some interest in the transformed mortal, and restores him to his human form.

The mortal is ready to pop the cork on some champagne. But thinking back to Tam Lin, one wonders what the Queen of Faeries' motives are here. Could she be taking an interest in her next sacrifice to Hell?

One strange aspect of "Allison Gross" is the presence of the man's sister Maisry, who appears each Saturday evening to groom the worm's hair with a silver comb. That is an odd thing to do to a worm, and seems to imply that Maisry can still see the man as human. She appears to have the ability to cure his enchantment with a kiss, but the worm-human again refuses to kiss "her ugly mouth." One wonders if this guy just has funny ideas about beauty. Or is there more to Maisry than meets the eye?

Maisry sees the man as human, not as a worm; she can see through the water-mirror of Faerie. It's possible that Maisry (which may be a nickname for Margaret) is a Faerie, or enchanted woman, who has the power to heal her mortal brother.

Northeastern European folklore has many songs about a sister-brother duo that travel into the Otherworld and back. Often in these songs, after returning from the Otherworld, the brother is invisible to all inhabitants of our world except for his sister, who has the Faerie sight. Here is a song from Estonia about the sister welcoming her brother back from the Otherworld. The brother is frozen, and the sister is the only one who can return him to a human existence:

> Come to the ground lovely brother
> Step on the ground dear brother
> My sister sweet birdie
> Swallow with a golden crown
> My fingers are frozen to reigns
> My feet are frozen to stirrups
> My dear young brother, Honey of my mind
> I shall heat the hot sauna
> And foment you with the birch whisk
> Defrost your fingers from reigns
> Release your feet from stirrups
> (Lintrop 2001, Volume 16)

Maisry seems to be like the sister in these Baltic songs. She alone can see her brother as human, and she combs his hair and maintains what she perceives as his human appearance. She wants to release him from the charm by kissing him, but as with Allison Gross, the brother resists kissing her "ugly mouth." He finally gives in to being healed from his curse by the Faerie Queen herself, who rides by on Hallow-even (Samhain) while leading the Wild Ride. We can guess what happens next. The tithe to Hell, a fate he might have avoided by having his sister Maisry heal him.

But, wait a minute: is it possible that Maisry is actually the Faerie Queen? In the Finnish and Estonian ballads, the sister has special powers: aside from her travels back and forth from our world to the Otherworld, she can predict the future by the cries of birds, and she carries an enchanted sword that she gives to her brother for his battles. In many ways, Sister sounds like the Faerie Queen. It's possible that the brother only sees in her his regular old sister Maisry until Hallowe'en, when she takes on her very powerful appearance as the Queen of the Fey. Then Brother realizes she is the Faerie Queen, and he'll allow her to heal him and take him into her train. Also in the Baltic ballads, the sister predicts the brother's death in battle. Perhaps in this case Maisry predicts her brother's death in the tithe. This would again be an instance when the Faerie mirror shifts human perception to reveal something we did not see earlier. The water mirror allows the brother to see his sister in a different light, as the queen she actually may be. Lastly, Maisry was a common nickname for Margaret, but could this Maisry have been Morgan, the Queen of the Fey?

The character Maisry appears in other ballads, always as an enchanted sister. In the next ballad to appear in the Child collection, "The Laily Worm and the Machrel of the Sea" (Child #36), we get a very similar story to "Allison Gross," except that the young man's father has married a very ugly sorceress, and it is she who has turned the young man into the titular worm, and his sister Maisry into a mackerel. Again, Maisry shows up every weekend to comb her brother's hair. In this telling, the father learns of his wife's curse and forces her to reverse it, then kills her for her malice. Here are the first few verses of the song:

> I was but seven year auld
> When my mither she did die
> My father married the ae warst woman
> The warld did ever see
> For she has made me the laily worm

That lies at the fit o the tree
An my sister Masery she's made
The machrel of the sea
An every Saturday at noon
The machrel comes to me
An she takes my laily head
An lays it on her knee
She kaims it wi a siller kaim
An washes't in the sea

The worm narrating the song says that as a human he has killed seven knights, and if his father were anyone else, he would kill Dad as well. His father realizes his fault in the situation, and confronts his wife. At first his wife lies, saying the two children have simply left home (an excuse in certain versions of *Hansel and Gretel*), but Dad perseveres. In these verses of the song, Dad forces Stepmom to undo the spell, then kills his evil wife:

He sent for his lady
As fast as send could he
'Whar is my son that ye sent frae me
And my daughter, Lady Masery?'
'Your son is at our king's court
Serving for meat an fee
An your daughter's at our queen's court'

'Ye lie, ye ill woman
Sae loud as I hear ye lie
My son's the laily worm
That lies at the fit o the tree
And my daughter, Lady Masery
Is the machrel of the sea!'
She has tane a siller wan
An gien him strokes three

And he has started up the bravest knight
That ever your eyes did see

She has taen a small horn
An loud an shrill blew she,
An a' the fish came her until
But the proud machrel of the sea:
'Ye shapeit me ance an unseemly shape,
An ye's never mare shape me.'

He has sent to the wood
For whins and for hawthorn
An he has taen that gay lady
An there he did her burn

EVIL STEPMOTHERS

Again and again the proverbial evil stepmother appears in Fairy tales. The mirror land of Faerie often has a situation where a good mother is replaced in the watery reflection by an evil stepmother or mother-in-law. The girl in this mirror-woman's care should be loved and nurtured, but is instead tortured and persecuted.

The evil stepmother is often an enchantress, and has powers of spellcraft and shape-shifting. In *Snow White*, she has the power to disguise herself and to receive prophesy in her magic mirror. In *Rapunzel*, she is a sorceress who takes Rapunzel as a changeling, traded for a head of her namesake cabbage, a plant that represents the girl's sexuality. In *Hansel and Gretel*, when the mother drives the children out of their home, they are taken in by another mother figure, an evil witch who tries to cook the children for dinner. Only Gretel's adult-like bravery saves them.

"Willie's Lady" has a wicked stand-in mother. In it, King Willie has sailed across the sea to find a wife and has brought the now-pregnant girl home to meet her new mother-in-law. But the elder woman does not like the new bride and places her under a spell: though she may come to term, she'll never give birth and will die with the baby inside her. Willie tries to placate his mother with gifts, but she won't budge. She wants Mrs. Willie dead. But like Gretel, the suffering bride thinks quickly. She instructs Willie to fashion a baby of wax with glass eyes and invite his mother to the fake baby's christening. There Willie stands close to the woman and hears her ask who was responsible for undoing a litany of spellbindings she has used. Willie unbinds each act, and his wife can finally give birth.

Here is the song, Child #6:

King Willie he's sailed over the raging foam
He's wooed a wife and he's brought her home

He wooed her for her long golden hair
His mother wrought her a mighty care

A weary spell she's laid on her
She'd be with child for long and many's the year
But a child she would never bear

And in her bower she lies in pain.
King Willie at her bedhead he do stand
As down his cheeks salten tears do run

King Willie back to his mother he did run
He's gone there as a begging son

Says, "Me true love has this fine noble steed
The like of which you ne'er did see

At every part of this horse's mane
There's hanging fifty silver bells and ten
There's hanging fifty bells and ten

This goodly gift shall be your own
If back to my own true love you'll turn again
That she might bear her baby son."

"Oh, the child she'll never lighter be
Nor from sickness will she e'er be free

But she will die and she will turn to clay
And you will wed with another maid."

Then sighing said this weary man
As back to his own true love he's gone again
"I wish my life was at an end."

King Willie back to his mother he did run
He's gone there as a begging son

Says, "me true love has this fine golden girdle
Set with jewels all about the middle

At every part of this girdle's hem
There's hanging fifty silver bells and ten
There's hanging fifty bells and ten

This goodly gift shall be your own
If back to my own true love you'll turn again
That she might bear her baby son."

"Oh, of her child she'll never lighter be
Nor from sickness will she e'er be free

But she will die and she will turn to clay
And you will wed with another maid."

Sighing says this weary man
As back to his own true love he's gone again
"I wish my life was at an end"

Then up and spoke his noble queen
And she has told King Willie of a plan
How she might bear her baby son

She says, "You must go get you down to the market place
And you must buy you a loaf of wax.

And you must shape it as a babe that is to nurse
And you must make two eyes of glass

Ask your mother to a christening day,
And you must stand there close as you can be
That you might hear what she do say"

King Willie he's gone down to the market place
And he has bought him a loaf of wax

And he has shaped it as a babe that is to nurse
And he has made two eyes of glass

He asked his mother to a christening day
And he has stood there close as he could be
That he might hear what she did say

How she spoke and how she swore
She spied the babe where no babe could be before
She spied the babe where none could be before

Says, "Who was it who undid the nine witch knots
Braided in amongst this lady's locks?

And who was it who took out the combs of care
Braided in amongst this lady's hair?

And who was it slew the master kid
That ran and slept all beneath this lady's bed
That ran and slept all beneath her bed?

And who was it unlaced her left shoe
And who was it that let her lighter be
That she might bear her baby boy?"

And it was Willie who undid the nine witch knots
Braided in amongst this lady's locks

And it was Willie who took out the combs of care
Braided in amongst this lady's hair

And it was Willie the master kid did slay
And it was Willie who unlaced her left foot shoe
And he has let her lighter be

And she is born of a baby son
And greater the blessings that be them upon
And greater the blessings them upon

The evil stepmother or evil mother-in-law motif is nothing new to us: as children we came to know it well in Fairy tales. In various versions of Snow White, she can be the stepmother or the biological mother. This tale is told throughout Europe; in fact, the name Snow White is a common girl's name in Slavic countries. The tale is often told very differently than the Disney version Americans know.

In some versions, the father, riding with his wife in his royal carriage, wishes he had a daughter; a girl as white as the snow he passes, with hair as black as the ravens he sees above him. He then finds a child on the road fitting just this description, and takes her into the carriage, claiming her as his own. This begins a jealous struggle between mother and changeling daughter. In other versions is the familiar switch, where the mother dies, leaving her daughter no money, and bequeathing the girl only beauty. A stepmother comes into the girl's life, marrying the father and jealously hating the daughter.

The motif also appears in Cupid and Psyche. In this story, Venus (Aphrodite) is the jealous mother of Cupid who hates her daughter-in-law for her beauty. She wants Psyche killed and only an act of the Gods can save the girl.

Psyche is a Nymph-girl, and Snow White has many Nymph qualities. For one thing, she is a changeling in some versions, found in the snow by a man riding in his carriage. We know she is Otherworldly because she can live among the Dwarves (in some versions these are ogres). Moreover, she sleeps with the Dwarves night after night in the form of a young girl (some versions state that Snow White is seven when her mother kicks her out), but does the work of a woman (ostensibly cleaning and cooking, but the other duties of a wife are implied).

There is also the hunter-rescuer element: the evil stepmother sends Snow White into the forest with a hunter, whom she instructs to return with the girl's heart (in some versions, her liver, which the mother will cook and eat, strengthening her tie with the cannibalistic robbers or ogres; in other versions, a bottle of blood corked with the girl's toe). But the girl, who appears juvenile, manages to dissuade the hunter from killing her by captivating him with her beauty. The Grimms' version runs: "Snow White was so beautiful that the huntsman took pity on her and said 'Just run off, you poor child.'" For Snow White to be considered so beautiful that the huntsman would disobey his own queen might be questionable, unless you realize we are dealing with a Nymph-girl: she has enchanted him with her beauty and sensuality, and the huntsman will not harm her. We also see the hare-girl motif here, since the huntsman kills a boar sow and brings its heart (or lungs and liver) to the queen as proof the girl is dead. Snow White has been exchanged for an animal, equating the girl with the boar sow; she is a Nymph who can take animal form (or at least she is equated with an animal in the mind of the hunter).

This exchange of an animal life for a human life, prompted by beauty or sexuality, has already been seen several times. In the story of Pwyll and Rhiannon, the couple's child is taken as a changeling and returned for a colt. In another *Mabinogion* story, Manawydan threatens to hang a mouse that turns out to be a Faerie King's wife. The Faerie must ransom the mouse to win his wife back. And Finn Mac Coul takes a deer as a wife, the beautiful Sadb, who bears him a son, Ossian. Over and over in the Faerie record are beautiful young women either seen as animals or traded for the lives of animals. Part of this has to do with the confused mirror-world of Faerie: animals sustain human life by providing food, clothing and companionship; women create human life and nurture the living. In the reflected water of the Faerie world, the two often become one, and men are lured to both the animal and the human girl, often having to trade one for the other. The Nymph Snow White is no exception.

Snow White's Otherworldly qualities are also in her name. As Maria Tatar points out in *The Annotated Brothers Grimm*, "Snow suggests cold and remoteness, along with the notion of the lifeless and inert, yet it also comes down from the heavens. And Snow White in the coffin does indeed become not only pure and innocent but also passive, comatose, and ethereally beautiful." (Tatar 2004, 240)

Snow White is young but seductive; she has the Otherworldly qualities of ethereal beauty, prolonged sleep (a state resembling death) and passivity; she remains childlike throughout the tale, yet captivates the prince who desires her sexually. Put all of these traits together, and what have you got? Yup, a Nymph.

We're not through with Snow White just yet; the next chapter looks at the tale from a different perspective.

Chapter 7

FAERIE PROPHECY

If Faeries can travel through the veil of mist or water, and if time is different on each end of the journey, can the Kindly Ones travel forward in time and witness events we have not yet experienced? Can they foretell our destinies by the use of the water reflection? Can they share this divination with us? In quite a few stories, the Enchanted Ones seem to have the uncanny ability to appear at the exact perfect moment, to see where a human is and what he or she is doing, and to know what is about to happen.

Do Faeries have the ability to divine the events of our world? Let's begin our examination of this idea with Snow White's stepmother.

The evil stepmother-Queen in *Snow White* has a magic mirror that can see both nearby and far away. When the Queen appears in the story, she is standing before the mirror asking the now-familiar question, and the mirror responding "You, O Queen, are the fairest of all." As the plot develops and Snow White riles up the Queen's jealousy, the mirror can see into the forest where the ethereal Snow White is hidden from sight. The mirror says:

"You are the fairest here, dear Queen
But little Snow White though far away

With the seven dwarves in her hideaway
Is now the fairest ever seen."

This type of divination, gazing into a mirror or a pool of water, is called scrying. It was a common divinatory method throughout Europe for many centuries. It would be a typical vehicle for the evil stepmother to use as her engine of divination.

Some stepmothers do not need an external divinatory method but rely on some extrasensory device. In *Rapunzel*, the enchantress seems to be psychically aware of the father-to-be stealing the plants from her garden, of the gender of the child that will be born, and she appears in the delivery chamber at the precise moment of Rapunzel's birth.

In these tales, the mother figure's divinatory visions become the central point of her struggle with her stepdaughter. The reflection of the Faerie water-mirror causes a powerful woman who is meant to nurture a child instead to attempt to destroy her, or to lock her in a tower and neglect her.

Not all Faerie diviners are women, and not all are stepmothers. "The Great Selkie" (Child #113; see chapter 4) collects the son he had sired with an "earthly nurse" (a mortal woman). The Selkie divines the future of the woman, himself and his child, saying:

And thee shall marry a proud gunner,
An a proud gunner I'm sure he'll be,
An the very first shot that ere he schoots,
He'll schoot both my young son and me.

In more common English, he tells her she'll marry a gunner (harpooner), who will fire a shot that will kill both the child and himself.

The Selkie has much in common with the Queen of *Snow White* in that his prophecy is his undoing. He can see that what he foretells will end up causing his destruction, but he goes through with it anyway, carrying the child away and freeing the nurse from his hold on her, allowing her to marry again. She will marry the Selkie's killer. In

Snow White, the queen's undoing is that she can communicate with the mirror. In the end, her obsession causes her death. Once her treachery is discovered, she is put to death by being forced to dance in red-hot iron shoes: iron to banish Faeries or other enchanted creatures, and fire to purify.

In a sense, Faeries and other enchanted creatures are pretty limited in who they are and what they can do. While they may have magical abilities that we find awesome, they are not capable of major transformation: the Selkie cannot stop himself from claiming his son; his counterpart, the female Selkie, cannot stop herself from leaving her family and returning to the sea once she has found her seal skin; and the Queen in *Snow White* cannot stop herself from hating her stepdaughter, though it consumes her. Faeries are captives to their identity, and this is what makes them helpful and harmful, good and bad, mysterious and enigmatic. In many ways we are like them, victims of ourselves. Yet we seem to find it easier to change (on the other hand, we die in eighty years or so, and they live unimaginably long lives when not subjected to harpoons or iron knives). For the Fey, though they are victims of their nature, this gives them a confidence and a passion that we may never understand or be able to affect ourselves.

BANSHEES (AGAIN)

One the best-known prophetic Faeries is the Irish Banshee. The Banshee is a Faerie woman (her name, Bean Sidhe, literally means that) who is attached to a particular family. Folklore says the Banshee is attached to the oldest Irish families, and these families include the Kavanaughs, O'Neills, O'Gradys, O'Connors and O'Brians. When a member of these families is about to die, the Banshee sings a mournful, wailing song. In Irish culture, the singing of a mournful song at a person's burial is called keening, but the Banshee would keen before the death occurred, foretelling the event. Young women were often forbidden by their families from marrying into clans that had Banshees, as these families were said to be cursed.

One story says that the Banshee combs her hair with a silver comb. Because of this, folklore warns never to pick up a comb one finds lying on the ground, or the Banshee might take you to the Faerie world. While there have been suggestions that this is an element of Mermaid lore mixed into the Banshee tales, it is also possible that the Banshee foresees death in the looking glass that accompanies the comb. Perhaps she is able to see through the water-mirror reflection into the Underworld and visualize a person who will take his or her place there.

There are many historical reports of Banshee sightings in Scotland and Ireland. In 1437, King James I of Scotland was said to have been approached by an Irish Banshee who foretold his murder. He was killed on February 21 of that year by a group of Scots led by Sir Robert Graham.

One more recent report of a Banshee occurred on the night of August 6, 1801, and was reported by a Sir Jonah Barrington, who was staying in the home of Lord Rossmore, Commander-in-Chief of the British forces in Ireland. In his book *Things I Can Tell*, the next Lord Rossmore relates Barrington's account of his father's strange death:

> At 2:30 am, Barrington and his wife were woken by a plaintive cry that seemed to be coming through a window from a grassy patch outside. The voice of a woman wailed or moaned, then called "Rossmore Rossmore Rossmore!"

The next morning, Barrington was told that Lord Rossmore had died at exactly 2:30 am. Barrington later wrote in his journal, "Lord Rossmore was dying at the moment I heard his name pronounced." (Rossmore 1912, 5)

It seems Banshees are so attached to their families that they will follow them to the New World. On February 5, 1878, Mary Marr, a Scottish American woman living in the Ohio River Valley, saw a ghostly woman riding a horse outside her window in the very early morning. She approached the rider, who told her, "I am here to tell you, Mary Marr, that Thomas Marr has just died. Say your prayers, Lady. I bid you well." Apparently her husband, Thomas, had died that night and his body had been washed away by the Little Kanawha River. The Banshee is still said to live in Marrtown, West Virginia.

Banshees are known not just as keening mourners attached to families but also as deer Faeries. chapter 4 mentioned that in County Cork, the An Chailleach Bhéarach could transform into a deer. In these Cork legends, the Banshee would take this form to commune with the dead. Recalling that deer are often at the start of contact between humans and Underworld creatures, like Pwyll and Arawn, or Finn Mac Coul and Sadb, it's quite possible that taking the form of the deer is one method for the Banshee to see through the veil into the Otherworld, and so predict the exact time of a person's death.

BIRD FAERIES

Another group of Underworld animals are birds, and many prophetic Faeries may take this form when foretelling the future. Throughout folkloric belief, enchanted birds can divine and act as omens for us.

Ravens are enchanted Underworld birds; in the *Mabinogion* are Bran and Branwen, the raven king and queen of enchanted Wales. Another Otherworldly voyager is named for the raven, Bran Mac Febal. Ravens are considered messengers who fly between our world and the Otherworld at will. Ravens are especially enchanted because they are carrion eaters; they eat dead creatures and then fly off. The ancient Celts felt that ravens would fly to the Otherworld, carrying the soul of their meal with them.

Here is an English rhyme that interprets the flight of ravens to foretell events:

One for sorrow
Two for joy
Three for a girl and

Four for a boy
Five for silver
Six for gold
Seven for a secret
Never to be told
(Traditional)

A ritual would be performed asking the enchanted birds for an answer to a question. The number of ravens flying overhead or landing nearby foretell the outcome, mood, gender of a baby and the accumulation of riches.

Ravens are sacred to Mab, the Faerie Queen, and also to Odin. And Branwen, or White Raven, communicated with her brother Bran (Raven) by sending an Otherworldly bird, a wren, to deliver her message. The wren is a shortened form of the bird's full name, bran's sparrow (or wren's sparrow, as Bran is pronounced sounding closer to *vran* or *wren* in many Welsh dialects. The *Mabinogion* refers to this giant Underworld king as Bran, or the blessed raven). The wren, aside from being Britain's smallest bird, is known as the bird of winter, and represents the Seven Year King and the winter God, or Father Christmas. In England today, the custom of killing a wren each Yule is observed, as it has been for countless centuries. Part of this morbid ritual involves foretelling the coming of spring. Young men sing a lovely song as they hunt the wren, then take the dead bird to each house in the village and exhibit his gruesome corpse. The song goes:

The wren, the wren, the king of all birds,
On St. Stephen's day was caught in the furze;
Though his body is small, his family is great,
So, if you please, your honor, give us a treat.
On Christmas Day I turned a spit;
I burned my finger; I feel it yet,
Up with the kettle, and down with the pan:
Give us some money to bury the wren.
(Traditional)

Notice the element of a boy burning his finger on a spit: this recalls the story of Cerridwen, where Gwion Bach gains all knowledge by burning his finger on the stew of wisdom. This story is also told of the Irish hero Cuculain (pronounced KOO-lane, "the Hound of Laine"). Cuculain fries up a salmon who has been feeding on the nuts of the hazel tree, the tree of wisdom. He burns his finger on the fish, puts finger to mouth, and becomes the wisest man in Ireland.

In another wren song from Pembrokeshire, the wren is referred to as "the king," and as his corpse is shown at each house, silver is given to the hunters to bring a prosperous growing season. Here is the song that these boys sing:

Joy health love and peace
Be all here in this place
By your leave we will sing
Concerning our king

Our king is well dressed
In silks of the best
In ribbons so rare
No king can compare

We have traveled many miles
Over hedges and stiles
In search of our king
Unto you we bring

We have powder and shot
To conquer the lot
We have cannon and ball
To conquer them all

Oh Christmas is passed
Twelfth Night is the last
And we bid you adieu
Great joy to the new
(Traditional)

It's interesting to imagine the little dead wren dressed in bright ribbons and a little silk chemise, but there you have it. The bird of the Underworld has returned to his home, carrying a message of hope that there will be a good spring. It is believed that in the spring the little bird will be reborn into the forest as a robin, letting the people of the community know that their prayers have been heard and that the spirits of their crops will return to their fields.

There is so much Otherworld lore centered around the tiny wren that whole books could be written on the diminutive critter and probably not mention all of it. The tiniest bird in England is protected at all times of the year other than the Yule season, and it is considered terribly bad luck to kill a wren or disturb its nest at any other time. A Welsh rhyme goes:

Y neb a dorro nyth y dryw/Nu chaiff iechyd yn ei fwy:
"Whosoever robs the wren's nest/shall never have health in his life."

Although the wren is called the king of winter, she is also called a queen, named Jenny Wren, and considered to be the wife of the robin. Each year the robin renews its red breast by killing the wren, sending it to the Underworld where it will reign as queen of winter. The robin's chest becomes red with his wife's blood.

The Druids called the wren "supreme among all the birds," and a wren feather in the pocket was believed to save a man from drowning (crossing the water passage to the Underworld). More than that, the Druids used the very complex song of the wren for divination.

At the core of all of these beliefs is the legend that the Faerie Queen took the form of a wren, at which time she was called Jenny Wren. The wren would then be considered Queen of the Underworld, and this is seen in the bird's Latin name: the wren belongs to the family Troglodytidae, which means "cave dweller." The wren crawls into caves and holes to hunt insects, which gives it an identity as a messenger between our world and the subterranean Underworld. It burrows into the mounds and hills where the Kindly Ones dwell. When the tiny wren crawls out of a burrow, it could simply be a mortal bird, but it could just as likely be a Faerie in the shape of the creature, even the Faerie Queen herself.

In the *Mabinogion* story of Branwen, Branwen was held captive in the kitchens of the Underworld king and needed to contact her brother Bran, the Blessed Raven. She did this by sending a wren as a messenger to Bran. What is not stated in the Welsh text is how the wren came to crawl through the kitchen window to serve Branwen. Indeed, that tiny bird must have known through its own divination that Branwen needed its help to serve as messenger between the Underworld where Branwen was held prisoner and the Overworld where Bran waited.

An old story says the wren became the king of the birds through cunning and Underworld connections. The birds decided they needed a king, and that whoever could fly the highest would be crowned. Each bird flew as high as he could, but the eagle flew the highest. When the mighty eagle was about to be declared king, a wren who had been hiding in his neck feathers flew out, climbing higher than the eagle.

Outraged, the birds declared that now the king would be the bird to fly lowest. The waders flew low indeed, but the wren crept into a mouse hole in the ground and yelled out, "I am king!"

The birds grew upset again, and asked the owl to watch over the hole and catch the wren when he came out. The diligent owl watched all night, but by morning he fell asleep and out crept the little wren and hid in the hedge. So now the owl will only come out at night, having been shamed by falling asleep during the day; and the crafty wren hides in the mouse hole and in the hedge, but is called king by all the birds.

The story again associates the wren with its underground dwelling and with the Underworld. Notice too that the wren usurps the place of the eagle, associated in Wales with the sun god Llew, and also the owl, the bird of prophecy. The wren trumps both, proving itself the supreme diviner and bird of wisdom.

In British currency, the wren graces England's smallest coin, the farthing, showing the great reverence the British have for their tiny king of the birds/queen of the Underworld.

OWLS

Another enchanted bird is the owl, connected with the Sirin and with the flower spirit Blodeuedd. The Greeks believed that owls, rather than ravens, could foretell the outcome of an event by their presence or numbers. In the *Iliad* and the *Odyssey*, Homer often mentions sightings of owls as omens. Even earlier, the Egyptians thought of owls as enchanted messengers of the Underworld, and the owl is the Egyptian hieroglyph for death. In the Bible, Ecclesiastes 10:20 says, "For a bird of the air shall carry the voice, and that which hath wings shall tell the matter." This seems to refer to the omen of an owl, though one tradition says it was a skylark that told Solomon that the Queen of Sheba would visit him.

Another Biblical owl is Lilith, who gets a lot of bad press, but maybe isn't such a bad girl after all. Perhaps she's just misunderstood. Lilith appears in the ancient Sumerian epic *Gilgamesh*, in which she is identified with the moon and with divination. She is also called "the maid who screeches," which is what owls do. Here is a passage from the "Huluppu Tree" tale, part of the prologue to the *Gilgamesh* narrative:

> A serpent who could not be charmed made its nest in the roots of the tree,
> The Anzu bird set his young in the branches of the tree,
> And the dark maid Lilith built her home in the trunk
> (Kramer 1938, lines 23–25)

Gilgamesh scholars translate "Anzu bird" as the owl, a bird of wisdom and prophecy. This passage identifies Lilith with the owl and the serpent, an identification that seems to set her up for some very bad PR from the Hebrews a few centuries later, when Lilith turns up in the Bible. The King James translation of Isaiah 34:14 says:

> The wild beasts of the desert shall also meet with the wild beasts of the island, and the satyr shall cry to his fellow; the screech owl also shall rest there, and find for herself a place of rest.

The "screech owl" (ל״ל) is also translated as the "night spirit," and both are supposed to refer to Lilith (לילית). Even without being a Hebrew scholar, you can probably see how similar the words are. Remember that Hebrew is read from right to left and compare the two spellings.

This is the only mention of Lilith in the Bible, but many Bible scholars think that because of the much earlier *Gilgamesh* text, Hebrews associated Lilith with the serpent of Eden in Genesis. The Sefer Zohar, a Kabalistic volume written quite a few centuries later in the Middle Ages, confirms the Hebrew view of Lilith as a demon and a serpent and calls her the female aspect of Samael, the Devil. Since this time, Jews have considered Lilith a seducer-murderer Faerie, or succubus, who is said to kill children and to appear to men in their dreams, seduce them and create children by their seed. Hebrews believed that Lilith could be warded off by circumcising their male children. Circumcision was believed to be a charm against death. In the story of Moses, Exodus 4:24–26, when God attacks Moses, his wife, Tzipora, circumcises their son and touches the bloody foreskin to Moses's head, saving him from death. To protect their progeny, Palestinian women make a "Lilith bowl," a ceramic with a maze on it, to capture Lilith if she should attack a sleeping infant. The Lilith bowl is left beside the child's cradle. (How similar is this to Irish folklore concerning charms against changeling infants?)

Despite her bad rap in the Middle Ages, the Sumerian and Hebrew folklore seems to tell us that Lilith is an Underworld owl Faerie that appears to men in dreams and foretells the future or imparts wisdom.

While she may be sexually motivated, like many other Nymphs, her owl-like insight and divination skills seem to come out while she is seducing men in a dream state. In *Gilgamesh* she is associated with the "World Tree" or "Tree of Life," and her wisdom may come from some very deep source represented in the Tarot or the Kabalah, systems based on the Hebrew Tree of Life. In certain Hebrew texts, Lilith is associated with Malkuth, the tenth Sephiroth or sphere on this Hebrew sacred diagram; a place of manifestation from thought into reality.

As far as being a baby stealer, we've seen this of Faerie Queens before. Lilith may have a Wild Ride legend that has been lost. She may also exact a tithe to Hell, remembered in the Hebrew reference to her being the female side of Satan. Being an owl, she is a night Faerie, connected with the moon and the night creatures. Night represents the unconscious mind and the dream state or trance state, so Lilith is said to visit men in their dreams. Night and sleep are symbolic of death and also orgasm (the French call orgasm "the little death"), so Lilith's reputation as a succubus and a seducer-murderer Faerie may come from an association with the death world or Underworld. Same with her rep as a baby stealer.

An area of the world that is chock-full of prophetic owl Faeries is eastern Europe. Gamayun, the Sirin and the Alkomost are Faerie creatures with the body of an owl and the head of a woman. The Gamayun and the Sirin can divine the future, but in each case the voice of the creature is so beautiful that when mortals hear her, they lose all sense of reality and follow her into the deep forest where they die (sounds familiar, doesn't it?). People would attempt to drive the bird women off by shooting a cannon or ringing loud bells. However, the creatures may foretell the future to the saints, predicting joys waiting for them in Paradise.

The Sirin in bird form is in an Estonian song called "The Brother's War Song." It tells of a bear-man who journeys into the Underworld to gather allies for a war, while his sister listens to prophecies of Sirins singing in a forest as birds:

What was there in the row of pines
Who in the row of hazel trees?
Cuckoo was in the row of pines
Nightingale in the row of hazel trees
The cuckoo was writing down letters
The nightingale scribed in the book
Whose turn it was to go to war
Whose turn to stay behind?
(Lintrop 2001, Volume 16)

In Poland, the Sirin is seen as another name for Vila (Weela), who can teach humans to converse with the birds (see chapter 10). This creature seemed to have an effect on the author Nabokov, who wrote his earliest published poems as Vladimir Sirin. She is indeed a muse of poets, and her enchanting voice can lull a writer into a creative trance.

A BIT MORE ABOUT FAERIE QUEENS

The same is true of L'Annawnshee, whom we saw in connection with King Henry. She is prophetic, giving humans (mostly men) the gift of the Faerie sight and inspiring poets and songwriters. Those inspired by her are said to be brilliant but to lead brief lives. Keats was very likely one of her poets. He wrote many poems about a shadowy Underworld beauty that both inspired him and whom he associated with his own looming death (*La Belle Dame Sans Mercy* being the best known of these). The bards of Ireland sought inspiration from L'Annawnshee, sleeping near rivers and streams to learn new songs from her watery voice.

Like L'Annawnshee, the Elf Queen is prophetic; she knew just where and when to find Thomas. And when Thomas returned from his seven years in the Faerie world, she had given him the gift of prophecy: he could foretell the weather and divined optimum times for harvesting and planting. This doesn't sound like very sexy information, but to Scottish farmers it was indispensable. To this day in Scotland, one can find almanacs sold that True Thomas allegedly wrote.

Along with Thomas's ability to foretell the future comes a strange curse: he can never tell a lie. For this he got the nickname of True Thomas. This is a true Faerie gift: both a blessing and a curse. Gifts from the Good People are like that. You may get something amazing, like back surgery, or something awful, like really bad back surgery. You take your chances with the Fey, and anyone who thinks it's a good idea to cavort with the Unseen People should go into it knowing this to be true.

Thomas also received the gift of the Faerie Sight. This means, quite simply, that unlike the rest of us Thomas could see Faeries wherever they might be. This is true of Tam Lin too, but in his case, the Faerie Queen did not intend for Tam Lin to have this gift (in fact, she did not intend Tam Lin to live very long past Hallowe'en). The Queen tells Tam Lin that if she knew this would happen, she'd have taken out Tam Lin's eyes and replaced them with "eyes of tree," or wooden eyes. The Faerie Sight is a type of divination that gives people the ability to see into the Faerie world, and so to see well beyond our own tiny reality and into a much larger reality. It allows one to see through the water-mirror of the veil between our world and the Otherworld. And isn't that what divination really is? The ability to see past our very limited sense of time and space, into a universe where time is not linear, and space is not confined to the small amount of area we can perceive at the moment.

It is interesting that the Faerie Queen did not foresee that Janet would rescue Tam Lin from the tithe. Likewise, the Queen in *Snow White* could use her mirror to find her stepdaughter, but could not foresee that she herself would be killed when Snow White was rescued and married. It seems that many Faeries are limited in what they can and cannot divine. There may also be only certain times of the year when Faeries have the power of prediction. Samhain or Hallowe'en, for instance, is a time long associated with divination and vision. The veil between our world and the Otherworld is thin then, as the spirits of the dead (crops killed in the harvest and animals killed in the hunt) pass between the two places. The Faerie Queen rides at this time because she will gather spirits to herself and bring them through the veil.

The Celts feared that at this time of the year, Death could easily come through the veil and take people at random. So they dressed as ghosts to fool Death into believing he'd already paid them a visit. They would also carve a skull from a wax turnip (we now use a larger gourd, a pumpkin) to mark a house as if Death had been there (similar to the Jews marking their doors with lamb's blood to ward off the Angel of Death during the tenth Egyptian plague, Exodus 11:1–12:36).

Spring, opposite autumn on the calendar, is also a time when the veil is thin: spirits resting in the Underworld travel back into our fields and forests to be reborn into the sprouting crops and newborn animals. As the snow and ice melts, streams and rivers surge with water, creating a crossing to and from Faerie.

In the Wiccan Rede, we find the line "where the rippling waters flow/cast a stone and truth ye'll know." This is a spell for finding the truth of a situation (as the Queen's mirror revealed the truth). The stone mentioned in the Rede is a lodestone, a magnetized iron stone. The water must be "rippling," or flowing freely, which occurs in spring and fall, after the thaw or during the autumn rains. A magnetized iron stone will upset or waken Naiads, river spirits in the rippling stream. So this is a Faerie spell, used to divine truth. Try it yourself sometime, and you'll see that it works.

In spring, Estonian young women try to divine which man they will marry by picking up trash from outside and placing it under their pillow; according to the tradition, they will dream of the man they are to fall in love with. This is exactly like the English ritual Keats describes in his poem *The Eve of Saint Agnes*, where his young woman heroine fasts all day, and believes that if she lays down to bed without looking behind her and lies with her hands beneath her head, she will dream of her future husband.

A very practical use for spring divination is to predict when the ice will thaw, and when one may plant. Most of us are no longer farmers, but you can imagine how important it must have been in an agricultural community to plant after the last frost, but early enough to reap a bountiful harvest. For this information, people observed animals. One animal observed today is the groundhog, which wakes from hibernation when the thaw begins. His decision to come out of his den or hit the snooze button lets farmers know when to begin planting. The custom of Groundhog Day rose from various European observances: Imbolc in Ireland, Oimelc in the Shetlands, and Candlemas across Catholic Europe. In each instance, animals were closely watched on February 2 to see how the weather would be for the next few weeks. An old rhyme goes:

> If Candlemas day be sunny and clear
> Expect two winters in one year

Groundhogs are an American mammal, and the custom of Groundhog Day originally applied to other creatures. The Romans had an early spring observance based on the hedgehog; in fact, many European cultures believe that hedgehogs can predict storms, and that they close the doors to their burrows when a storm is coming. Likewise the Irish observed the hedgehog, the Germans watched the badger, and various Northern European peoples looked to the bear. Each are burrowing animals considered especially enchanted because they delve beneath the ground, under hills and mounds where the Fey dwell. Let's take a look at some lore surrounding each of these enchanted burrowers.

HEDGEHOGS

Throughout the Isles, Faerie lore connected with these spiny little critters abounds. The Irish call them *graineeogs* ("ugly ones") and believe them to be Witches in animal form. Shakespeare referred to hedgehogs as Faerie creatures, grouping them with animals the Fey kept watch for when guarding the Queen. In A *Midsummer Night's Dream*, Act Two, Scene 2, the Fairies sing:

> You spotted snakes with double tongue,
> Thorny hedgehogs, be not seen;
> Newts and blindworms, do no wrong;
> Come not near our Fairy Queen.
> (Shakespeare, A *Midsummer Night's Dream*, Act II,
> Scene 2, 9–12)

In fact, it is commonly believed in Cornwall and Scotland that Pixies can assume the form of hedgehogs. When they do this, they are called Urchins. They are believed to do mischief in this form, but can foretell the future. There are many stories of humans who have found Urchins by the wayside and, believing them to be mortal children, nurtured them, only to find that they are actually Pixies.

Gypsies also believe hedgehogs to be enchanted, and they refer to them as Hedge-hursts. Scottish Gypsies have tales of hedge-hurst children born to mortal parents as the result of a curse. Gypsies have been known to eat the little creatures; European Gypsies consider eating a hedgehog to be a cure for stomachaches and snakebites.

The Grimms collected an odd story called *Hans the Hedgehog* that has all of this hedgehog folklore within it. A human man and woman give birth to an Urchin as a result of a curse the father brings on himself, and their spiny offspring moves between the Otherworld of the deep forest and the human world of town and castle. The story goes like this:

A man laments that he has no child, and would even prefer a child who looked like a hedgehog to being childless. Sure enough, his wife bears a son that is half-human and half-hedgehog. The child, Hans, takes his father's pigs and rides off on a shod cock to live in the forest, where he takes up the bagpipes to pass the time.

A king, trying to find his way through the forest, hears the bagpipes and asks Hans to help him find his path home. In return, he promises his daughter to Hans. But after Hans helps the king and returns to his pigs, the king returns to his castle and assures his daughter that he will never honor the promise he has made to the hedgehog boy.

In time, another king loses his way in the forest and hears the bagpipes. Hans helps him, and this king promises his daughter in earnest.

Hans goes to the court of the first king and finds that the king has ordered that if Hans ever shows up, he is to be shot at. But he evades the gunners and takes the king's daughter. As they are leaving the castle, Hans the Hedgehog sticks his spikes in the girl and sends her home wounded and bleeding, telling her she is being punished for her father's dishonesty.

Hans then visits the second king who welcomes the hedgehog boy as a son and prepares a feast for the promised wedding. The daughter is afraid of Hans's spikes on their wedding night, but Hans assures her she will not be hurt. As they enter the bedchamber, he peels his hedgehog skin off and burns it. At first he is ghastly and scarred, but a doctor rubs him with salve and Hans becomes a handsome young man. The two consummate the marriage and live happily ever after.

So this hedgehog is an Urchin who becomes a prince through his visit to the forest Otherworld (complete with a huge pog of pigs), and then his marriage to a girl who proves honest. Like many Faerie creatures, this enchanted being may take animal form or human form but must remain human when he marries a mortal. He also is able to divine which female is deserving of her royal title, proving one to be deceitful and the other sincere. Each time a king promises Hans his daughter, Hans does not accompany the king, but returns to the Otherworld forest where he has the power to foretell his future with the girl. Before arriving at the first king's castle, he is aware that he will be met with violence and that the girl will prove unfaithful.

BEARS

Another type of burrowing beast is the bear, and this beast is often a prophetic changeling creature as well. In *Snow White and Rose Red*, the enchanted bear became Rose Red's lover and was able to arrive at just the right moment to rescue her from the Dwarf, an act that required the skill of divination. Bears are all over the Grimms' tales, especially in the story of *Goldilocks*. While her tale is very watered down, it has all the elements of a Nymph/changeling tale: a trip into the forested Otherworld; a secluded house with enchanted beings inside, in this case bears; and a struggle to free herself from this world and return to the mortal world. *Goldilocks* compares to such tales as *Mr. Fox* and *The Robber Bridegroom*; it has simply taken on a much more childish character in its modern setting.

In Northern European folklore, the bear is looked to for predicting weather patterns to guide both planting and hunting. Tribal Russian people such as the Mansi and Khanty have a tradition of gathering for Bear Feasts. People sing songs, tell stories and predict the planting forecast for the coming year. One element of these stories is a bear character that can divine the future. Here is a Bear Feast story about a woman, a bear, a brother and sister, and a very bad marriage:

> There were a sister and a brother who lived together. The brother said it was wrong to live this way. He moved away and made a wife for himself out of a cedar-tree. The sister went looking for her brother and found him. While the brother was out, she chopped the cedar woman to splinters which she buried under a pile of shingles. Then she put on the cedar woman's clothes and lay down in her place. So she lived with her brother. Soon a son was born to them.
>
> One day the boy heard a voice saying, "Your mother killed me and buried me under a pile of shingles." The boy told his father what he had heard. Learning the truth the man flew into a rage and killed both his sister and his son.

Spring came. The blood of the little Mos'-woman fertilized a plant called *porgy* (hogweed). The weed was eaten by a passing she-bear. When the time came, the she-bear gave birth to two bear-cubs and a little girl, the first Por-woman. One day the bear told her daughter, "Tomorrow people will come and kill me as well as your brother and sister. When people cook my meat, take care you do not eat it. When night arrives, come to the back of the house." Everything came to pass as the bear had said. At night the girl went to the back of the house where her mother taught her what should be done with the meat and bones of the killed bear. The girl brought her mother back to life. The she-bear gradually rose up to the skies, becoming the constellation of the Little Bear (Ursa Minor). Her daughter, however, become the mother of all Por-people. (Lintrop 2001, Volume 3)

One aspect of this tale explains a relationship between two Ob-Ugric tribes, the Por and the Mos. These people live on the Siberian plains in central Russia in an area called Khanty-Mansi, along the Ob River.

The story starts out with a brother-sister pair. Many times in tales of enchanted beings, brother and sister pairs are two aspects of the same being (like the Greek brother and sister Apollo and Diana, the sun and the moon or day and night). The brother and sister pair come up a lot in Northeastern European folklore, and they represent a journey to the Otherworld across ice or water (see chapter 6). In this story, the brother and sister start out as lovers. Looking at a familiar tale, the story of Blodeuedd, there's a similarity: in that tale; Gwydion impregnates his sister Arianrhod using a wooden staff. Later the issue of that brother-sister union, Llew Llaw Gyffes, marries a maiden created for him by Gwydion from nine flowers of the forest. Since both Llew and Blodeuedd were sired by Gwydion, they too are a sexually involved brother and sister. The brother-and-sister-as-lovers theme is in other mythologies too, such as the Egyptian folkloric record.

Apparently in this case the brother has a fit of remorse over lying with his sister and decides to fashion a wife from a cedar tree. Again, a similarity to Blodeuedd. In both stories, a young man needs a wife and makes one (or one is made for him) from local vegetation. Both Blodeuedd and the cedar wife are obviously Faeries, specifically Nymphs, with a strong connection to the Otherworld through the flowers from which they have shape-shifted to human form. As mentioned, Blodeuedd is created by Gwydion, Llew's father, so she and Llew are actually brother and sister. It seems like the lovers in this sort of tale are meant to be brother and sister, since here the sister kills the Cedar Nymph and assumes her place. The incident of the brother growing livid and killing his sister and his child is not uncommon in folklore: remember that Hansel and Gretel's mother tried to kill them.

Now the whole hacking your family to bits thing seems like it would be really bad (I don't recommend it). But in this case it seems destined, and ultimately the brother-sister union in this tale creates an enchanted bear-girl that births a new tribe.

Because we're talking about divinatory burrowers, let's look at the prophecy of the she-bear in the tale. She divines that she will be killed and gives her daughter instructions that must be carried out so that the she-bear may enter the Otherworld. Because the daughter does as she is instructed, the she-bear completes her transition; afterwards she is still visible to her daughter as a constellation. This is very like the tale of the Selkie; although the Selkie mother leaves her husband, her children may still speak to her and visit her in seal form. The daughter may now depend on her celestial Fey mother to impart predictions about weather and seasonal changes.

There is another tale in which a bear-human brother is tied to the Otherworld through a tryst with his sister, one that may be a good deal more familiar: the tale of King Arthur.

Arthur (pronounced Art-ur) is Welsh for "Bear-man." Like the bears in the Ugric tales, Arthur is meant to be seen as Otherworldly, earthly and celestial at the same time. King Arthur was born in ful-fillment of prophecy, and was tied to the Otherworld through his childhood with Merlin and through his tryst with Morgan. In Chi-valric tales, he quested for the Holy Grail, the wine cup of the Last Supper. But in earlier tales he was questing for Cerridwen's cauldron of rebirth or Bran's cauldron of immortality. (Arthur was so con-nected to the legend of Bran that one myth says that centuries after Bran's singing head was buried to defend England against enemies, Arthur dug up Bran's head to show that he alone was now the protec-tor of England.) Both Bran's and Cerridwen's cauldrons bring the gift of prophecy to their owner. Finally as protector of England, Arthur is a celestial bear being, watching Britain from the heavens. The an-cient Britons believed Arthur rode a chariot through the night sky: their name for the constellation we call Ursa Minor was "Arthur's Chariot."

There is a Baltic myth very much like Arthur's. In this story, a bear-man named Oter, who was raised by foster parents after being orphaned, uses a magic sword to cut down the World Tree, the great tree at the center of creation. Often in these tales Oter rises from the sea: in Baltic lore this indicates that he has come from the Un-derworld. Also like Arthur, Oter has an Otherworldly sister who can predict the future. Once again, like the pair in the Ugrian bear tale and like Arthur and Morgan, we have a sister-brother pair who must destroy a magical center of the world to restore order.

Throughout these tales is a thread of predicting the seasonal cy-cles. Arthur is the bear-man, the Seven Year King who dies and is re-born, reflecting the crops in the field and the prosperity of the land. He is the Bear partly because he dies (hibernates or journeys to the Otherworld) and will rise again (awakens).

HANSEL AND GRETEL, BIRDS AND BEARS

In each of the brother-sister stories and songs from the Baltic region and Siberia, a brother-sister pair journeys between our world and the Underworld, and destroys some central feature there (like the World Tree) to restore balance. Each of these stories has an element of prediction or divination, and some enchanted animal.

Hansel and Gretel is a familiar tale but seems to be a simplification of these much older brother-sister tales. While this Grimms story was obviously made very harmless and sweet compared to the more raw forms of the story, it has many elements found in these older Baltic and Siberian tales.

The Grimms' version begins with the line "Hard by a great forest dwelt a poor wood-cutter with his wife and his two children." This line makes us believe the woman is Hansel and Gretel's natural mother. In fact, the role of the wife is very ambiguous: the story flip-flops between calling her the children's mother and their stepmother. Maria Tatar suggests that the original telling named her as the children's birth mother, but that the Grimms changed her to a stepmother to explain her hatred of the children. (Tatar 2004, 74)

The children's names are both common German names. The original story was called *Little Brother and Little Sister*, very like the Baltic stories called *Brother and Sister*. What's also interesting is the name *Gretel*: it is short for Margaret. Maisry is also a nickname for Margaret, and we've already seen Maisry as a prophetic sister character.

In the story, a famine has come on the land. Apparently medieval Germany suffered several times of famine and starvation was common. The mother figure, worried about running out of food, convinces the father to take the two children deep into the woods where they will perish, and she and her husband will no longer need to feed them. But the children are so hungry they cannot sleep, so they overhear the conversation. Sleep is often connected to prophetic vision—here night, the time of sleep, allows the children to receive the warning. Sleep is also connected with death: if the children had slept through the night, they would have been unaware of their impending death.

Hansel collects white stones, which the story says "glittered like real silver pennies." (Hunt, *Household Tales*, 1884, Tale 15) Coins or metallic runes were a very common form of divination in German magic, and Hansel may have been predicting that he would be able to rescue himself and his sister. He strews the pebbles on the trail behind him. Sure enough, the first time they are left in the forest, the children are able to follow this trail and return home.

They are taken out the next day without the chance to collect stones. As they walk, Hansel looks back at the house. When his father asks why, Hansel explains, "I am looking back at my little pigeon which is sitting on the roof, and wants to say good-bye to me." (*Ibid.*) Birds occur several times in this tale, and each time a bird is mentioned, it is at a point when the children are journeying between worlds. In this case, the pigeon watches them enter the forest, which we know is the Underworld.

This time Hansel strews bread on the ground: bread is the food they commonly eat and is a symbol of their mother's fear of starvation. Now birds eat the bread, and the children can no longer follow the trail home. Successfully abandoned this time, the hapless children wander for a while, lost in the forest. Then the story tells us: "When it was mid-day, they saw a beautiful snow-white bird sitting on a bough, which sang so delightfully that they stood still and listened to it. And when its song was over, it spread its wings and flew away before them, and they followed it until they reached a little house, on the roof of which it alighted; and when they approached the little house they saw that it was built of bread and covered with cakes, but that the windows were of clear sugar." (*Ibid.*) Again, a bird has guided them to an enchanted destination. Notice they listen to the entire song before following the bird: bird song can communicate prophecy, and enchant humans. Enchanted, the children follow the animal to the house made of sugar.

The woman living in the house appears when they eat the walls and windows of her home. This is very like Tam Lin or the Beast, summoned by some alteration of their environment. The woman feeds the children and comforts them, but we learn she actually means to eat them. Compare this to Mr. Fox or *The Robber Bridegroom*, where innocent mortal women enter the forest home of enchanted creatures in a quest for love, and the creatures plan to terrorize and eat them.

The "witch," who is much more characteristic of a seducer/murderer Faerie, locks Hansel in a wood shed to fatten him up, and sets Gretel to doing household chores. In time she prepares to eat both children.

The fact that both the stepmother and the witch make plans to kill the children links the two women, and we get the notion that they are really the same person. Remember that the stepmother in *Snow White* entered the forest posing as a peasant selling apples, and Snow White did not recognize her. Compare this also to the bear story, where the sister poses as the cedar wife. Each of these women has the ability to shape-shift, and uses it to assume an identity that their prey sees as less threatening (or in this case, way more nourishing). Here the stepmother poses as a woman who lives in a house made of food, the one commodity the children lack in their home; she also feeds them when they first come to the house.

Now Gretel tricks the witch into crawling into her own oven: "She pushed poor Gretel out to the oven, from which flames of fire were already darting. 'Creep in,' said the witch, 'and see if it is properly heated, so that we can put the bread in.' And once Gretel was inside, she intended to shut the oven and let her bake in it, and then she would eat her, too. But Gretel saw what she had in mind, and said: 'I do not know how I am to do it; how do I get in?' 'Silly goose,' said the old woman. 'The door is big enough; just look, I can get in myself!' and she crept up and thrust her head into the oven. Then Gretel gave her a push that drove her far into it, and shut the iron door, and fastened the bolt." (*Ibid.*) Like the woman in "Reynardine" or *The Robber Bride Groom*, Gretel has used the witch's own savagery against her. Notice also the specific mention of the door being iron; Gretel knows the material will subdue the witch's power.

The children finish eating the house, then help themselves to the witch's valuables. They enter the forest again, but this time they come to a stream. They fear they cannot cross, but a duck paddles by and Hansel is able to summon the duck to ferry them across: "The duck came to them, and Hansel seated himself on its back, and told his sister to sit by him. 'No,' replied Gretel, 'that will be too heavy for the little duck; she shall take us across, one after the other.' The good little duck did so, and when they were once safely across and had walked for a short time, the forest seemed to be more and more familiar to them, and at length they saw from afar their father's house." (*Ibid.*) A bird assists them again and they cross water. It may be beating a dead horse (or duck) at this point to point out that their escape from the Underworld and their return to the mortal world involves a journey over water.

When they arrive home, the story takes this inexplicable turn: "The man had not known one happy hour since he had left the children in the forest; the woman, however, was dead." (*Ibid.*) The narrative offers no cause for the woman's death, but we can see that her sudden expiration happens to exactly coincide with the death of the forest witch in the enchanted world. We can assume the two women are one and the same; one aspect tries to starve the children, the other aspect tries to force the children to eat so much they grow fat, so that she may eat them. The children share the witch's jewels with Dad, and they live, well, you know how.

Like the pair in Baltic stories, Little Brother and Little Sister enter the Underworld together. Once there, they can communicate with birds, which guide their steps. In "The Brother's War Song" above, the sister can understand the prophecy of the birds that divine which soldiers will die in the war. Here, the birds lead the children both into danger and out again, predicting their initiation and safe escape.

An element in the Northeastern European tales is that the brother destroys a central part of the Underworld. In *Hansel and Gretel*, it is the house made of food, which the brother twice insists that he and Gretel eat: once when they arrive and again when the witch has expired. Hansel/Brother must destroy this central feature of the Underworld to restore balance in the human world (the death of the stepmother and the nurturing environment of their home). Through the prophesy of the birds, Gretel leads him into the Otherworld and back again so that he can accomplish this.

Hansel is cast in the role of Underworld Bear-man, like Brother and King Arthur. Gretel, like Sister, is able to divine the song of birds and rid the world of the danger it is in (the witch/mother). In the older tales, Sister must welcome Brother back into the mortal world by defrosting him. In this tale, Gretel welcomes Hansel back this way: "Gretel emptied her pinafore until pearls and precious stones ran about the room . . ." (*Ibid.*), ensuring that Brother can resume his place in our world. Neither he nor his family will ever starve again.

BADGERS

A good deal of European bear lore that predicted weather was transferred by the Germans to badgers. Also a burrower, the badger is well known in Germany, England, Japan and Russia as a prophetic creature. The English rhyme concerning Candlemas day is told in German this way:

> The badger peeps out of his hole on Candlemass Day,
> If he sees the sun shining he draws back into his hole
> (Chambers 1869, 102)

A lot of Russian and Siberian lore is common to Japan as well, as the Japanese and Siberian people have common ancestry. In Japan, the badger is a spirit called the Tanuki, which predicts the death of men and peers into the future. The Tanuki could be a good friend, and many Japanese stories tell of badger creatures giving gold to priests (as a gift to the gods).

The English also have a tradition that badgers can predict death, as shown in this rhyme:

> Should one hear a badger call,
> And then an ullot [owl] cry,
> Make thy peace with God, good soul,
> For thou shall shortly die.
> (Traditional)

Our tradition of black cats crossing one's path leading to ill luck seems to be based on the badger doing so in British lore. But in Scotland, a badger tooth in the pocket brings good luck, especially at gambling.

In each of these cases, an enchanted burrower is observed to foretell the future, and each animal is believed to be a Pixie or enchanted creature. The magical aspect of these traditions never made it to the United States, where the groundhog is simply an animal that can sense when the weather is changing. Pixies, Urchins and Tanukis seem to have remained in the Old World, foretelling the future quietly and staying hidden from our view.

That seems to be the way in our modern society. Faeries have slipped into new roles, inhabiting new stories, our culture creating new niches for the Kindly Ones. Let's look at the way we see Faeries now, and what our view of the Otherworld says about us.

Chapter 8

~~~

THE CHANGING ROLE OF FAERIES

Do you believe in Faeries? I do. You might ask why a grown man would believe in the Kindly Ones. After all, you'll say, they are figments of our imaginations, a fantasy, boogie-men. They are Disney characters. They are the creatures of Fairy tales, itself an expression that implies untruths or fantasies. In our modern lore, Faeries are no longer menacing or eerie. They have gone from towering to diminutive, from frightening to trivial. Fairies have dwindled from threatening creatures to cartoons for children. While every man, woman and child once knew about Tam Lin and Mab, was wary of eating Faerie food and knew the dangers of sleeping too close to the Wild Ride on Hallowe'en, our culture entertains our children with tales of Tinker Bell and cute Faerie Godmothers. While our great-grandparents knew that a woman who had just given birth must sleep with iron beneath her bed, we look down our noses at the quaint superstitions surrounding November Eve.

But consider that folklore, saga and myth have spoken of the Fey for thousands of years. These stories go so far back in time that we cannot trace them to their beginnings. They go back to the first meetings between Celts or Germans settling Europe, and the Picts that they found there; to the Saami and the Lapps meeting the Fin-folk; to the Khanty and the Mansi finding the ancient races of the Siberian Plains. Why keep these stories alive, and pass them down from generation to generation, if they were simply not true?

Something in Fairy tales and Faerie folklore must touch us deeply, must have a ring of truth, for our culture to carefully preserve these stories in songs, books, tales and movies. Even if the Faeries are no longer scary; even if the food will no longer keep us in the Faerie world; even if Faeries look more like Tinker Bell than Tam Lin, some-thing keeps us coming back, keeps us teaching our children, holds us in their spell. What is it, and why do we let it continue in a culture that "doesn't believe"?

Our European, Asian and African ancestors were farmers and hunters, trappers and traders, gatherers and herders. They spent most of their lives outdoors. In a normal day, they observed the many fac-ets of the natural world, from animals grazing to plants blooming, from rain and snow falling to the way sun lit a flower at any point in the day. They were keenly aware of changes in the natural world, and they responded quickly to these. When they became aware of any force of nature, seen or unseen, they did not choose to accept or deny it, but merely reacted to it in the way that best ensured their survival and well being. When they experienced the influence of Faeries, they learned how to deal with these Otherworldly neighbors. They learned of the evils of the Faerie world, and protected themselves as best they could. They kept their children safe, they placated the Fey when they had to, and they interacted with the Good People in ways that were amenable for both worlds. Their Faerie lore, in songs and stories, offered them a glimpse into the enchanted world that they believed existed all around them, at all times.

We know from this folkloric record that ancient people took Faer-ies seriously. Vikings who settled England warned their daughters to avoid haunted places. They taught their children to lie flat on the ground or throw iron in the path if Odin should ever ride by with his pack of Hell Hounds. Their sagas told of the feast halls of Faerie,

and of humans who had married into that race. There was no sugges-
tion of humor or disbelief there. They believed that the Fey and their
own race married and mated, to their race's joy or sorrow.

The invading Normans came to know the Fey, and accepted gifts
of chalices from them. They may very well have taken Fairies as lovers, or at least so their songs tell us.

In Estonia and Siberia, people listened to the birds for divination,
and hoped to meet a beautiful woman in green robes who could
teach them the deep meanings of the birds' songs. People gathered
at the Bear Feast and sang the oldest songs about the tiny men who
visited from a distant Faerie world over the water, and about Brother
and Sister who fought battles in that world.

Deep belief in the Good People continued right up until the very
precipice of the Industrial Age. Shakespeare, writing in the relatively
recent Renaissance, presented his audiences with very realistic Faeries
and made no apologies for doing so. His Puck tampered with peoples'
lives, his Oberon fumed over a changeling, and his Ariel assisted his
master Prospero in every way against the demonic Caliban. Shakespeare never had to explain these creatures to his audience. Like the
writer himself, his audiences had grown up on Faerie myth and legend, and knew that when Bottom ate and drank of the Faerie Queen's
dinner, terrible things would happen. They were fully aware of how
Titania's ward had come to be a changeling, and watched with great interest the struggle between Oberon and Titania for the fate of the boy.
And they knew that come sunrise, all the enchantment and confusion
laid upon four Pixie-led lovers might disappear without a trace.

But industrialization changed people's lives dramatically. In France,
Germany, England and America, people left their farms. They settled
in cities where factories afforded jobs and careers. They no longer
spent hours of their days in nature, but in dingy clothing mills and gas
lantern-lit factories. Life became faster paced and more difficult. They
no longer lived in a society where everyone did essentially the same
work and lived the same lifestyle. Now they could compete for better
jobs and better pay. Many grew bitter and frustrated at their place in
the economic world that industrialism had created.

This new world left very little room for magic. People became prag-matic, and many lost their ties to the old songs, customs and rituals their parents had known from centuries before. But at the same time, for the offspring of those doing well financially, childhood became a longer process. Where children had assumed farm work by the age of five or six, and married by fourteen, now the children of middle-class families had many years of innocence before them. Many did not take on any work until their teens, and did not marry until their twenties. The nursery became a place of mystery and childish enchantment. People became very interested in the quaint beliefs of their ancestors, through stories that seemed to be disappearing. These stories were read to eager children, usually in a sanitized form, rather than the way they were collected by men like the Grimms.

At this time, people thought of writing stories based on the old beliefs. Removed from a culture that truly believed, Faeries could be-come an analogy of faith, characters in a quest novel, or pretty figures in a book or play to delight children and make adults long for their youth. Audiences were not meant to believe these things as truth, but simply to suspend disbelief and be entertained.

In the three hundred years between Shakespeare and J. M. Bar-rie, Faeries had become the delight of children, tiny creatures that meant humans no harm. Audiences in 1904 laughed when Tinker Bell appeared on stage as a tiny light and a ringing bell. They had no problem accepting that this was how Faeries looked. And in 1920, Arthur Conan Doyle had no trouble believing that Elsie Wright and Frances Griffiths, two teenaged girls from Bradford, England, had photographed themselves with cutesy, dancing, winged Faeries. After Doyle's publication of the photos in *Strand* magazine, The British pub-lic reacted badly, showing a general disbelief in Faeries. One critic, a scientist named Major Hall-Edwards, wrote this letter to the *Birming-ham Weekly Post*:

On the evidence I have no hesitation in saying that these pho-tographs could have been 'faked'. I criticize the attitude of

those who declared there is something supernatural in the circumstances attending to the taking of these pictures because,
as a medical man, I believe that the inculcation of such absurd
ideas into the minds of children will result in later life in man-
ifestations and nervous disorder and mental disturbances . . .
(Doyle, 1922, 78)

He not only dismisses the existence of Faeries, but states that
allowing children to believe in them will lead to insanity. (In
1981, Wright and Griffiths admitted to faking the photographs
that had fooled Sherlock Holmes's creator, though they insisted they had seen Faeries in the English forests. In a 1985 TV
interview, Elsie said "Two village kids and a brilliant man like
Conan Doyle, well, we could only keep quiet.").

As the belief in actual Faeries began to fade, Victorian society began
to view Fairy tales and myth as instructive, allegorical story. "Reynardine," for instance, could be viewed as a cautionary tale of how un-
checked sexuality could lead young women into serious trouble. In a
society where speaking about sexuality was unseemly and disrespect-
ful, using Faerie stories and folk songs to educate young audiences
about the dangers of sex was considered more comfortable for listener
and teller. In "Tam Lin," a girl could see clearly the complications of
chasing the seducer, while at the same time praising Janet's heroism in
fighting for the man she loved. Many folk songs about the struggles of
love between modest young women and seductive bad boys, usually
sailors, became popular in the late eighteenth and early nineteenth
centuries. Couching these struggles in Faerie terms made them en-
joyable, frightening and ultimately memorable. Remember meeting
Little Red Riding Hood and the wolf when you were three? You might
not have understood the sexual implications of Red getting into bed
with her seducer, but you knew she should not have done it!

Then came a time when scholars began to view the Kindly Ones as
a psychological study. Why did people need to hear these stories? What

purpose did they serve? Sigmund Freud, the first doctor to study the workings of the human mind, viewed mythology as a landscape of the psyche, using characters from classical myth to demonstrate the patterns of thought he detected in the human psyche: Nymphomania, Oedipal complex, Psyche herself as a roadmap to the sense of self. Freud's students, Carl Jung and Bruno Bettelheim, wrote papers and books about why the child's mind needed Fairy tales and mythic stories to fully develop. While these scientists did not believe in Faeries, they believed deeply in our need to understand the Fey, if only through fantasy. Bettelheim, for instance, believed that the water-mirror of Faerie allowed children to safely examine the injustice they encountered in their lives and their relationships with parents and siblings.

Because they had become the domain of children, the stature of the Good People continued to diminish. Around this period, Kate Greenaway began painting idyllic depictions of Faeries dancing in garden greenery, untouched by the drudgery of the Industrial Revolution. In the 1920s, Cicely Mary Barker created the Flower Fairies, childish dancing beings whose dominion was common garden blooms. Barker's work, heavily inspired by Greenaway, placed into the minds of English and American culture the idea of the dancing, childish, tiny Faerie.

These creatures were a fantasy that people who had been through an unspeakably horrible war and a Great Depression needed desperately to help give their children a message that the world could still be innocent and beautiful. Perhaps the message ran, "You won't see these delightful creatures dancing in your own flower garden, but here in this book you can imagine them, and know that life can be lovely." It was during this time, the 1920s and 1930s, that publishers released books of Fairy tales and nursery rhymes by the dozens, with plates by such notable Faerie illustrators as Arthur Rackham and Edmund Dulac (the rock stars of the Golden Age of Illustration). In their illustrations, Faeries and humans were always costumed in Renaissance or Victorian garb, the clothes of long ago and far away.

By the end of World War II, a new designation arose: teenager. For the first time in history, a child between thirteen and eighteen was not expected to marry and establish a career, but was expected to attend high school sock hops, listen to rock and roll, and consume mass quantities of milkshakes.

This enormous change in social status of the young brought about new sets of beliefs, and new attitudes toward what was and was not appropriate for children. Teens who had been marrying and reproducing two decades earlier were now shielded from learning the "facts of life." Innocence among children was considered vital and necessary, and was now expected to last not eight or ten years, but eighteen years. Now an eight-or ten-year-old who might have been given over to an apprenticeship a scant fifty years earlier was considered a mere child who must be sheltered from the world. A twelve-year-old, who would be focused on who he or she might marry a few decades earlier, had no cares now other than homework and pop stars, and of course, the relatively new medium of pop star=making culture: cinema.

Enter Walt Disney, animator and marketing genius. Disney was the right man at the right time for the new era of the two-decade childhood. Using Faerie material from the Grimms and other collections that children were already familiar with, Disney created a new lexicon of Faerie lore: cartoons. Using characters based on the art styles of Barker and Greenaway, Dulac and Rackham, these Fairies were intimate and familiar to children. Gone were the sexual elements of Tam Lin and Nymphs. Faeries were fantasy creatures now, good like the Faerie Godmother of Cinderella, or evil like the Sea Witch. Like Ariel the Mermaid and the sanitized Nymphs and Satyrs of *Fantasia*, they loved the way humans love. Gone was the threat of being pulled beneath the sea in a lover's embrace, or falling in love with a Nymph and being left forever alone with the memory of Faerie music and the delicious touch of that Otherworldly vixen. Humans in Disney films never go mad or end up dead because of Faerie love. Even Ariel gets the prince and stays alive, unlike the ending of the tale told by Hans Christian Andersen.

In this age of industry and computers, when life for most of us is safe and even a little boring, Faeries evoke the nostalgic longing for childhood. They were the celluloid companions we cherished in our long childhood years, the dolls we shared with our playmates, the dreams we dreamed when growing up seemed far away and unimaginable. We all had those two decades in Neverland, when the Darlings' window was far off, in another world, and we could play endlessly with Tinker Bell. We now cherish the hours our own children spend making friends with the Little Mermaid and the Faerie Godmother.

But for those of us who believe, despite the two decades of childhood, despite the warnings that these are fantasies that will somehow damage our minds, despite the so-called proof of our own eyes and ears, we know that there is a good deal more to the story. They may serve as Victorian warnings against following your most primal urges; they may serve as celluloid companions and nostalgic reminders of childhood; they may entertain our children for hours so that we can get that elusive bath or nap; but behind all the prettiness and happy endings, behind the cute dancing children with wings, behind the sweet Nymphs and Satyrs sheltering in each other's embrace from Zeus's rainstorm, we know they are really there, in all of their terror and awe. They still appear in our songs. We still tell their stories. We use them as characters in our books, in our movies. We make them appear sweet and cute, but as adorable and docile as they seem, they still try to kill the Wendy bird. They go on appearing in our dreams, bringing us prophecy or despair. We still warn of them, even when we collectively agree they just couldn't possibly exist.

So go ahead, see them as adorable creatures. See them as figments of an overactive imagination. See them as characters from Fairy tales. That's fine. I will still pay attention to those darting figures in my peripheral vision. And when I hear the songs, I will heed the warnings.

Don't say you weren't warned as well.

Chapter 9

MODERN FAERIE STORIES

I have mentioned that I believe Faeries exist. Since you're reading this, you might too. Or at least you're keeping an open mind. If you do concede the possibility, you're not alone. But there are a lot fewer of us than there used to be.

As I've also mentioned, a hundred years ago, perhaps even less, it was considered common and normal to believe in the existence of the Fey. Any sober adult would acknowledge their existence and their place in our lives. It was customary among the most upstanding citizens to leave milk and rum in the corners of the house for the Good People, to call out to the Wee Folk and bid them good health in order to ward off any ill effects they may consider visiting upon us.

Even sixty years ago, this was common practice. But today, we live in a world where Faerie belief is considered silly, quaint, old-fashioned or even ridiculous. Strange as that sounds to we who believe, the iconoclasts of our society do not notice the evidence that is all around us. Like the doctor who humbugged Arthur Conan Doyle, most people in the modern world would scoff at any mention of the existence of Fairies.

Yet in the midst of this disbelief is still a constant presence of Faerie references. People who would never admit to believing in the Fey use words and phrases, tell stories, and hold beliefs that owe to the Otherworld. There's almost a subconscious undercurrent of insistence on Faerie belief. And why not? People in every corner of the world believed in the Good People for so long that it became a huge part of our ideology. The stories persist. Let's explore a few of them.

FAIRY TALES

This book has looked at tales collected by Wilhelm and Jacob Grimm, James Francis Child, William Butler Yeats and several other respected and learned collectors of folklore. These tales, rhymes and songs have been around for centuries, changing as our language changes, mixing with other sets of songs and stories, and passed on over the centuries from adults to children.

Over the years, a large collection of different kinds of stories have been carelessly chucked into the melting pot of "Fairy tales." A good number of them have no Faeries or magical creatures of any kind in them at all. Some are fables, some nonsense rhymes, some folk wisdom. But true Fairy tales have certain common elements, including:

- A belief in magic and magical creatures.

- A sense that our daily world is adjacent to an Otherworld or Faerie world, and that certain people and beings can pass between the two worlds.

- An acceptance of certain standard characters in the context of any tale of this type (Faerie Godmothers, Elves, giants). These characters are so accepted that they need no explanation or interpretation.

- A belief that transformations can commonly occur (shape-shifting between animal and human form, sleeping spells, beans growing overnight).

- A notion that humans can beseech Otherworldly beings for aid, and can be aided by them at any time (i.e., crying over one's misfortune will summon one's Faerie Godmother).

- A belief that these Otherworldly ones are singularly interested in human affairs: that certain ones create good to make a "happily-ever-after" ending. Or, conversely, that certain standard characters, like wolves and stepmothers, are concerned with darkening the affairs of humans.

We accept these notions because we have heard these stories since we were infants. We came to a childish understanding of our world based on these magical scenarios. We accepted that any human who cried out to magical beings for help would be helped. We were firm in the notion that giants, talking wolves and evil sorceresses who had married our fathers would and could threaten our lives at any moment. We had great confidence in such gadgets as spinning wheels and talking mirrors, even though we'd never seen one and really had no idea of their practical workings (how many modern people have even seen a spinning wheel?).

The stories took hold in our minds and became more real than particular aspects of our adult lives. Having worked as an educator, I know that the average American adult has tremendous difficulty finding Bolivia on a map, cannot tell you which war was fought to gain America's independence (or from whom that independence was won), and would hem and haw if asked whether Arkansas was east or west of them at that moment. But every person I know can tell you what became of Sleeping Beauty after she ate the poisoned apple, what Jack traded for magic beans, and why the Little Mermaid wanted to become human.

Because of this, references to these tales abound in our adult society. Every woman in the dating scene knows the reference in the saying "you have to kiss a lot of frogs before you find your handsome prince"; everyone who struggles to make a living dreams of "spinning straw into gold" or of "finding the golden goose"; a large corporate chain presents itself as having "the Midas touch"; mothers waking their children refer to a child as "sleeping beauty"; the list of references to these tales of our childhood goes on and on.

So why, in a culture so dead set on not believing in Faeries, do these tales continue to inhabit our childhoods and remain in our adult consciousness? Why do nonbelieving adults keep passing these tales to their children?

Bruno Bettelheim, in his excellent book *The Uses of Enchantment*, delves into the psychological reasons why "Fairy tales" remain with us. Using Jungian psychology, he explores the myriad fears, doubts, questions and phobias we experience as children, and shows how the tales the Grimms collected address those issues for us during our formative years. He makes a very good argument for the continued use of Fairy tales as entertainment for children. Bettelheim does this so well, I don't have to do it here.

But I also think that we, as a culture, believed so strongly for so long in the existence of the Good People that we cannot simply dismiss them. On the very deepest level, we do not want to take the frightening chance that we are pissing off a scary, malevolent race of magical creatures with our disbelief. But for many, our conscious minds cannot accept those same beliefs. So we diminish them. We shrink Fairies from Tam Lin-size to Tinker Bell. We trivialize them, making them "the stuff of childhood," acting careless toward them, while at the same time ensuring their survival by carefully passing them on to our children.

Many people hold beliefs to be true that are in sharp contrast with each other. You will find many a staunch sober Christian who would tell you belief in Faeries is insane, who also feels that his or her children must be taught Fairy tales or they will be deprived of a happy childhood. In relating these tales, the storyteller revisits his or her own cherished experiences of the Fey and other magical creatures. The time spent in this world of Faerie magic, so real and so relevant to the storyteller for a good part of his or her life, must be passed on, and remembered vividly. Why? Because it is a set of beliefs, no matter how illogical to the modern person, that must be cherished and respected. On some level, it is quite real and omnipresent.

Following are some very common magical creatures that inhabit our real-life world and their Faerie origins.

THE TOOTH FAERIE

Every kid looks forward to a visit from the Tooth Faerie. When I was a kid, this mercurial creature might leave a Mercury dime. Now it's up to a dollar, or perhaps a five in a more prosperous household. Interesting how this particular Faerie keeps track of inflationary buying power. This childhood ritual, played out in homes across America and Europe, is an old tradition, dating back to the Middle Ages (when the tooth was buried in the ground). But does this sweet ritual have a dark, morbid origin?

The idea of a Faerie giving gifts is common throughout the folkloric record. The shoemaker received prosperity in his business from Elves (Kobolds, really), for example. The next section discusses the best-known magical gift-giver on earth.

What is interesting about the Tooth Faerie is the exchange of a gift for a piece of the child's anatomy. The losing of a tooth represents growth. The child is outgrowing his or her "baby teeth," and will now grow "adult teeth." The fact that this rite of passage is marked not just by a gift of money but by such a gift from a magical creature is fascinating.

Throughout folklore, Faeries often exchange gifts of natural objects for human lives or control over humans. The merchant in *Beauty and the Beast* exchanged his daughter for a rose; Janet made a similar exchange with Tam Lin, exchanging her virginity and vows of love for a "double rose." In *Rapunzel*, a man exchanges his unborn daughter for a plant that his wife craves (Lamb's Lettuce, called Rapunzel in Germany). Faeries see the natural world as their domain, and when humans pick certain flowers, the Good People exact a price. This price is more often than not a human life to command as they will; a changeling, in one form or another.

In *Sleeping Beauty*, the tale begins with Faerie gift-giving. Several Faeries visit the christening of Sleeping Beauty, offering gifts of blessings (talent, beauty and wit). One Faerie, who was slighted by not being invited, curses the girl to die when the thorn of a spindle pricks her. Another Faerie alters the curse so that the pin prick will result in a century of sleep, ended upon the arrival of the girl's intended husband. In the Grimms' version, briars grow around the sleeping girl and kill or maim any prince who tries to find Sleeping Beauty, but they part in the path of the true lover. So these enchanted plants, which caused the sleep in the first place, also give the gift of a human: Sleeping Beauty's betrothed.

In the tale of *Sleeping Beauty*, the gift of a lover is given to the girl as she sleeps. That element is common to the lore of the Tooth Faerie. In fact, adults tell children they must be asleep or the Tooth Faerie will not visit.

Sleep is symbolic of death. The sleeper is unaware of the world around her and is utterly vulnerable. There are many folkloric references to sleep as if it were death: in *Sleeping Beauty*, the beauty was supposed to die but instead sleeps for a hundred years; in *Rip Van Winkle*, the title character sleeps for a hundred years after drinking Faerie beer and wakes up to find that he has been taken for dead; Snow White falls asleep after eating the poisoned apple (actually a tomato in French) and is presumed dead and placed in a glass casket (glass represents the mirror of Faerie, and the passage over water into the Otherworld). Rhiannon is asleep when her child Pryderi is taken changeling. In each tale, a human is taken changeling or casualty by the magical world, and sleeps while events transpire around them. Sleep is a magical state that connects us to the Otherworld, and during which death hovers about us.

Chapter 7 showed the connection between the enchanted realms and our world in the burrowing beasts: bears, hedgehogs and badgers. The Tooth Faerie herself was an enchanted burrower, a mouse, in French, Spanish and Italian traditions.

The Tooth Faerie ritual, like rituals of the singing of lullabies and the exchange of gifts with the magical world, comes from a time when people were acutely aware that death and magic hovered about them constantly, and that at any moment these unseen forces could come crashing down.

Growing up in New York City, within a large Jewish community, I was well aware that many of my friends went through an odd ritual. When their mother or grandmother cooked a chicken, she would first wave it over the boy's head, reciting a prayer. Then she'd throw the chicken in the pot.

Throughout Jewish scripture, the idea of trading the life of the oldest son for an animal sacrifice occurs. In Genesis 22, Abraham is told to kill his oldest son, Isaac (in the Muslim, faith the same story is told involving Abraham's other son, Ishmael). As Abraham is about to make the sacrifice, an angel stops him, giving him a ram to sacrifice instead. Further on, in Exodus 12, the Hebrews escape the plague of the death of the firstborn son by sacrificing a lamb and painting its blood on their doors as a sign to the Angel of Death. In Leviticus 23, the Jews are instructed to sacrifice a lamb each year to commemorate this escape from the plague. And in Corinthians 5 and several other verses, Jesus is referred to as the Passover lamb. Among the other things Jesus might be, he is the firstborn son of Mary, and he allows himself to be the sacrifice to his God rather than allowing the lamb itself to be substituted.

What appears throughout both the folkloric record and the Judea-Christian record (derived over many centuries from both revelation and from folklore) is the belief that human life may be taken by Otherworldly beings, and that plants and animals may be substituted for the taking of human life. This is a dark, morbid knowledge that surfaces again and again: in Pagan religion, in the folklore that carries memories of Paganism and in Jewish and Christian belief. In every system of faith, there is the notion that death hovers over us, and we must trade some living organism or some physical part of ourselves to stave off that spirit of death, or that Faerie being that would claim our lives.

The Tooth Faerie is a memory of this. While she has been reduced in size, stature and fearsomeness, we teach our children that they must give to the Otherworld a piece of themselves so that their lives will be spared. In exchange, they will receive a gift from the Faerie creature: a shiny coin.

The coin is an important feature of the exchange. We live now in a culture where paper money has more buying power than coins, but this is culturally a new development. Paper money was not used in the United States until the Civil War, and only then because people were hoarding coins for their "melt value" (whichever side won would accept the melted silver and gold as currency). For centuries before this, money was in copper, brass, silver and gold coinage, and it is important to us as believers that coins are used in the Tooth Faerie exchange.

The giving of coins as a Faerie gift is well known in folklore. In the *Mabinogion*, Gwydion gives Pryderi a bag of coins for his pigs. When Pryderi sees the coins in the light of morning, they have become leaves and twigs. The Welsh have the same story of the Tylwyth Teg, the Fair Family, who bargained at market with coins that later turn to leaves. Brian Froud speaks of this tradition as well, attributing it to Irish Faeries. The coin also represents the coins placed on the eyes of the dead, a payment to the ferryman who will row the dead person into the Underworld. The tooth coin symbolizes that journey (since it is associated with the child's head, like the coins placed on the eyes) and bargains against it. The coin used in the tooth ritual is a charm for health and fortune from the Faerie.

Coins are also related to rune stones and other divinatory tokens. We still use the "heads or tails" divinatory method involving a coin, and the Chinese I Ching involves reading coin characters. This tradition is also seen in the use of the wishing well. People all over the world throw silver coins into flowing water or into a wishing well, hoping for magic to aid them and bring good fortune. Naiads, Faeries of wells, springs and streams, have always been thought to grant wishes and bring fortune, either good or bad. Coins seal the bargain.

So the dark exchange of a child's tooth for her continued health and good fortune should—in fact, must—involve a coin rather than a paper bill to work as intended. Chapter 10 explains that the Fey like shiny coins, and for them to exchange coins for lives or for discarded human body parts is a blessing.

At the bottom of this cutest of childhood traditions is a sinister trade. A child must give a piece of herself, her tooth, to the Faeries. In return, she will be allowed to grow to adulthood. As a token of this exchange, the child is left a Faerie coin. The exchange must be made while the child sleeps, the time when the Fey have their greatest power over our lives.

Pleasant dreams, kiddies.

CHRISTMAS TRADITIONS

Christmas is a Christian holiday, perhaps the most important of the year (with the possible exception of Easter. Don't worry, we'll get to that one too). But Christmas, which Catholic Rome brought to Pagan Europe, is steeped in Pagan tradition, and the Good People continue to exert their presence in the Yule celebration.

Santa Claus

The face of Christmas, Santa Claus is known throughout Europe and the Americas as the Christmas gift giver. But who is Santa Claus, really?

The figure of Santa Claus comes partly from the Greek bishop Saint Nicholas ("Jolly Old Saint Nick" of song) who had a reputation for giving gifts to the poor. He was especially known for giving dowries to destitute girls so they could be married rather than being forced into prostitution. Saint Nicholas wore a beard and canonical robes, facts which may have influenced Thomas Nast's original drawings that first reflected the jolly bearded Santa we know today.

But the figure of Father Christmas, as he is called in Europe, or Sinter Klaas is much older than jolly Saint Nicholas. Throughout northern Europe, Father Christmas visits homes at the Winter Solstice, leaving gifts. Some think the tall, bearded man is based on the Norse God Odin, who flies through the skies in a sleigh or upon an eight-legged horse named Sleipnir, accompanied by the ravens Huginn and Muginn. One tradition says that children would leave stockings of oats and sugar out on Yule eve for Sleipnir, and Odin would thank these children for offering his horse food by leaving candy in return.

The association with the Pagan God of the returning sun continued through the ninth century, when the Venerable Bede, an author, monk and scholar, commented upon the belief that humans could consort with Otherworld creatures on that occasion. He states of the December holiday that it was a "feast day of the pagan god Jul, when it was possible to couple with the spirits of the dead and with demons that returned to the surface of the earth . . ." (Veyne 1987, 432) In other words, like Samhain (Hallowe'en), ancient Europeans believed that they could consort with Faeries at the Yule feast.

Among the Faeries that visit at Yule are goat spirits. Imagine waking up on Yule morning and being greeted by a giant goat that shouts, "Are there any good children here?" In Finland, Joulupukki visits children at Yule (Joulu). This Otherworld creature, whose name means "Yule Goat," rides a sleigh drawn by reindeer and enters each house with those words. Being part goat, the Joulupukki has a long white beard and his goat call would sound like a laugh (hence an association with Santa's jolliness and appearance). But the loveable Joulupukki has a dark side. In early Finnish folklore, the Yule Goat would demand presents in return for warding the spirit of death away (just like the Tooth Faerie). People called Nuuttipuk-kis (Night Goats) would also visit people's homes on the Solstice and eat leftover food. (Creepy, don't you agree?). The goat-footed spirit or demon is a common Faerie appearance throughout Europe, resembling Pan, the Fauns, the Glastig and other shape-changing Faeries. Finding them at the basis of Yule lore is no surprise. Finding them gorging themselves on leftovers in your refrigerator might be a bit of a shock, though. Night Goats may be at the bottom of the "leaving cookies for Santa" tradition.

In Lapland, people looked forward to a visit from the Yuletumpta, a Gnome or Elf that rides a sleigh through the town, giving gifts to good children. As pleasant as that sounds, he is accompanied by a black Gnome or Elf that carries a rawhide whip to strike bad children. This adds a whole new dimension to "you'd better not shout, you'd better not cry."

The Yuletumpta and the Joulupukki both make their homes in Lapland, in the far north. This tradition explains the American belief that Santa lives in the North Pole. And the Yuletumpta's dark Elf companion forms the basis of our tale of the Elves that help Santa by making presents. Also Gnomes, like Dwarves, are creatures of the earth (in modern Paganism, Gnomes are associated with the element of Earth). They are diggers, mining metals to make weapons (in Norse mythology, the Gnomes or Dwarves make the swords and hammers used by the Gods). So it is no surprise that Santa's home in the North Pole is said to be deep underground.

In what is perhaps the most famous portrayal of Father Christmas in our modern culture, Charles Dickens characterizes the Spirit of Christmas Present as a huge Gnome-like being that visits Ebenezer Scrooge in his sleep. In keeping with Faerie folklore, Scrooge experiences days and even years in the course of one night, and is vulnerable in sleep to emotions he would not succumb to in wakefulness. The spirit has evil helpers, Ignorance and Want, hidden beneath his green robes, mimicking Santa's Elves. The spirit is a gift-giver, but like the original Joulupukki, he demands gifts from Scrooge in return: generosity and enjoyment of life.

The figure of Santa Claus is a very similar figure to other Faeries, especially those associated with the Wild Ride, the journey between worlds, and the giving of gifts both good and bad. Santa comes when children are asleep, representing a state of death. In fact, the holiday comes in the very dead of winter, when trees are leafless and life has disappeared from the Earth. In that death state, Santa has the ability to travel between our living world and the Otherworld of death and frost. His gifts are an assurance that life will return in the spring. In this sense Santa is much like the Tooth Faerie, warding off death and assuring life. In America, he enters through the chimney, but there is really no rational explanation of Santa's entry; being Elfin, he may enter a home at will and leave as he pleases. He comes through the door between the worlds, riding the river of blood referred to in "True Thomas" (perhaps this is why in some tales he is dressed in red robes). He also visits all homes on earth in one night, a feature of Faerie lore in which time is experienced differently in Faerie than in our world. He is an enchanted creature that remains unseen yet leaves his presence felt everywhere. He is the quintessential Faerie.

As leader of the Wild Ride, and as a bearded, robed figure of the night, we return to the association of Santa with Odin. Not the God Odin, but the Faerie figure that leads the Wild Ride and terrorizes mortals; a great creature, bearded, perhaps antlered, clad in green robes and riding a giant eight-legged horse. While Santa has been sanitized and made cute and friendly, think about the notion we were raised to believe: a huge, magical man with a great beard in green robes (red robes in the U.S.) enters your house on Yule night, takes your food and leaves gifts. Creepy, yes? Even a little terrifying. What if he finds you there, awake? A small, defenseless child? This is why the legend insists that the children must be asleep during Santa's visit. Just like the legend of Odin and the Wild Ride. When the Faerie train rides through the night, and time is suspended, we mortals had best be in the deathlike state of sleep to endure the visit, or we will perish in sunless winter frost . . . Merry Christmas.

The Christmas Tree and the Mistletoe

Dryads, tree spirits of the Oak and several other trees, have an influence of regeneration and good fortune upon humans. Nowhere is this belief more evident than in the tradition of bringing trees and the mistletoe plant into the home on Yule.

The evergreen tree represents the promise of life, showing that even though the winter has taken life from the forest and the fields, the greenery will return. In the folklore and psychology of Faerie, sleep and death are analogous states. The forest is sleeping, appearing dead, during the cold European winter. The Dryads sleep, hibernating through that dark season.

In mythic terms, Persephone, Goddess of nature and growth, has slipped into the Underworld, where she will reign as queen beside Hades until the spring. She is now queen of death, presiding over the spirits of that gray world. Life has left the earth with her.

But the evergreen remains alive, green and vibrant in harsh winter. The spirit of that tree does not sleep, or die, when the snow blankets the ground. So it has been a custom for centuries to bring this living tree spirit into the home, signaling a compact between the Dryads of the forest and the members of the household that life will return in the spring, in every sense. The crops will grow to feed the family; the animals of the forest will return for hunting; the sun will warm the earth again; and life will quicken in willing human women.

Decorating the tree with light is another sign of this compact. The light of the sun, and mythically the influence of the Sun God, are brought into the home by lighting candles (and now Christmas lights) upon the tree. And gifts are placed beneath the tree (and as O. Henry poignantly pointed out, there is a sacrifice made by each member of the household in the giving of gifts: the tradition that led to the analogy between the Yule Gnome or Yule Goat and the charitable Saint Nicholas).

But the greatest Faerie presence is represented by the hanging of mistletoe in the home.

Mistletoe is a parasitic plant that grows on several host trees, the best known being the oak. The mistletoe stays green year round and bears a white berry in winter. Birds are drawn to the berries, and so the mistletoe is known to attract several varieties of birds, especially thrush and wrens, both of which are sacred birds in European lore (especially the wren, England's tiniest bird, which is associated with the God of Winter, to wit, Jul or Father Christmas).

Throughout Europe the mistletoe has been considered a sacred tree, bringing gifts good and bad. The Druids (whose name has the same root as Dryad) reverenced the mistletoe, which they called "all-heal," and Druids used mistletoe berries as an internal medicine, an aphrodisiac and a hallucinogen. The plant was a symbol of the sacrifice of the Seven Year King and cutting down the mistletoe represented castrating the Young God. Mistletoe is symbolic of Hercules, who is a Seven Year King figure in Greek myth, and also of Gwion Bach, the servant of Cerridwen who is killed by that Goddess and then reborn as the bard Taliesin.

The Druids would sacrifice a white bull each year in place of the seven-year ruler. Pliny the Elder, a Roman who wrote volumes about the customs of the Gauls (Celts), states:

> The Druids (for so they call their Magi), have nothing more sacred than the mistletoe, and the tree on which it grows, provided it be an oak. They select particular groves of oaks, and perform no sacred rites without oak leaves, so that from this custom they may seem to have been called Druids according to the Greek derivation. They call it All-Heal in their own language; and having prepared sacrifices and feasts under the tree with great solemnity, they bring up two white bulls, whose horns are then first bound. The priest, clothed in a white gar-

ment, ascends the tree, and cuts it off with a golden pruning knife, and it is received in a white sheet or cloth. Then they sacrifice the victims, and pray that God would render his own gift prosperous to those on whom he has bestowed it (Smiddy 1871, 88–89).

Like the mistletoe berry itself, the blood of the sacrificed white bull was used as a hallucinogen whose enchantment produced prophetic visions. The Irish text *The Book of the Dun Cow* tells that a priest would drink the white bull's blood, and "would see in a dream the shape and appearance of the man who should be made king, and the sort of work in which he was at that time engaged" (Graves 1952, 106).

In Norse myth, a mistletoe arrow kills Baldur. His mother, Frigga, had made a deal with each tree in the forest not to kill her son, but had forgotten the little Mistletoe (in *The White Goddess*, Graves suggests that the mistletoe appears childish compared to other trees, so seemed harmless to Frigga). Loki, using a mistletoe arrow, kills Baldur. But the Gods resurrected Baldur (as the sun is resurrected at Yule), and so the mistletoe became a symbol of Baldur's rebirth, and a symbol of the death and rebirth of the Seven Year King. Because of this, Frigga commanded that whenever enemies meet under a sprig of mistletoe growing in the forest, they must put their weapons down and make a truce. In time, this extended to people meeting under the mistletoe and kissing in friendship.

Mistletoe as a symbol of the resurrection of the sun is pretty important in Scandinavia, since that part of the world is on the Arctic Circle and winter brings a thirty-five-day night. The mistletoe, invested with mythic solar energy, is a symbol of fertility, and the berries are taken as an aphrodisiac. In Scandinavia and northern Scotland, it is custom to place mistletoe under a bed when a woman is attempting to become pregnant. After the birth, the mistletoe is placed under the crib to protect the sleeping infant.

The Christmas tradition of hanging the plant and kissing beneath it seems to have come to England and the United States from the Norse lands. There, a sprig of mistletoe is hung in a barn or farmhouse, and under it, no girl may refuse a kiss from a boy. However, after each kiss the boy must remove a berry from the sprig. When all the berries are gone, the girl may refuse further kisses (or she may place a new sprig under her bed, we suppose). When the tradition got to Britain, the picking of a berry in exchange for a kiss was forgotten. But that is a vital part of the tradition, as it represents the exchange of gifts with the spirit of the plant.

The entire tradition of the spirit of the mistletoe fits every Faerie gift-exchange tradition. First, the plant (and its Faerie) is associated with winter and night, the time of sleep and death. During sleep, humans are vulnerable to Faerie enchantment, and the passage of time is unrelated to waking time. Indeed, in the far north, home of the mistletoe traditions, winter night is seven weeks long. This is very like the time muddle of a journey into the Faerie world.

During this winter's night sleep, the mistletoe Faerie is awake and aware, as seen by the green of the plant and its blooming white berries. The berries are hallucinogens, so they create a state in humans like that of roaming in the Otherworld (it has been suggested that the traditions of Santa Claus flying and dropping down the chimney come from the experiences of humans taking mistletoe berries while acting as Joulupukkis during the Yule celebration). They are also protective of humans, as seen in the tradition of placing them under a sleeping infant.

The mistletoe Faerie exchanges gifts with humans. In exchange for its berries, it demands human sexuality (the kissing and the various other activities under its provenance). In this respect, this Faerie is very like Tam Lin or the enchanted creatures of the Grimms, exchanging a gift of the natural world for sexuality and protection. Humans are willing participants in the exchange, kissing and engaging in sex under the mistletoe or with the plant under their bed. The

Faerie is then asked to protect the child born from this arrangement, essentially forming a symbolic changeling exchange during the infant's sleep to protect it from the real thing (kind of the way a vaccine gives you a tiny case of the disease it is protecting you from).

But the mistletoe Faerie, like other gift-givers, can give bad gifts as well as good ones. Her berry is poison if taken wrong or if too much is ingested. She can be a killer, as Baldur found out. So she is a seducer-murderer as well as a life-giver.

The fact that this Faerie is female is hinted at by the Druids, who cut the mistletoe with a moon-shaped sickle, sacred to the Moon Goddess and so to all things female and regenerative. Her gift-giving and seducer-murderer qualities also give us the impression that she is female, as well as the fact that she struggles with Frigga for the death of Baldur, a mythic connection with that Goddess or a competition for Baldur's sexual attention. Finally is the generative qualities of this Faerie, the ability to quicken childbirth and serve as surrogate protector of babies. Like the Faerie Queen herself, Mistletoe can exchange a human child for a Faerie infant, though she only does so in sleep because of her compact with the humans involved. But as a hallucinogen she is able to bring a human into the Faerie world, giving him visions and destroying his time sense. There she may kill him or allow him to travel back, at her whim.

So the next time you find yourself with some hottie under the Yule mistletoe, think carefully.

EASTER TRADITIONS

The hare has a sexual connotation and Nymphs will take the form of a hare in the forest. The hare, or rabbit, is at the center of many folkloric traditions, and the Easter bunny is a sanitized memory of this sexual Faerie creature.

In "The Bonny Black Hare," a Nymph girl lures a hunter by transforming from hare to woman. Part of this was meant to show the transformation from young girl to sexual woman, as Nymphs often do in folklore and myth. Spring is the time of year when the ground turns from the barren, "chaste" visage of "pure" or "lily white" snow (adjectives used to describe young girls), to the lush, fertile earth that will bear grains and fruit (again, allusions to sexual women who bear children). The hare exemplifies this too, for this little critter looks innocent and adorable, like a young girl, but in the spring the hare becomes insatiable, mating almost constantly and then bearing her litter. Are you at all surprised that that Nymphs like to take this form?

Many of our words for the sexual organs of a woman are references to the hare. In Scotland, the hare is called a *coney*. This became *cunny*, yielding our rather abrasive word for the female part. Victorian Scots called pet rabbits the same thing we call a pet cat, a pussy, and this little euphemism stuck as well. These words should not be taken as obscene, but as sacred words referring to sacred sexuality, alluding to rites like the Bacchanalia. The Church, in waging a propaganda war on folklore, Paganism and Faerie belief over a thousand years has stripped these words of their sacredness and made them derisive and vulgar.

But the Church could not eliminate these elements from the spring celebration. In fact, the Pagan roots of Easter are evident in the name, which comes from various Goddess names, including Oestara, a Norse Goddess of spring, and Ishtar, the Semitic Goddess. The biblical Ester is Hebrew for Ishtar. Ester assumed a place of esteem in the Old Testament where she is seen as a matriarch rather than a Goddess. From her name, we get Easter.

The Nymphs of spring, in the guise of the hare or rabbit, busily spread their happy sexual Faerie energy through the forest, glade and field, ensuring the growth of crops and the renewal of animals and people. They seduce humans and imbue them with sexual passion, needed to keep humans in tune with the natural world, which is bristling with reproductive energy as the crops and fruit trees grow and blossom. In England and other parts of Europe, Beltane (early May) was celebrated by young men and women going into the fields to make love, placing themselves in tune with the renewing energy of the crops and the forests. The folk song "Wild Mountain Thyme" speaks of this ritual:

> Oh, the summer time is coming,
> And the trees are sweetly blooming,
> And the wild mountain thyme
> Grows around the blooming heather.
> Will you go, lassie, will you go?
>
> And we'll all go together
> To pull wild mountain thyme
> All around the blooming heather,
> Will you go, lassie, go?
>
> I will build my love a bower
> By yon clear and crystal fountain,
> And all around the bower,
> I'll pile flowers from the mountain.
>
> If my true love, she won't have me,
> I will surely find another
> To pull wild mountain thyme
> All around the blooming heather.
> (Traditional, Arr. Klein 1995)

In this song, a young man sings about the Beltane rite, preparing to take the young woman of his fancy into the heather fields for their sexual romp. He will build her a bower, a small shelter of thyme and grasses over a wooden framework, to celebrate the growth of the season as they lay together. These rites were often a bit orgiastic, and the singer says that if the object of his love won't have him, another young woman will take her place.

These celebrations are very old ones, begun in ancient Greece and even earlier, as the Bacchanalia. Nymphs attending Bacchus would dance about him in the spring, celebrating the just-blooming vines;

Bacchus would get excited, and he and the Nymphs would romp and drink, creating a sexual rite that placed them into a trance. In this state, Bacchus could open the gates between the worlds and allow the spirits of the crops killed in last year's harvest to enter our world and inhabit the growing vines of this year's fields. Without this rite, the crops would have no spirit and would not taste good or make fine wine. (This belief may be the origin of the word *spirits* in reference to liquor.)

This rite was seen throughout Europe for centuries, but fell by the wayside in most places under the scrutiny of Victorian morality. The ritual can be seen in the original release of the movie *The Wicker Man* (1973), in which a Scottish police officer investigates an alleged crime in a town that still practices the old Pagan rites. But for the most part, these practices are no more.

But people could not altogether give up the spring rites. The hare continues to bless the Easter celebration, carrying with it the sexuality of the Nymphs that attend Bacchus and spread the sexual energy through the fields that will ensure we eat this year. The next time you see an adorable child in an Easter dress receive a pet rabbit on that holiday, think about our Nymph girl and about a few choice dirty words.

HALLOWE'EN TRADITIONS

Nowhere is our connection with the Otherworld more evident than in the celebration of Hallowe'en. The name we use, *Hallowe'en*, comes from All Hallows Eve, shortened to Hallowe'en. It is the evening when we reverence our hallowed dead. The original celebration comes from the Celts, who believed that when the harvest ended, the Faerie Queen led the Wild Ride through the forest. This celebration was simply called autumn, which in Gaelic is Samhain (pronounced SOW-en). Because the dead spirits are journeying from our world to the Otherworld, the veil between the worlds is thin. This means that souls of the living can be claimed. Children asleep in their beds who find themselves too close to the Wild Ride can become changelings. And Death can come and take souls as he pleases.

To combat the second problem, the crafty Celts would carve a scary skull out of a wax turnip, and place it on a pole near their doors. This jack-o'-lantern would deter Faeries and other spirits that had come to claim the sleeping kiddies. They would also send a troupe of dancers through the streets dressed as ghosts and ghouls so that Death would believe he'd already visited the town and would move along without claiming any souls.

These led to our modern Hallowe'en traditions of carving a jack-o'-lantern out of a pumpkin and of dressing as young pop stars.

While we celebrate Hallowe'en on October 31, the true holiday falls on November 1. The Celts considered the day to start at sunset (which is the custom of Jews as well), so the celebration begins at sunset on October 31, which by Celtic reckoning is when November 1 begins. In ancient times, Samhain simply fell on the last day of the harvest, whatever day that was. So Samhain is a moveable feast, falling on whatever the appropriate day happens to be. The Pagan celebration was probably standardized to November 1 by Gerald Gardner, the Englishman who modernized the practice of Wicca in the mid-twentieth century.

Hallowee'n is a day when Faeries have great power to roam our world. In "Tam Lin," our changeling hero tells Janet that her rescue of him on Hallowe'en will be aided by Fey who side with true love. "But tonight is Hallowe'en/The Faerie folk do ride/Those that would let true love win/At Miles Cross they do hie." And in "Allison Gross," the Faerie Queen appears on Hallowe'en to unfetter the worm-man from the tree to which Allison Gross has chained him.

Hallowe'en has always been the time associated with the tithe to Hell. The Faerie Queen sacrifices a human, a price she must pay for the privilege of living in the Faerie Lands rather than being driven into Hell. That this tithe is paid on Hallowe'en comes from ancient traditions of the sacrifice of the Seven Year King, which was usually done as the harvest was gathered in. This custom reinforces our connection of Hallowe'en with death and ghosts.

The worst Faerie offenders at this time of year are Pixies, those mischievous little goat-boys of the forest. In late autumn, Pixies like to appear around dusk as bright lights. Humans seeing these lights tend to be enchanted and follow the illumination wherever it leads them. Since it's easy for them to slip in and out of their world at this time of year, Pixies can come into the forest, take on the bright appearance, then lead some mortal into the Otherworld as he or she follows them. This is called being "pixie-led." People who are pixie-led into the Otherworld are seldom seen again.

The Glastig are also very powerful at Hallowe'en, as this is the time of the hunt. The same can be said of the Faeries Herne and Odin. Odin's Hunt is a late autumn event, and anyone wandering unfamiliar forests at this time should be careful of loud sounds of hounds and bells.

FAERIE EXPRESSIONS

Many expressions or sayings in our common speech come from Faerie belief. Here are some examples:

Knock on wood (or in England, touch wood): Dryads live in trees and are thought to bring both good and bad luck. We saw their presence in our lives with the Yule tree and the mistletoe. In ancient times, people thought they could call on the Dryad spirit for luck, or to counteract a curse or bad thought. So they would knock on or touch wood, especially oak, to ask the blessing of the tree Faeries. This custom is still quite active today. I once knew a young woman who carried a small piece of oak in her purse so that she could knock wood whenever she felt she needed to.

A little birdie told me: Certain Faeries can teach us to communicate with birds, such as the Sirin and Vila. Faerie birds can foretell the future. People use this expression to mean that information came to them from a source they won't divulge, with the implication that Faeries gave them the information.

Wailing (or howling) like a Banshee: This is usually used when someone is shouting or singing in an annoying way. It can also be used for someone singing loudly and out of tune. It comes from the belief in Banshees, discussed in chapter 7. It is said in Scottish that Banshees can wail so loudly that they can break glass. The song of a true Banshee, however, is beautiful and very sad, and her type of mournful singing is called *keening*.

Impish: This term describes an adorable but mischievous child and is one of many terms that come from names of mischievous Faeries. An Imp is a small Faerie with a reputation for trouble. *Puckish* is also used to describe someone doing mischief with a sly grin, and for the same reason. The name Puck derives from *booka* or *Pookah*, which means goat. Folklore is full of mischievous goat Faeries, like the Joulupukki. Pan, the goat-footed God, was the namesake of J. M. Barrie's charming, troublesome hero, Peter Pan.

Urchin: A cute but mischievous child may also be described as an Urchin. The term is often applied to orphans or street children. While this term is used to name a spiny sea-creature, the original comes from Pixies that resemble spiny hedgehogs. In folklore, Urchins might allow themselves to be found by humans and raised as mortal children, but ultimately their Faerie nature would surface. The fact that Urchins would often be found on roadsides led to the use of the term for street children or orphans. In the tale of *Snow White*, one version states that Snow White was an Urchin, found on the roadside by the king and queen.

Gremlins: This Faerie, which lent his name to both a series of movies and a car, lives in engines and machines and tries to destroy them. As early as World War II, pilots would blame engine failure on Gremlins. To this day, mechanical difficulties are blamed on these little critters.

You have to kiss a lot of frogs to find your prince: One of many phrases in common use that comes from Grimms and other collections of Fairy tales. In this case, from *The Frog Prince*. While the girl in *The Frog Prince* was not looking for a mate or husband, the phrase applies to modern young women who are braving the dating scene.

Enchanted: Literally this means placed under a magical spell. It is used when meeting someone who seems lovely or charming, and is often said in French, *enchanté*. The original means being placed under an enchantment by a Faerie being. The implication is that you are meeting someone who has the ability of a Faerie to place a spell on you, or to seduce you.

Siren song: Something that attracts a person so strongly he or she cannot resist it. The phrase comes from the Sirens, Nymphs who would sit on rocks in the ocean and sing so beautifully that sailors could not resist steering toward them and crashing their ships on the rocks.

Brownies: A branch of the Girl Scouts named both for the color of the uniform and an association with the Faerie critters. The official Brownies story involves a changeling child; a human child would not help her family work, so she asked an owl to exchange her for a Brownie. The owl tells her to go to a pond at night and peer into the water. There she will see a Brownie. The Brownie she sees is her own reflection. In fact, the investiture of a Brownie pin comes with a recreation of this Faerie ritual: the fledgling Brownie must enter a magical forest, or wood, accompanied by standing Brownies. At the center of this forest is a "pond," a mirror surrounded by earth and leaves. The girl is then blindfolded and spun while the owl's poem is recited by the troop leader. At the end of the poem, the blindfold is removed, and the girl sees herself in the pond. At this point in the poem the girl must respond to her reflection:

Leader: Twist me and turn me and show me an Elf, I looked in the water and saw. . .
Girl: Myself!

As if this ritual did not carry enough Faerie magic, the pin is then applied upside down. The girl must perform three good deeds before the water-mirror of Faerie can be used to righten the pin, at which point the girl may wear it right side up. She is now a fully invested Brownie, a changeling child who will help her family in all of their work.

Chapter 10

GETTING TO KNOW THE FAERIES IN OUR WORLD

You've now read a book pointing out a good deal of bad dealings between humans and the Fey. They do not play well with people. If you haven't noticed that, I suspect you simply weren't paying attention. I'm not really sure what else I can say to dissuade you from ever trying to hobnob with Hobgoblins, but there are always those few who don't listen well.

Sure, there are a few times when things worked out. Janet and Tam Lin. If you're a pregnant young woman who does not mind hanging out at eerie river crossings on dark nights and having the occasional changeling man turned into a fierce lion while lying naked on top of you, then by all means, pursue a long-term relationship with the Faerie of your choice. The frog prince? Even as an analogy, kissing frogs is icky. Imagine doing it to the real thing.

Sometimes interaction with the Good People is necessary or even desirable. They inhabit our houses and yards, foretell events and carry off our shiny valuables, so sometimes we have to hold conversations with them. As my former girlfriend would say, sometimes you "need to have the talk."

So here are some times and places to "have the talk," and some ways in which you might have it. None involve picking roses on the grounds of haunted castles.

PROTECTION FROM FAERIES

Many of us who believe and who work with unseen forces find ourselves in the presence of the Good People in ways we may find annoying, hurtful or just plain bad. Below are some examples of things that might happen if various types of Faeries hover around your space:

- Shiny objects such as keys and change go missing.
- Objects are moved and turn up in places you did not put them.
- You hear noises in walls and under furniture.
- Slithery little things slither just on the periphery of your vision.
- You may hear voices or music that you cannot account for (no, you are not insane).
- You may become easily distracted, lose time and have strange random thoughts that seem uncharacteristic.

If any of these things happen to you, you may wonder if you're going psycho. There's a fairly good chance you are not, especially if you work magic, believe in the Fey, talk to the Good People or live in a very old wooden house.

If you think Faeries share your space and you want to gently urge them to leave you alone or stop "sharing" your stuff, there are things you might do.

Never speak harshly to Faeries. Call them by names such as the Good People or the Kindly Ones. Ask them to respect your space so that you and they can get along peacefully. Remember that they most likely have lived in the house or building that you think of as home for a very long time; or they believe that you invited them to live there.

Here are steps you can take to gently urge them to consider moving out:

1. Tie a piece of red thread around your doorknob, dresser drawers and on your bedpost. Red thread is a very old charm used to banish enchantment. It only has to be there to work, and can be placed as inconspicuously as you like.

2. If you have access to rowan wood, place a small piece under your bed or over your door jamb (the wooden frame around your door). In North America, rowan is known as mountain ash. Even the tiniest piece will work.

3. Carry iron objects on your person. An old iron skeleton key bought in a junk shop, antique shop or vintage store and worn on a chain around your neck is perfect. Carbon steel and stainless steel have a good deal of iron in them, so a steel pocket knife or a nail will do the trick. Some wrist watches are also made with steel bands. Nickel, copper and brass used to mint U.S. coins do not have any iron in them, so these are not good for this purpose (in fact, some Faeries love to steal them). Some non-U.S. coins have a steel or iron core, including the British one and two pence, the German five and ten pfennig and the Canadian nickel. (At the time of this writing, the United States is considering a steel core penny and nickel.)

4. Leave gifts for the Fey in your life. Small articles of clothing (such as well-made doll clothing) might work, especially hats. Marbles and old brass keys, coins and old small toys might also work. Even a rolled-up piece of aluminum foil looks very shiny to a Faerie. Loudly state "this is for the Good People" when you leave the object in some hidden corner of a room or below a porch or doorway.

If you do not want your Faerie friends to leave but would rather deal with the little surprises they inspire, the next spell might be useful.

A SPELL FOR FINDING LOST OBJECTS

Keys missing? Glasses not where you left them? Coins disappearing from that little spare change jar you leave on the kitchen table? Certain types of Faeries love shiny objects and carry them away to hoard them. Brownies, Gnomes, and Kobolds are among the worst offenders. These are all household Faeries, and they are very complex creatures.

If you have a missing object, especially a metallic object such as a car key, here is what you should do: Take something shiny and round, like a marble or a glass or metal bead (a small rolled-up tinfoil ball will work in a pinch); hold up the object and loudly announce, "If you return my keys (change, contacts case, whatever), you may have this." Then place the ball or bead under a clear glass or Mason jar where the Fey can see it but cannot get it. In very short order you will find the lost object. Then simply lift the glass and toss the ball or bead into a corner of the room.

Kobolds, by the way, can be very helpful little beings. They are the stars of the Grimms' tale *The Shoe Maker and the Elves*. In that story, they proved lifesaving to the titular shoemaker. In that story, Kobolds can be dismissed by giving them gifts, especially clothing (J. K. Rowling knew this and used it in a Harry Potter book with the character Dobby). While this is helpful knowledge, once you get accustomed to living with Faeries, you may find it useful to keep them around.

While your point of view may be that Faeries live in your house, their point of view is just the opposite, especially in older houses: you are the interloper, and they are the residents. In Brian Froud's book *Faeries*, Froud relates a story that took place in New Jersey in recent times. A man cut down a large tree in his yard (which he felt he had every right to do, as it was his yard). After felling the tree, a tiny man appeared to him, cursing in a foreign language. The little man explained that this tree had been his home for a very long time.

Faeries are very innocent of human politics and would not consider rent or mortgage as a right of ownership. To the Faerie, possession is nine-tenths of the law, and living in a place, whether a house, tree or stone, entitles the tenant to claim the place. Here humans and Faeries are in disagreement. But if you are going to deal with the Fey, you must consider their point of view on these matters. It may be very impolite to attempt to remove the Good People from your home or property by leaving gifts for them, and you may find they could have been a useful ally in some future time of need, so my advice is, don't do it.

The Germans would try to lure the Kobolds into their homes by carving laughing Kobolds out of wood or wax (wood is especially potent as the Kobolds are thought to be tree spirits). Boggarts and Nixies are lured in similar ways. In one German legend, a Kobold can be lured into a home by visiting an ant hill at noon on Saint John's Day and seeing a bird on the ant hill. The bird will become a Kobold and may be carried into the house in a burlap bag.

Having a Faerie creature of this type was thought to bring wealth and fertility into the home. Women trying to conceive would be especially desirous of Fey house guests, and might leave milk laced with a bit of rum in small bowls in the house corners. In Ireland, these beliefs apply to Pixies and Nixies, even though these creatures also can be mischievous; they might bring grain and gold into a house. A family that received unexplained gold or extra earnings would attribute it to a new Kobold moving into the house.

Kobolds and other small Faeries have been known to help with housework. In German lore, Kobolds are often seen as resembling children of three or four years old and will work hard alongside a housewife or servant doing such tasks as washing clothes or dishes. Tales of Robin Goodfellow, a British Sprite, involve Robin doing both mischief and good and helping favored housewives with these sorts of cleaning chores. Other legends say that Kobolds will tidy up a home or stable after the human owners have gone to bed for the night.

A few rules for keeping Kobolds, Nixies and Brownies: They are very sensitive, and you must never scold them or tease them or they will leave (remember the Faerie wife who exacted a promise never to tease her of her Faerie origins?). They also expect to be fed at the same time and in the same place each day, usually in the evening. They like beer, rum in milk and table scraps. If you move to a new home, it is likely that the Kobold will move with you.

TALKING TO BIRDS

Some people are born with the gift of speaking to birds. I wouldn't believe that if I had not seen it myself. My wife walks through the forests and a bird will land on a branch, chatter to her, fly to the next branch, chatter some more and keep the conversation going for a mile or more. Same bird, not oddly similar birds. Really, I only believe it because I've seen it.

Now perhaps you would like to be able to speak to birds. It can be done.

In the forests of Poland is a Faerie called Vila. She is an enigmatic Faerie, known throughout eastern Europe all the way into Siberia. In some places she is said to be a shape changer, taking the forms of various animals. In some places she is thought to be a seducer-murderess, but I think that's just bad PR. In Poland, it is believed that by enacting a certain ritual, you may induce Vila to teach you the language of birds.

First, gather three things: a horseshoe, a hank of hair from a horse's mane or tail and a piece of horse manure (the last one is, I agree, the ickiest).

Now walk to the deep forest and place these items in a circle around you. Dance around the circle three times, then stand with your bare foot on the horseshoe (ideally when performing this rite you should be "barefoot" all over; I'll leave that to your discretion).

Standing with your foot on the object, call out three times to Vila (pronounced WE-la in Polish).

Your ritual is done, but you're not. At any time after this, while you are walking through the forest, a very beautiful woman with long flowing hair will greet you. Depending on who is telling the story, she may either be naked or clothed in a white or golden gown. Whichever turns out to be the case, try not to appear shocked or envious. Greet her as a sister and offer her food and drink. That's Vila, and now she will teach you the language of birds.

Vila is a mysterious creature. She is known throughout Europe as Vila, Wila and Veela. Aside from being beautiful and sometimes naked, she is quite a singer and her voice seduces men. In some stories she is part of a group of water Nymphs, the Vila, who live in lakes and clouds. These Nymphs can cause storms and take delight in drenching lonely travelers. In another myth, the Vila (or Weela) are girls who died before their wedding day and seduce young men only to break their hearts, never knowing true love. In each of these stories, the Vila are associated with birds and with the sky. In one story, the Vila are referred to as Sky Women.

J. K. Rowling refers to the Vila in her Harry Potter books, where she calls them Veela. They accompany the Bulgarian Quidditch team in book four of that series, and appear as fire-throwing bird women.

HELP FROM THE DRYADS

Dryads are tree Nymphs known throughout Europe. The syllable *dry* refers to the oak tree and the word Dryad is linguistically connected to the Celtic word Druid (priests who reverence trees, especially the oak). Dryads are associated with quite a number of trees: Melaia live in ash groves; Hamadryads are seen as living in any group of trees; and in the myth of Daphne, that Nymph is turned into the spirit of the laurel when she is unpleasantly pursued by Apollo. In Japan, the tree Nymph is known as Kodama, and the Scottish have a male tree spirit called the

Ghillie Dhu. In the case of all Dryads, harming trees without doing certain rituals first leads to very bad things happening.

Tree Nymphs are usually shy and helpful creatures, and if you approach them with a good deal of serenity and respect, they can be coaxed into helping you. The help may be to find your way when you're lost or to accomplish what you desire (prosperity, for instance, or health; asking Nymphs for help with love and romance is probably not a good idea).

The spell for asking a Dryad for help is an easy one.

Find a tree that you feel very connected to. It should be one you visit often, and sit near, climb, gather nuts from or just like to look at and touch. Oak, ash and laurel work best, but thorn trees, willow, birch and chestnut are good too.

Cast a circle around the tree by walking clockwise three times. Repeat the words "weave the enchantment well" as you walk, saying the phrase once for each revolution.

Now stand close to the tree, touching it or leaning against it. Say, "Lovely spirit of the tree, grant the wish I ask of thee." Hold in your mind the request you are making, and if it's for something physical, like money, hold a token of the wish (a coin, for instance) while you speak the phrase. (Use a silver, nickel or copper coin such as a U.S. half dollar or dollar. Old U.S. half dollars up until 1964 were silver, so that would be best. Do not use an iron coin!)

Leave the tree a gift, such as a hair from your head, a thread from your clothing or a wet kiss (really! Your spit is part of you, and the Dryad will be happy you offer it). Or leave the coin behind.

Now back away from the tree, thanking the Nymph for her help. Do not take down the circle you've cast, as it will be needed for the creature to work her magic. Also, once you leave the spot, do not look back. This is a standard of working magic. Remember Orpheus.

Once you get what you've asked for (and remember, Faeries work in their own timeframe, not yours, so be patient!), return to the tree or grove and leave a thank-you gift. This could again be hair or clothing, a kiss, or a coin or marble. Gifts of drink and food work well too, especially sweets.

This seems like a very simple spell, maybe even a little naïve, but it works (I've tried it many times). The Nymph will probably want a favor from you in return someday, so bear that in mind when doing this spell, and remember again that "someday" could mean tomorrow or twenty years from now.

FAERIE INSPIRATION

The Druids would sleep by a brook or stream for inspiration from Naiads. This works for us today as well.

Whether you are a musician, writer or artist, student, computer programmer or nurse, you might find yourself being stuck for an idea. It happens to everyone. You can ask Faeries for help.

Go to a stream or fast-running brook. The faster the water is running, the better. Cast a magical circle by walking three times around an area and saying, "Weave the enchantment well" once each time you go around. Now lay down on a comfy blanket or sleeping bag, letting the water lull you to sleep. When you wake up, a new idea or inspiration may dawn on you.

Doing this spell often helps you listen. It may not work the first time but keep at it. It might take a little practice. Fairies of that brook may take a time or two to bond with you. Bringing gifts will help. Shiny objects, marbles, food or drink are always good. Do not throw copper pennies in water, as the copper will leech out and pollute the area.

Chapter 11

THE END

Fairy tales usually end like that: "And they lived happily ever after. The end." But that's not how it really is with Faeries. They are out there, watching, seeing great humor in what we do and how we act. It's probably of no consequence to them that most humans don't believe in them anymore. After all, they've been here a lot longer than we have, and they'll probably be here long after we're gone. Whoever they are, wherever they come from, once you untangle the memory of Picts and the tales of the old gods from their stories, you're left with them, the Kindly Ones, the Good People. They live in our world when it pleases them, they take the children who catch their eye, and they make love to the young women and young men they find enticing.

And it's not like they did this long ago and somehow stopped. I'm convinced they do it all still. They are there, watching patiently for those of us who can see them, who know they are lurking, who leave milk with a little rum mixed in on the back porch.

It happened to me when I was young, maybe a bit into my twenties. I was walking through the forested area of Staten Island, New York, as I often would. The forest wasn't very big or dense, just a patch of green a few city blocks wide. An egret fished in a little pond there, and I'd look at it every chance I got. Lovers used the groupings of trees for privacy, though the fact that I know that shows how little privacy they actually got. And Witches, myself included, would do full moon rituals in the deepest thickets.

Maybe it was the lovers hidden among the thickets or the energy of rituals or the egret. Maybe it was because Staten Island, like the rest of New York, is old and magical, with energy I've seldom felt anywhere else (and I've visited a lot of places). But that day I stood near a copse of trees, and when I turned, there he was. He had small eyes and a huge crooked nose. His hat was silvery red, if that's really a color, which I suspect it's not for most people. He just looked me over and then sank back into a bole of an old tree. He knew I'd seen him, and he'd certainly seen me. He was content at that.

So when you walk down the street, sit in your yard or weed your garden, know that they are watching. They have their own reasons for doing so, and just maybe, if you are either very lucky or perhaps very unlucky, you'll see one. And maybe experience a bit more. Just try to remember the warnings.

And if you are one of the lucky ones, perhaps you will live happily ever after.

The end.

THE VOYAGE OF BRAN MAC FEBAL

Irish bards or storytellers told *The Voyage of Bran Mac Febal* for centuries before it was written down in AD 700–900 by monks. It was translated several times. Here is a translation made in 1895 by Kuno Meyer:

'Twas fifty quatrains the woman from unknown lands sang on the floor of the house to Bran son of Febal, when the royal house was full of kings, who knew not whence the woman had come, since the ramparts were closed.

This is the beginning of the story. One day, in the neighborhood of his stronghold, Bran went about alone, when he heard music behind him. As often as he looked back, 'twas still behind him the music was. At last he fell asleep at the music, such was its sweetness. When he awoke from his sleep, he saw close by him a branch of silver with white blossoms, nor was it easy to distinguish its bloom from that branch. Then Bran took the branch in his hand to his royal house. When the hosts were in the royal house, they saw a woman in strange raiment on the floor of the house. 'Twas then she sang the fifty quatrains to Bran, while the host heard her, and all beheld the woman.

And she said:

'A branch of the apple-tree from Emain
I bring, like those one knows;
Twigs of white silver are on it,
Crystal brows with blossoms.

'There is a distant isle,
Around which sea-horses glisten:
A fair course against the white-swelling surge,
Four feet uphold it.

'A delight of the eyes, a glorious range,
Is the plain on which the hosts hold games:
Coracle contends against chariot
In southern Mag Findargat.

'Feet of white bronze under it
Glittering through beautiful ages.
Lovely land throughout the world's age,
On which the many blossoms drop.

'An ancient tree there is with blossoms,
On which birds call to the Hours.
'Tis in harmony it is their wont
To call together every Hour.

'Splendours of every colour glisten
Throughout the gentle-voiced plains.
Joy is known, ranked around music,
In southern Mag Argatné

'Unknown is wailing or treachery
In the familiar cultivated land,
There is nothing rough or harsh,
But sweet music striking on the ear.

'Without grief, without sorrow, without death,
Without any sickness, without debility,
That is the sign of Emain—
Uncommon is an equal marvel.

'A beauty of a wondrous land,
Whose aspects are lovely,
Whose view is a fair country,
Incomparable is its haze.

'Then if Airctech is seen,
On which dragonstones and crystals drop
The sea washes the wave against the land,
Hair of crystal drops from its mane.

'Wealth, treasures of every hue,
Are in Ciuin, a beauty of freshness,
Listening to sweet music,
Drinking the best of wine.

'Golden chariots in Mag Réin,
Rising with the tide to the sun,
Chariots of silver in Mag Mon,
And of bronze without blemish.

'Yellow golden steeds are on the sward there,
Other steeds with crimson hue,
Others with wool upon their backs
Of the hue of heaven all-blue.

'At sunrise there will come
A fair man illumining level lands;
He rides upon the fair sea-washed plain,
He stirs the ocean till it is blood.

'A host will come across the clear sea,
To the land they show their rowing;

Then they row to the conspicuous stone,
From which arise a hundred strains.

'It sings a strain unto the host
Through long ages, it is not sad,
Its music swells with choruses of hundreds—
They look for neither decay nor death.

'Many-shaped Emne by the sea,
Whether it be near, whether it be far,
In which are many thousands of motley women,
Which the clear sea encircles.

'If he has heard the voice of the music,
The chorus of the little birds from Imchiuin,
A small band of women will come from a height
To the plain of sport in which he is.

'There will come happiness with health
To the land against which laughter peals,
Into Imchiuin at every season
Will come everlasting joy.

'It is a day of lasting weather
That showers silver on the lands,
A pure-white cliff on the range of the sea,
Which from the sun receives its heat.

'The host race along Mag Mon,
A beautiful game, not feeble,
In the variegated land over a mass of beauty
They look for neither decay nor death.

'Listening to music at night,
And going into Ildathach,
A variegated land, splendour on a diadem of beauty,
Whence the white cloud glistens.

'There are thrice fifty distant isles
In the ocean to the west of us;
Larger than Erin twice
Is each of them, or thrice.

'A great birth will come after ages,
That will not be in a lofty place,
The son of a woman whose mate will not be known,
He will seize the rule of the many thousands.

'A rule without beginning, without end,
He has created the world so that it is perfect,
Whose are earth and sea,
Woe to him that shall be under His unwill!

'Tis He that made the heavens,
Happy he that has a white heart,
He will purify hosts under pure water,
'Tis He that will heal your sicknesses.

'Not to all of you is my speech,
Though its great marvel has been made known:
Let Bran hear from the crowd of the world
What of wisdom has been told to him.

'Do not fall on a bed of sloth,
Let not thy intoxication overcome thee,
Begin a voyage across the clear sea,
If perchance thou mayst reach the land of women.'

Thereupon the woman went from them, while they knew not
whither she went. And she took her branch with her. The branch
sprang from Bran's hand into the hand of the woman, nor was there
strength in Bran's hand to hold the branch.

Then on the morrow Bran went upon the sea. The number of his
men was three companies of nine. One of his foster-brothers and
mates was set over each of the three companies of nine. When he

had been at sea two days and two nights, he saw a man in a chariot coming towards him over the sea. That man also sang thirty other quatrains to him, and made himself known to him, and said that he was Manannan the son of Ler, and said that it was upon him to go to Ireland after long ages, and that a son would be born to him, even Mongan son of Fiachna—that was the name which would be upon him.

So he sang these thirty quatrains to him:

'Bran deems it a marvellous beauty
In his coracle across the clear sea:
While to me in my chariot from afar
It is a flowery plain on which he rides about.

'What is a clear sea
For the prowed skiff in which Bran is,
That is a happy plain with profusion of flowers
To me from the chariot of two wheels.

'Bran sees
The number of waves beating across the clear sea:
I myself see in Mag Mon
Red-headed flowers without fault.

'Sea-horses glisten in summer
As far as Bran has stretched his glance:
Rivers pour forth a stream of honey
In the land of Manannan son of Ler.

'The sheen of the main, on which thou art,
The white hue of the sea, on which thou rowest about,
Yellow and azure are spread out,
It is land, and is not rough.

'Speckled salmon leap from the womb
Of the white sea, on which thou lookest:

They are calves, they are coloured lambs
With friendliness, without mutual slaughter.

'Though (but) one chariot-rider is seen
In Mag Mell of many flowers,
There are many steeds on its surface,
Though them thou seest not.

'The size of the plain, the number of the host,
Colours glisten with pure glory,
A fair stream of silver, cloths of gold,
Afford a welcome with all abundance.

'A beautiful game, most delightful,
They play (sitting) at the luxurious wine,
Men and gentle women under a bush,
Without sin, without crime.

'Along the top of a wood has swum
Thy coracle across ridges,
There is a wood of beautiful fruit
Under the prow of thy little skiff.

'A wood with blossom and fruit,
On which is the vine's veritable fragrance,
A wood without decay, without defect,
On which are leaves of golden hue.

'We are from the beginning of creation
Without old age, without consummation of earth,
Hence we expect not that there should be frailty,
The sin has not come to us.

'An evil day when the Serpent went
To the father to his city!
She has perverted the times in this world,
So that there came decay which was not original.

'By greed and lust he has slain us,
Through which he has ruined his noble race:
The withered body has gone to the fold of torment,
And everlasting abode of torture.

'It is a law of pride in this world
To believe in the creatures, to forget God,
Overthrow by diseases, and old age,
Destruction of the soul through deception.

'A noble salvation will come
From the King who has created us,
A white law will come over seas,
Besides being God, He will be man.

'This shape, he on whom thou lookest,
Will come to thy parts;
'Tis mine to journey to her house,
To the woman in Line-mag.

'For it is Moninnan, the son of Ler,
From the chariot in the shape of a man,
Of his progeny will be a very short while
A fair man in a body of white clay.

'Monann, the descendant of Ler, will be
A vigorous bed-fellow to Caintigern:
He shall be called to his son in the beautiful world,
Fiachna will acknowledge him as his son.

'He will delight the company of every Faerie-knoll,
He will be the darling of every goodly land,
He will make known secrets—a course of wisdom—
In the world, without being feared.

'He will be in the shape of every beast,
Both on the azure sea and on land,

He will be a dragon before hosts at the onset,
He will be a wolf of every great forest.

'He will be a stag with horns of silver
In the land where chariots are driven,
He will be a speckled salmon in a full pool,
He will be a seal, he will be a fair-white swan.

'He will be throughout long ages
An hundred years in fair kingship,
He will cut down battalions—a lasting grave—
He will redden fields, a wheel around the track.

'It will be about kings with a champion
That he will be known as a valiant hero,
Into the strongholds of a land on a height
I shall send an appointed end from Islay.

'High shall I place him with princes,
He will be overcome by a son of error;
Moninnan, the son of Ler,
Will be his father, his tutor.

'He will be—his time will be short—
Fifty years in this world:
A dragonstone from the sea will kill him
In the fight at Senlabor.

'He will ask a drink from Loch Ló,
While he looks at the stream of blood,
The white host will take him under a wheel of clouds
To the gathering where there is no sorrow.

'Steadily then let Bran row,
Not far to the Land of Women,
Emne with many hues of hospitality
Thou wilt reach before the setting of the sun.'

Thereupon Bran went from him. And he saw an island. He rowed round about it, and a large host was gaping and laughing. They were all looking at Bran and his people, but would not stay to converse with them. They continued to give forth gusts of laughter at them. Bran sent one of his people on the island. He ranged himself with the others, and was gaping at them like the other men of the island. He kept rowing round about the island. Whenever his man came past Bran, his comrades would address him. But he would not converse with them, but would only look at them and gape at them. The name of this island is the Island of Joy. Thereupon they left him there.

It was not long thereafter when they reached the Land of Women. They saw the leader of the women at the port. Said the chief of the women: 'Come hither on and, O Bran son of Febal! Welcome is thy advent!' Bran did not venture to go on shore. The woman threw a ball of thread to Bran straight over his face. Bran put his hand on the ball, which clave to his palm. The thread of the ball was in the woman's hand, and she pulled the coracle towards the port. Thereupon they went into a large house, in which was a bed for every couple, even thrice nine beds. The food that was put on every dish vanished not from them. It seemed a year to them that they were there—it chanced to be many years. No savour was wanting to them.

Home-sickness seized one of them, even Nechtan the son of Collbran. His kindred kept praying Bran that he should go to Ireland with him. The woman said to them their going would make them rue. However, they went, and the woman said that none of them should touch the land, and that they should visit and take with them the man whom they had left in the Island of Joy.

Then they went until they arrived at a gathering at Srub Brain. The men asked of them who it was came over the sea. Said Bran: 'I am Bran the son of Febal,' saith he. However, the other saith: 'We do not know such a one, though the Voyage of Bran is in our ancient stories.'

The man lept from them out of the coracle. As soon as he touched the earth of Ireland, forthwith he was a heap of ashes, as though he had been in the earth for many hundred years. 'Twas then that Bran sang this quatrain:

For Collbran's son, great was the folly
To lift his hand against age,
Without any one casting a wave of pure water
Over Nechtan, Collbran's son.

Thereupon, to the people of the gathering Bran told all his wanderings from the beginning until that time. And he wrote these quatrains in Ogam, and then bade them farewell. And from that hour his wanderings are not known.

GLOSSARY OF FAERIES, PEOPLE AND PLACES

Faeries, Fairies or Fey exist all over the world, and have been known in many cultures by many names. They may be an older race of people, a race of enchanted beings or a race of creatures from a parallel world. Probably all three are accounted for in Faerie lore. This glossary includes beings discussed in this book, along with their pronunciations and alternative spellings.

Aine (Irish; AN-ya or EN-ya): An Irish name for the Faerie Queen, Aine was believed to have married mortals and borne half-human children. One of her human husbands was the Earl of Desmond.

Alfheim (Norwegian; Elf Home): Norwegian, Danish and Swedish land of the Elves. Mentioned in the Norse *Saga of Thorstein* and other sagas and myths.

An Chailleach Bhéarach (Irish; En KI-eech BEAR-ak, the Old Woman of Bear Island): Title of the Banshee when she transforms into the form of a deer.

Arawn (Welsh; ar-AWN; also Arrawn): A character in the *Mabinogion*, a Welsh Underworld king who takes the form of the human Pwyll for a year and a day while Pwyll journeys to the Underworld. Usually thought to be antlered.

Arthur (Welsh; Bear-man): An enchanted king of England and Wales, dates unknown. Arthur was born in fulfillment of prophesy, raised by foster parents, and had relations with the Faerie Queen, called Morgan Le Fay in the legends. He is a Seven Year King figure, dying for the prosperity of the land, and being reborn at some future time. He is called the Once and Future King.

Bacchanalia (Greek): The feast of Bacchus or Dionysus, attended by dancing, frenetic Nymphs.

Banshee (Irish; BAN-she; Woman of the Mounds; also Beansidhe): An Irish or Scottish cattle Faerie said to keen or sing mournfully when a member of a certain family is near death. Banshees are said to connect themselves to the oldest Irish and Scottish families, and their song may warn of an unexpected death.

Barghest (English; BAR-guest): A Demon Dog of Yorkshire, mentioned in the writing of Sir Walter Scott.

Barrie, James Matthew (Scottish, 1860–1937): Scottish novelist and playwright, Barrie is famous for writing both the play and the novel versions of *Peter Pan*. His work gave us Tinker Bell, a tiny mischievous Faerie who haunts Kensington Gardens in London.

Bettelheim, Bruno (Austrian-American, 1903–1990): Psychiatrist and writer who analyzed Grimms' Fairy tales from a Freudian perspective. His book *The Uses of Enchantment* (1976) was a brilliant study of how children respond to the darker material in Fairy tales.

Black Shuck, The Doom Dog (Cornish, Welsh): One of many Hell Hounds or Demon Dogs that haunt the British countryside. The name comes from the Saxon *scucca*, meaning "demon."

Blodeuedd (Welsh; BLOOD-weth or Blu-DI-weth. Flower Face; also Blodwedd, Bloodwedd, Bleudwedd): A Welsh Faerie made from nine flowers of the forest, who shape shifts into an owl. The owl is called Blodeuedd in Welsh.

Bran, Bendigai Vran (Welsh; Raven, Blessed Raven; also Bendigaivran): Giant raven God or spirit who fought a battle against a king of the Underworld. Spoken of in the *Mabinogion*. Also associated with the wren, called the *Cutty Vran*, wren's sparrow or bran's sparrow.

Bran Mac Febal (Irish; Raven; Bran son of Febal): Human who is summoned by an Otherworld maiden to voyage over the Western Ocean to the Isle of Women.

Branwen (Welsh; White Raven; also Bronwen, Bronwyn): Sister of Bran, mother of Gwern. Branwen is a princess trapped by an Underworld king and held prisoner in the *Mabinogion*. She trains a wren to speak, and he carries her cry for help to her brother Bran, who fights a war for her release.

Brownies: House Fairies, usually quite small, sometimes mischievous.

Carter Hall (also Carterhaugh): Scottish locale spoken of in several folkloric ballads, thought to be haunted by Faeries.

Cerridwen (Welsh; KER-id-wen; also Kerridwen): An enchanted sorceress who has a cauldron of rebirth. She can transform into several animals. Her second child became Taliesin, the great Welsh bard.

Child, Francis James (American; 1825–1896): American folklorist and mathematician who collected hundreds of Scots-English ballads, many concerning Faerie lore and Faerie visitations. His collection is published as *The English and Scottish Popular Ballads* (First printing, 1882–1898).

Cro Sith (Scottish): A Faerie horse.

Daoine Sidhe (Irish; DWEE-na SHE): Underworld Faeries from the folklore of County Ulster in Ireland. Warlike Faeries who feast, fight, drink and who often kidnap human women. Some legends say they are the great heroes of Ireland, the Fenians, forced to live underground as the result of losing a war.

"Demon Lover, The": An English ballad of an Otherworldly lover seducing a woman.

Doyle, Sir Arthur Conan (English; 1859–1930): Novelist and pioneer in crime fiction, Doyle established relationships with several researchers into the truth of the existence of Fairies, and published an article in 1920 concerning the Cottingley Fairies, a case in which two teenaged English girls claimed to be able to photograph small dancing Fairies. Though Doyle was known as a brilliant writer for his Sherlock Holmes novels and stories, he was ridiculed for believing what turned out to be a hoax.

Each Uisge (Scottish; EACH WE-sweg): A Faerie horse that rises from saltwater. It will carry a rider to his death by drowning.

Elf, Elves (Germanic): A Germanic and Norse name for a race of Fairies. Elves may be associated with the ancient race of people or enchanted beings that the earliest Norse found when they arrived in Europe. Traditionally Elves are as tall as humans and are often warlike. Modern tales have made Elves out to be small and cute. The modern legend of Santa Claus states that Elves make his toys.

Evil Stepmother: Many Fairy tales and folkloric sources have a surrogate mother who acts as a destroyer rather than a nurturer to the children in her care. Often both she and the children are enchanted creatures with magical powers. In some material, she is a mother-in-law.

Fairport Convention: Popular English rock band performing from the late 1960s to the present, known for collecting English and Scottish folk songs and performing them in a modern rock format. They are considered the first English folk-rock band. Perhaps best known for their seminal 1969 album *Liege & Lief*, considered the first performance of British folk music in a psychedelic rock format. Notable alumnae who are well-known as folk musicians include Sandy Denny (solo career, now deceased), Martin Carthy, Richard Thompson (both guitarists with brilliant solo careers), and Ashley Hutchings (after leaving Fairport, cofounded a number of folk rock groups, including Steeleye Span, Morris On, and the Albion Country Band, all of whom work with traditional music in a rock format).

Faun (Greek, Roman; also Faunus): A type of shape-shifting Faerie that takes the form of a human or a deer. A well-known Faun in literature is Tumnus, a character in C. S. Lewis's *The Lion, the Witch and the Wardrobe* (1950).

Fey (also Fay): Common name for the Faerie folk, used as a woman's name that was popular at the turn of the twentieth century. The actress Fay Wray (1907–2004) is well known for her role as Ann Darrow in *King Kong* (1933). Probably derived from the German *Fa'an* or *Fein*, Fair Folk.

Finfolk: Saami and Shetland name for Selkies, a type of sea Faerie.

Finvarra (Irish): King of the subterranean Sidhe, or warrior Faeries. Known for kidnapping mortal women and subjecting them to Faerie music, causing them to forget the mortal world and become his lovers. One mortal woman he became involved with was Ethna.

Fliadais (Irish; Flee-a-DAY-us): Irish deer Goddess or Faerie. Similar in appearance to the Greek Artemis.

Froud, Brian (English; b. 1947): Well-known illustrator of Faerie books. Froud's books on Faerie lore are extremely popular, and have influenced the way modern fans view the Fey.

Glas Gaivlen (Scottish): A Faerie cow.

Glastig (Scottish; also Glaistig): Seducer-murderer Faerie who herds deer, and may take the form of a deer or some other animal.

Graineeog (Irish, Ugly One): Irish term for an enchanted creature posing as a hedgehog. These creatures are known to predict bad weather and the coming of summer.

Greenaway, Kate (English; 1846–1901): A well-known illustrator famous for paintings of children and of childlike, adorable Faeries. An award medal in her name was established for illustrators of children's books in 1955.

Grimm, Jacob (1785–1863) and Wilhelm (1786–1859); together known as the Brothers Grimm: German scholars, linguists and folklorists, famous for collecting tales of Faeries and enchanted beings from the German and French countryside. The stories they collected are often called Grimms' Fairy tales.

Gwri Golden Hair (Welsh; HWAR-ee): Name given to Pryderi by his foster parents in the *Mabinogion*.

Gwydion (Welsh): In the *Mabinogion*, a Welsh enchanted being who is a great bard and warrior. He sires two sons, Dylan and Llew Llaw Gyffes, with his sister Arianrhod. He creates Blodeuedd out of flowers as a wife for Llew.

Hedge-hurst (Romany): Gypsy term for an enchanted creature that appears as a hedgehog.

Herne (English; Hern, Herne the Hunter): A God or Faerie, or both, that haunts the forest around Windsor Great Park in Berkshire. Herne is an antlered being who leads the Wild Hunt. Shakespeare refers to Herne in *The Merry Wives of Windsor* as the spirit or ghost of a forester who was hanged from an old oak tree.

Hildaland (Orkney Scottish): A disappearing reappearing island in the Orkneys, inhabited by Selkies or Finfolk. Humans are captured and forced to dwell there as mates to their enchanted captors.

Huntley Bank: Scottish locale, known in several ballads as a Faerie dwelling. The site of a meeting between Thomas Learmont of Erceldoune and the Elf Queen.

Imp: Small English Faerie, usually childlike. The term is often applied to misbehaving children.

Jenny Green Teeth: An English Faerie said to murder children.

Kelpie (Scottish and Cornish): A Faerie horse that lives in both land and water. Also called the Cro Sith.

L'Annawnshee (French-Irish; Lan-AWN-shee; Faerie of the Underworld; also Leannawnshee): A Faerie woman said to inspire artists and poets, but who takes their lives early in return for their artistic brilliance. Also known as a seducer-murderer Faerie. Associated with Keats's *La Belle Dame Sans Merci*.

Leprechauns (Irish): Irish term for a type of mischievous Faerie, often well dressed and very energetic.

Lilith (Hebrew from Sumerian, לילית, lil-EET): A prophetic Faerie who appears as an owl or a serpent in early Sumerian text (such as the *Gilgamesh* epic). Kabalistic Jews consider her a succubus and associate her with the serpent of Eden in Genesis. Some Jews believe that circumcising male children kept them from being harmed by Lilith as babies, or seduced by her as men. Palestinian women sing lullabies to protect their children from Lilith.

Llew Llaw Gyffes (Welsh; KLEW Klaw Giffs, the Little Lion with the Steady Hand; also Lleu Llaw Gyffes): Welsh sun god or sky Faerie spoken of in the *Mabinogion*. Llew or Lleu was born under a triple curse that he could never have a name unless his mother named him, could never be near arms unless his mother armed him, and could never marry a mortal woman. He was fostered by his uncle Gwydion, and married Blodeuedd, a Faerie made of flowers who took the form of an owl.

Lorelie (German): One of several seducer-murderer Faeries living in German rivers, especially the Rhine. Like Sirens and Mermaids,

Lorelie are impossibly beautiful, and may attract male victims by singing or grooming. A common name for German women, it was recently given a boost in popularity by a character on the television show *The Gilmore Girls*.

Mab (Welsh/English; Young Girl or Young Queen): English name for the Faerie Queen. Mab commands horses, dogs and ravens, and leads a Wild Ride through the English forest each Samhain or Hallowe'en. She must sacrifice a human every seven years in what is called the tithe to Hell in order to allow the Faeries to remain in the Faerie world.

Mabinogion (Welsh; MAB-in-O-gee-un, Tales of the Young Lord): A Welsh text comprised of several ancient folkloric tales of Faeries, Gods and Goddesses, and humans who make pacts with various kings of the Underworld. Some of the oldest Arthurian material is found in the *Mabinogion*. Eleventh-century monks first recorded the text from much older sources. Translations into English include editions by Lady Charlotte Guest (1812–1895), Jeffrey Gantz and Patrick Ford.

Manawydan (Welsh; man-OO-den): In the *Mabinogion*, Manawydan is an enchanted mortal who battles Otherworld enemies who have taken the form of mice. Second husband of Rhiannon, stepfather of Pryderi, father-in-law to Kigva.

Merfolk: English name for Selkies.

Moddey Dhoo (Manx): A Hell Hound or Demon Dog of Man, said to haunt Peel Castle.

Morgan Le Fay (French; Morganna of the Faeries): A name for the Faerie Queen in the Arthurian tales. Morgan was said to be Arthur's half sister, though the two had relations and Morgan bore a son, Mordred, who later killed his father.

Niamh of the Golden Hair (Irish; also Neve, Neive, Neev or Nev): Queen of the Faerie world, wife of Ossian. This Faerie name is a popular name for girls in Ireland and of Irish descent, such as the actress Neve Campbell.

Nixie (German and Saxon English): Water Nymphs or Sprites, sometimes harmful. Nixies will often exchange their babies for human children.

Nymph (Greek): One of a multitude of female Greek Faeries who take various animal shapes, but when in human form are seen as impossibly beautiful young women. Though some will die to protect their chastity, others are hypersexual; the term *nymphomania* was coined based on their mythology. The author Vladimir Nabokov (1899–1977) also used their myth in coining the term *nymphet*, meaning a very young (i.e., preteen) flirtatious or sexual female. Types of Nymphs include Naiads, Dryads, Nereids, Hamadryads, Hyades, Leimakids, Alseids, Muses and many others. The name Nymph may be a comparison between a budding flower and a woman's sexual organ.

Oestara (Norse; probably from Sanskrit, o-STAR-ah): Norse name for the Goddess of spring, associated with such Middle Eastern Goddesses as Astarte, Ishtar and Asherah; also a celebration in her honor observed by modern Pagans on Spring Equinox.

Odin (Old Norse; also Wodin): Name for a God in Old Norse myth, and also of a Faerie that leads a Wild Hunt. A good deal of our perception of Santa Claus is based on images of Odin. Our weekday Wednesday is named in honor of Wodin.

Orfeo (English): An enchanted king who does musical battle with the Faerie King for the return of his wife. Probably based on the Greek myth of Orpheus and Eurydice.

Ossian (Irish; O-sheen, Little Deer): Son of the great Irish hero Finn Mac Coul and a deer woman named Sadb, Ossian journeyed to Tir N'an Og to marry Niamh of the Golden Hair, the queen of that land.

Oupis, Loxo and Hekaerge (Greek): Three maidens who attend Artemis. Each died defending her chastity and was given eternal life as a Nymph. Greek women honor the three in certain rituals, often by leaving offerings of their hair.

Picts: A race of aboriginal people known to the earliest Celtic settlers of Ireland and Wales. The Picts may have been an enchanted race or simply a race of humans very close to nature. From their name are derived the words Pixie and Piskey.

Pixie (Irish, Cornish; also Piskey): Any of several mischievous shape-shifting Fairies found throughout Europe. Their name may derive from Pict, the Celtic name for an aboriginal or enchanted race found in ancient times throughout Europe.

Pookah (POO-kah): an English or Irish Faerie, mischievous and tricky, associated with Puck. The name probably comes from *buka* or *booka*, Greek for goat or pastoral animal. Pookahs often take the form of goats or horses.

Pryderi (Welsh; Pri-DEER-e, Anxiety): Welsh king, son of Pwyll and Rhiannon. When Pryderi was born, he was taken by a Faerie creature to the Underworld. Later he was returned in exchange for a horse colt. Pryderi battled Underworld creatures all of his life, and was killed in a dispute with Gwydion over a pog of pigs gifted to him by the Underworld king Arawn. Spoken of in the *Mabinogion*.

Puck: English Pookah, used by Shakespeare as an alternate name for Robin Goodfellow. A mischievous Faerie of the English forest.

Pwyll (Welsh; POOSH, Thought): In the *Mabinogion*, a Welsh king who makes a pact with the Underworld king Arawn. Married to Rhiannon, father of Pryderi.

Rackham, Arthur (English; 1867–1939): A pioneering illustrator well known for his paintings of Fairies. Rackham illustrated a myriad of well-known books, including editions of *Alice's Adventures in Wonderland*, *A Midsummer Night's Dream* and many Fairy tales and fables.

Reynardine (French; Fox-man): A traditional song involving the Scottish legend of Mr. Fox, a seducer-murderer Faerie that alternates between the forms of a fox and a man.

Rhiannon (Welsh; ree-AHN-en): Welsh Underworld horse Faerie, married to Pwyll to create a bond between humans and the Underworld. Mother to Pryderi. Rhiannon was thought to have eaten her son (he was actually taken by an Underworld Faerie), and her punishment was to act as a horse for seven years. Later she was kidnapped by a Faerie and held as a changeling.

Robin Goodfellow: An Imp or Pixie of the English forest, very mischievous and dangerous. Robin appears in Shakespeare's *A Midsummer Night's Dream* as a servant of Oberon, the Faerie King. His name comes from a bird, known in folklore as the King of Summer.

Sadb (Irish; SAV): A woman transformed into a deer, wife of Finn Mac Coul, mother of Ossian.

Samhain (Irish; SOW-ane or SO-vane: winter); Irish name for the final harvest, called Hallowe'en in America. The Irish reckon the New Year to begin at the end of the old year's harvest, so Samhain is the Irish New Year.

Seely Court (Irish): The Irish Faerie court, presided over by a Faerie Queen. These are the benign Fey; the malicious Fey are known as the Unseely Court.

Selkies (Saami, Danish, Irish, Scottish and Manx; also Selky, Selchie, Silkies): Faeries that take the appearance of seals when in the sea, and of humans when on land. They often breed with and marry humans, but break their hearts when they are drawn back to the sea after living as humans for many years. Sometimes called Mer-folk or Finfolk.

Shoopiltee (Shetlands): A Faerie horse of the Shetlands. Similar to the Norwegian Nokken.

Sidhe (Irish; SHEE, Mound Dweller): The Irish name for the Faerie race, probably derived from an early aboriginal European people whom the Celts called the Picts, who lived in underground dwellings.

Siren: Three bird-women who lured sailors to their death with their beautiful voices. Seen in Homer's *The Odyssey*, 12:52.

Sirin (Russian): Owl-women Faeries whose singing could be used by saints to fortell the future. Those not trained to undertand them could go insane listening to their song.

Sleipnir (Old Norse; SLAPE-near): Odin's eight-legged horse.

Spenser, Edmund (English; c. 1552–1599): English poet who wrote *The Faerie Queene*, an epic poem said to be an allegory for Queen Elizabeth I.

Sprite: One of a number of mischievous, energetic Faeries.

Steeleye Span: English band, performing from the late 1960s to the current time, well known for collecting English and Scottish folk songs and performing them as pop rock. Started by Fairport Convention alum Ashley Hutchings and folk legend Martin Carthy. The band has won several awards for its performance of traditional British music. The band name is taken from a character in a folk song.

Tam Lin: According to a well-known ballad, a human taken by the Faerie Queen when he fell from his horse in battle. Tam Lin (which may be a Scottish pronunciation of Tom Lane) is rescued by his lover, Janet.

Tanuki (Japanese): Japanese term for a prophetic Faerie that appears as a hedgehog.

Tewaz (Old Norse): Saxon name for Odin, from whom we get our word Tuesday.

Thomas Learmont of Erceldoune, True Thomas (Scottish; c. 1220–c.1298): Scottish lord, poet and prophet who was believed to have ridden with the Queen of Elfland to the Otherworld.

Teirnon Twryv Vliant (Welsh; Man of Thunder; also Teirnyon): In the *Mabinogion*, foster father of Pryderi; probably a Welsh thunder God.

Tir N'an Og (Irish; TEER nah NOG, Land of the Young or Land of Youth; also Tir Na Nog): The Irish name for the Faerie world, reachable by riding a magical white horse over the Western Ocean.

Titania (English from Russian): Shakespeare's name for the Faerie Queen. In A *Midsummer Night's Dream*, Titania has taken a changeling child as her special charge, which has incited a fight with her husband Oberon.

Tithe to Hell (also Tiend to Hell): Legend of a sacrifice of a human life paid every seven years by the Faerie Queen, perhaps based on ancient memories of the sacrifice of the Seven Year King. Legend says that the Faeries are only allowed to live in the Faerie world by tithing human lives to Satan.

Tuatha De Danaan (Irish; too-ATH-a dee DAN-an, People of the Goddess Danaan or Dana): An ancient race of Irish Faeries or heroes, depending on who you ask, who settled Ireland and fought legendary wars. They are said to live still under the earth.

Urchin (English): A shape-shifting Faerie that may take the form of a hedgehog. Urchins will often pose as mortal children to be taken in by human families.

Vila (Russian; Ukrainian; also Weela, Wila, Veela): Eastern European Faerie that inspires poets but may also murder them. She befriends worthy women and teaches them the language of birds. She is a Nymph and appears as a horse or an impossibly beautiful young woman, either naked or in white or gold robes.

Xana (Spanish): Spanish name for Nixies or similar water Sprites. Xana will exchange their infants for human children.

BIBLIOGRAPHY

Ashliman, D. L. *German Changeling Legends.* Pittsburg, PA: University of Pittsburgh, 1996.

Barrie, J. M. *Peter Pan.* New York: Holt and Company, 1987.

Best, R. I., and R. Baumgarten, trans. *The Book of the Dun Cow.* Dublin: Library of the Royal Irish Academy, 1870.

Bettelheim, Bruno. *The Uses of Enchantment: The Meaning and Importance of Fairy Tales.* New York: Random House, 1976.

Brand, John. *The Popular Antiquities of Great Britain.* London: Reeves and Turner, 1905.

Briggs, Katherine. *British Folk Tales.* England: Dorset Press, 1989.

———. *The Vanishing People: Fairy Lore and Legends.* New York: Pantheon, 1978.

Bronte, Charlotte. *Jane Eyre, An Autobiography.* London: Service & Paton, 1897.

Callimachus. *Hymns and Epigrams. Lycophron. Aratus.* Trans. A. W. Mair and G. R. Loeb. London: William Heinemann, 1921.

Campbell, John Gregerson. *Superstitions of the Highlands and Islands of Scotland.* Glasgow: James MacLehose and Sons, 1900.

Carthy, Martin. *Sweet Wivelsfield* (musical recording). Dream (Decca) Records, 1974.

Chambers, Robert. *The Book of Days*. London: W. and R. Chambers, 1869.

Child, F. J. *English and Scottish Popular Ballads*. New York: Dover, 1965.

Comyn, Michael. *Laoidh Oisín air Thír na nÓg*. English trans. Michael Comyn. Dublin: Tralee, 1863.

Doyle, Sir Arthur Conan. *The Coming of the Fairies*. New York: Hoder & Stoughton, 1922.

Duffy, Maureen. *The Erotic World of Faery*. London: Hodder & Stoughton, 1972.

Ellis, S. M. *Mainly Victorian*. London: Hutchings and Company, 1924.

"Folktales in Pre Industrial England." http://www.socyberty.com/Folklore/Folktales-in-Pre-Industrial-England.180861.

Ford, Patrick K., trans. *The Mabinogion*. Berkeley, CA: University of California Press, 1977.

Freud, Sigmund. *Moses and Monotheism*. New York: Random House, 1955.

Froud, Brian, and Alan Lee. *Faeries*. New York: Harry N. Abrams, 1978.

Gantz, Jeffrey, trans. *The Mabinogion*. New York: Dorset, 1976.

Gardner, Gerald B. *Book of Shadows*. Unpublished.

————. *The Meaning of Witchcraft*. York Beach, Maine: Weiser, 2004.

————. *Witchcraft Today*. New York: Citadel Press, 2004.

Glob, P. V. *The Bog People: Iron Age-Man Preserved*. Ithica, NY: Cornell University Press, 1975.

Graves, Robert. *The White Goddess*. Third ed. London: Faber & Faber, 1952.

Grimm, Jacob. *Deutsche Mythologie*. Fourth ed. Trans. by D. L. Ashliman. 1877.

Grimm, Jacob and Wilhelm Grimm. *Children's and Household Tales*. Trans. Margaret Hunt. 1884

————. *Household Tales*. London: George Bell, 1884. http://ebooks.adelaide.edu.au/g/grimm/g86h/

Guest, Lady Charlotte, trans. *The Mabinogion*. London: Bernard Quaritch, 1877.

Hartland, Edwin Sidney. *The Science of Fairy Tales*. New York: Scribner & Welford, 1891.

Holy Bible, The. King James version. Chicago: Spencer Press, 1947.

Homer. *The Odyssey*. Trans. Samuel Butler. Online at http://classics.mit.edu/Homer/odyssey.mb.txt

Hunter, Jennifer. *Magical Judaism*. New York: Citadel Press, 2006.

Johnson, Robert. *Hellhounds on my Trail* (musical recording). Dallas, TX: Columbia Records, 1937.

Jones, W. H. S., Litt. D., trans. *Description of Greece* by Pausanias. London: William Heinemann Ltd., 1918.

Keightly, Thomas. *The Fairy Mythology*. London: H. G. Bohn, 1860.

Klein, Kenny. *The Flowering Rod: Men and their Role in Paganism*. Megalithica Books, 2009.

———. *High Grows the Barley* (musical recording). Kansas City, Blackthorn Records, 1995.

Knightly, Charles. *The Perpetual Almanac of Folklore*. London: Thames & Hudson, 1987.

Kramer, Samuel Noah. *Gilgamesh and the Huluppu-Tree: A Reconstructed Sumerian Text*. Chicago, IL: University of Chicago, 1938.

Lawson, John Cuthbert. *Modern Greek Folklore and Ancient Greek Religion*. Cambridge: Cambridge University Press, 1910.

Leland, Charles G. *Aradia, Gospel of the Witches*. London: C.W. Daniel Co., 1984.

Lewis, C. S. *The Chronicles of Narnia*. American ed. New York: Harper Collins, 2001.

Lintrop, Aado. "Bear Feast Songs." *Electronic Journal of Folklore*, vol. 3, 2001.

———. "The Great Oak and Brother-Sister." *Electronic Journal of Folklore*, vol. 16, 2001.

Matthews, Caitlin. *Mabon and the Guardians of Ancient Britain*. Rochester, VT.: Inner Traditions International, 2002.

Monaghan, Patricia. *The Red-Haired Girl from the Bog: The Landscape of Celtic Myth and Spirit*. Novato, CA: New World Library, 2004.

Nabokov, Vladimir. *Lolita*. New York: Vintage, 1991.

Pausanias. *Description of Greece*. Trans. W. H. S. Jones and D. Litt. London: William Heinemann Ltd., 1918.

Rees, Alwyn, and Brinley Rees. *Celtic Heritage*. London: Thames and Hudson, 1961.

Rossmore, Lord. *Things I Can Tell*. London: Eveleigh Nash, 1912.

Ryall, Rhiannon. *West Country Wicca*. Washington, D.C.: Phoenix Publications, 1990.

Scott, Sir Walter. *The Lay of the Last Minstrel*. Chicago: Scott, Foresman and Co. 1899.

Shakespeare, William. *A Midsummer Night's Dream*. Chicago: Scott, Foresman and Co., 1910.

———. *The Complete Works of William Shakespeare*. Cambridge, MA: Massachusetts Institute of Technology, 1993. http://shakespeare.mit.edu/

Sharpe, Cecil J. *The Sword Dances of Northern England*. London: Novello, 1951.

Sheba, Lady. *The Book of Shadows*. St. Paul, MN: Llewellyn, 2004.

Smiddy, Rev. Richard. *An Essay on the Druids, the Ancient Churches, and the Round Towers of Ireland*. Dublin: W. B. Kelly, 1871.

Squire, Charles. *Celtic Myth and Legend*. London: Gresham, 1905.

Tatar, Maria, ed. *The Annotated Brothers Grimm*. New York: W. W. Norton and Company, 2004.

Veyne, Paul. *A History of Private Life*, vol. I. Cambridge, MA: Harvard University Press, 1987.

Whittle, Mark. "Primordial Sounds: Big Bang Acoustics." http://www.astro.virginia.edu/~dmw8f/sounds/aas/press_release.txt

Wolf, Naomi. *Promiscuities: The Secret Struggle for Womanhood*. New York: Fawcett Columbine, 1997.

Yeats, W. B. *The Celtic Twilight*. Mineola: Dover Publications, 2004.

Zell-Ravenheart, Oberon, and Morning Glory. *Creating Circles and Ceremonies*. Franklin Lakes, NJ: Career Press, 2006.

INDEX

TO WRITE TO THE AUTHOR

If you wish to contact the author or would like more information about this book, please write to the author in care of Llewellyn Worldwide and we will forward your request. Both the author and publisher appreciate hearing from you and learning of your enjoyment of this book and how it has helped you. Llewellyn Worldwide cannot guarantee that every letter written to the author can be answered, but all will be forwarded. Please write to:

Kenny Klein
℅ Llewellyn Worldwide
2143 Wooddale Drive, Dept. 978-0-7387-1883-5
Woodbury, Minnesota 55125-2989, U.S.A.
Please enclose a self-addressed stamped envelope for reply,
or $1.00 to cover costs. If outside U.S.A., enclose
international postal reply coupon.

Many of Llewellyn's authors have websites with additional information and resources. For more information, please visit our website at http://www.llewellyn.com